JAMES FOR[REST]

MOUNTAIN MAN

446 MOUNTAINS.
SIX MONTHS.
ONE RECORD-BREAKING
ADVENTURE.

C**⊕**NWAY

LONDON • OXFORD • NEW YORK • NEW DELHI • SYDNEY

CONWAY
Bloomsbury Publishing Plc
50 Bedford Square, London, WC1B 3DP, UK

BLOOMSBURY, CONWAY and the Conway logo are trademarks of Bloomsbury Publishing Plc

First published in Great Britain 2019
First paperback edition 2020

Copyright © James Forrest, 2019, 2020
Maps © John Plumer, 2019

James Forrest has asserted his right under the Copyright, Designs and Patents Act, 1988, to be identified as Author of this work

A catalogue record for this book is available from the British Library

Library of Congress Cataloguing-in-Publication data has been applied for

ISBN: PB: 978-1-8448-6605-2
ePub: 978-1-84486-562-8
ePDF: 978-1-84486-564-2

2 4 6 8 10 9 7 5 3 1

Typeset in Berling LT Std by Deanta Global Publishing Services, Chennai, India
Printed and bound in Great Britain by CPI Group (UK) Ltd, Croydon CR0 4YY

MIX
Paper from
responsible sources
FSC
www.fsc.org   FSC® C013604

To find out more about our authors and books visit www.bloomsbury.com
and sign up for our newsletters

The Alfred Wainwright quote on pages 3 and 242 is from *A Pictorial Guide to the Lakeland Fells, Book One, The Eastern Fells* (Frances Lincoln, London, 2005); the Alastair Humphreys quote on page 69 is from *Microadventures: Local Discoveries for Great Escapes* (William Collins, London, 2014).

Every effort has been made to contact the copyright holders of material reproduced in this book. If any errors or admissions have inadvertently been made, they will be rectified in future editions provided that written notification is sent to the publishers.

CONTENTS

Maps..iv
Foreword by Anna McNuff vi

Prologue 1
1 Navigationally Challenged............................... 5
2 Back on Track... 14
3 Organised Chaos 22
4 Calamity James.. 33
5 A Double-Edged Sword................................. 44
6 Day Tripper... 56
7 Sleeping Wild 65
8 Spies, Elephants and a Porsche 74
9 Hitch'n'hiking 86
10 A Strange Double Life................................. 101
11 The Mind of a Peak-Bagger........................... 107
12 A Cloud in the Heavens............................... 117
13 The Bog of Eternal Stench 128
14 Chasing Aliens 139
15 Sleeping in a Swamp 160
16 Liam's Mangoes 171
17 Dodging Bombs 180
18 Boy Racers and Middle-Finger Salutes 190
19 Mapless and Clueless 208
20 A Handsome Crag 220
21 The Final Summit..................................... 227
22 Afterwards 243

Epilogue 249
How to Plan Your Own Epic Adventure 266
Glossary 279

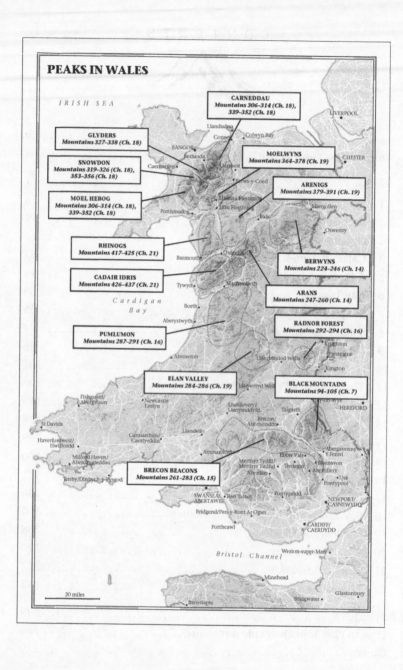

PEAKS IN WALES

IRISH SEA

CARNEDDAU
Mountains 306–314 (Ch. 18),
339–352 (Ch. 18)

GLYDERS
Mountains 327–338 (Ch. 18)

SNOWDON
Mountains 319–326 (Ch. 18),
353–356 (Ch. 18)

MOEL HEBOG
Mountains 306–314 (Ch. 18),
339–352 (Ch. 18)

MOELWYNS
Mountains 364–378 (Ch. 19)

ARENIGS
Mountains 379–391 (Ch. 19)

RHINOGS
Mountains 417–425 (Ch. 21)

CADAIR IDRIS
Mountains 426–437 (Ch. 21)

BERWYNS
Mountains 224–246 (Ch. 14)

ARANS
Mountains 247–260 (Ch. 14)

RADNOR FOREST
Mountains 292–294 (Ch. 16)

PUMLUMON
Mountains 287–291 (Ch. 16)

ELAN VALLEY
Mountains 284–286 (Ch. 19)

BLACK MOUNTAINS
Mountains 94–105 (Ch. 7)

BRECON BEACONS
Mountains 261–283 (Ch. 15)

Cardigan Bay

Bristol Channel

LIVERPOOL

Llandudno
Conwy · Colwyn Bay
BANGOR
Bethesda
Caernarfon
Llanrwst
Betws-y-Coed
Blaenau Ffestiniog
Porthmadog
Llan Ffestiniog
Bala
Llangollen
Oswestry
CHESTER

Barmouth
Dolgellau
Tywyn
Machynlleth
Borth
Aberystwyth
Aberaeron

Knighton
Presteigne
Llandrindod Wells
Kington

Llanwrtyd Wells

Fishguard/
Abergwaun
Newcastle
Emlyn
Llandovery/
Llanymddyfri
Talgarth
Brecon/
Aberhonddu
HEREFORD

St Davids
Carmarthen/
Caerfyrddin
Llandeilo
Haverfordwest/
Hwlffordd
Milford Haven/
Aberdaugleddau
Ammanford
Tenby/Dinbych-y-Pysgod
Merthyr Tydfil/
Merthyr Tudful
Aberdare
Ebbw Vale
Tredegar
Abergavenny/
Y Fenni
Blaenavon
Abertillery
Usk
Pontypool

SWANSEA/
ABERTAWE · Port Talbot
Bridgend/Pen-y-Bont Ar Ogwr
Pontypridd
NEWPORT/
CASNEWYDD
Porthcawl
CARDIFF/
CAERDYDD

Weston-super-Mare

Minehead

Glastonbury

20 miles

Barnstaple
Bridgwater

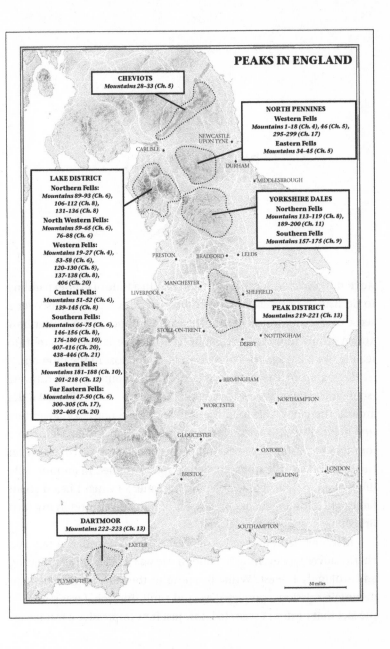

PEAKS IN ENGLAND

CHEVIOTS
Mountains 28–33 (Ch. 5)

NORTH PENNINES
Western Fells
*Mountains 1–18 (Ch. 4), 46 (Ch. 5),
295–299 (Ch. 17)*
Eastern Fells
Mountains 34–45 (Ch. 5)

LAKE DISTRICT
Northern Fells:
*Mountains 89–93 (Ch. 6),
106–112 (Ch. 8),
131–136 (Ch. 8)*
North Western Fells:
*Mountains 59–65 (Ch. 6),
76–88 (Ch. 6)*
Western Fells:
*Mountains 19–27 (Ch. 4),
53–58 (Ch. 6),
120–130 (Ch. 8),
137–138 (Ch. 8),
406 (Ch. 20)*
Central Fells:
*Mountains 51–52 (Ch. 6),
139–145 (Ch. 8)*
Southern Fells:
*Mountains 66–75 (Ch. 6),
146–156 (Ch. 8),
176–180 (Ch. 10),
407–416 (Ch. 20),
438–446 (Ch. 21)*
Eastern Fells:
*Mountains 181–188 (Ch. 10),
201–218 (Ch. 12)*
Far Eastern Fells:
*Mountains 47–50 (Ch. 6),
300–305 (Ch. 17),
392–405 (Ch. 20)*

YORKSHIRE DALES
Northern Fells
*Mountains 113–119 (Ch. 8),
189–200 (Ch. 11)*
Southern Fells
Mountains 157–175 (Ch. 9)

PEAK DISTRICT
Mountains 219–221 (Ch. 13)

DARTMOOR
Mountains 222–223 (Ch. 13)

CARLISLE

NEWCASTLE
UPON TYNE

DURHAM

MIDDLESBROUGH

PRESTON   BRADFORD   LEEDS

MANCHESTER   SHEFFIELD

LIVERPOOL

STOKE-ON-TRENT

NOTTINGHAM

DERBY

BIRMINGHAM

NORTHAMPTON

WORCESTER

GLOUCESTER

OXFORD

BRISTOL   READING   LONDON

SOUTHAMPTON

EXETER

PLYMOUTH

50 miles

FOREWORD

BY ANNA MCNUFF

Adventure is *the* antidote for modern life. In a time of ever-expanding to do lists, it offers a pocket of calm that allows us to rediscover a sense of awe and wonder about the world around us. No matter how grown up and important we might have become, adventure taps into feeling like a kid again – content, carefree and lost in the moment.

Having spent the past decade cycling, swimming and running (sometimes in fancy dress, sometimes in bare feet) over 20,000 miles around the globe, I've seen the transformative power of adventure first-hand. I've also spent long periods of time in between those journeys to far-flung places slumped over a laptop or collapsed on the sofa and so, often, it's smaller escapes crammed in around daily life that are responsible for keeping me sane. So when I heard about James's mission to embark on a series of mini adventures in my own British back yard, I was intrigued.

I first 'met' James when he stepped on stage to deliver a talk at a charity adventure evening in London. He was funny, self-deprecating and strikingly honest. While listening to the story of his one-man mountain mission, completed around a full-time job, I was struck by the fact that he didn't seem to know just how impressive a feat it was.

It's clear that James is not a person who chooses to take an easy path through life, and there's a real bravery in that. He has repeatedly hauled himself from the rut of everyday existence and sought adventure. It's hard enough to gain momentum to go on a single adventure, but to do it week in, week out – that takes a unique kind of strength. It's akin to lifting multiple, slippery atlas stones in World's Strongest Man. (Although, given that James bears a resemblance to popstar Will Young, he's doesn't fit the bill for a usual competitor.)

All too often, adventure seems like something that happens in a distant, far off land. A hazy dream that sits just beyond our reach. It can be seen as something that 'other' people do. People who are free from the shackles of family life or don't need to hold down a full-time job. What James does so beautifully in *Mountain Man* is that he opens up a space for you to place yourself in his ill-fitting, damp, borrowed women's hiking boots.

He shows us that, for less than the cost of a family package holiday, you can create a truly memorable experience, close to home. Guided by his immersive descriptions of the landscape, I was able to see a country that I had written off as familiar through fresh eyes. I got lost in his adventure as if it were my own. When he was cold, I was cold. When he was brimming with joy, I felt the warmth of it bursting from the page, and when he took simple pleasure in cramming fistfuls of peanut butter into his mouth – I tasted that too.

When you turn those final pages and reach that 446th peak with James, I know there will be no doubt in your mind. Adventure will feel closer than it ever has done before. The only question that remains is where and when you'll choose to begin a journey of your very own.

PROLOGUE

My name is James and there is nothing extraordinary about me. I'm not some sort of super-human, all-action adventurer. I have no idea how to abseil down a precipice, or forage for berries, or navigate in mist. I can't build a shelter or tie useful knots or run ultra-marathons. I'm scared of most animals and my legs go wobbly if I stand too close to a cliff edge. Dark nights freak me out and I can barely sleep in my tent unless it's perfectly horizontal. Oh, and I can't even grow a rugged beard. Rubbish credentials for an adventurer.

There was nothing extraordinary about my adventure, either. I didn't wrestle a bear, or dodge bullets in a war-ravaged country, or survive a near-fatal accident. There were no poisonous spiders or hostile bandits. I didn't triumph over horrific personal demons or have any life-changing epiphanies. I never once had to sever a boulder-trapped limb to free myself from a ravine. All I did was put one foot in front of the other on my days off from work.

But that ordinariness is exactly why my adventure *was* extraordinary. It proved that you can integrate something truly adventurous into your everyday life. You don't need to be rich, or have 12 months off work, or travel halfway across the world, or be Ranulph Fiennes. You don't need technical skills or expensive kit. With a little outdoorsy grit and adventurous spirit, anyone can go on a big adventure – including you.

In 2017 I climbed all four hundred and forty-six 2,000ft mountains in England and Wales in just six months – the fastest-ever time. Solo and unsupported, I walked over 1,000 miles, ascended five times the height of Everest and slept wild under the stars over 25 times. And I did it all while holding down my job, moving house and, somewhat miraculously, keeping my personal life just about under control.

The mountains taught me a simple but transformative lesson too: if you disconnect from technology, you reconnect with something innate and natural. In an internet-obsessed world of Instagram likes, Netflix binges and bursting email inboxes, we have lost our way. But if you turn off your phone and go climb a mountain, life is happier. Priorities realign, everyday worries dissipate, and closeness to nature and landscape is rekindled. Your reality becomes wholesome, humble, uncomplicated and fulfilling. It is joyous and liberating.

You learn to savour the simple pleasures in life – the pitter-patter of rain on your tent, a hot drink on a summit, the stillness of a forest, the wind in your hair, the crunch of the rocks below your feet – while simultaneously becoming immune to the stresses and anxieties that plague everyday life. After all, when you're watching the sky swirl a thousand shades of pink as the sun sets over silhouetted mountains, you really don't care about your burgeoning to-do list at work; and when you're hiking along an airy sun-drenched ridgeline, you truly can switch off from the incessant noise of online life; and when you're feeling like the king of the world on top of an exposed summit, you quickly realise how meaningless and fruitless our technology addictions really are.

Conversely, spending time in the mountains *is* meaningful and fruitful. Every walk I've completed has been time well spent – time for wilderness and solitude, for self-reflection and quiet, for escapism and nature. Every mountain has brought me boundless happiness. To non-believers this might seem a sentimental exaggeration but I stand by the statement. Being in the mountains is good for the soul. Why? Because, in the poetic words of the great fellwalker Alfred

Wainwright: 'I was to find ... a spiritual and physical satisfaction in climbing mountains – and a tranquil mind upon reaching their summits, as though I had escaped from the disappointments and unkindnesses of life and emerged above them into a new world, a better world.'

So what are you waiting for? Grab your boots, turn off your phone and go explore that better world.

CHAPTER 1

NAVIGATIONALLY CHALLENGED

I've always been pretty terrible at navigation. On countless occasions I've been well and truly lost in the mountains, wandering around aimlessly, descending into the wrong valley or taking the wrong turn off a summit. One year on the GR20 in Corsica, my friend Joe and I even walked for two full days in the wrong direction, nearly starving ourselves in the process but justifying our schoolboy error with the get-out clause 'It's all part of the adventure'. Back in the mountains of Britain I've fared little better. Put it this way, if it wasn't for the GPS-tracking capabilities of the OS Maps app, I'm pretty sure I'd be face down in a gully in the Rhinogs of North Wales right now, with a bemused feral goat nibbling at my rotting body.

My ability to navigate life was, for many years, similarly feeble. I didn't know where I was going or what I wanted. I lost focus of my passions. I made bad decisions. I chased material goals that never satisfied. I marched steadfastly towards one ambition only to realise I'd taken a wrong compass bearing and was heading in completely the wrong direction. My journey to the start line of this peak-bagging challenge was, therefore, neither straightforward nor guaranteed. I could so easily have never made it.

I grew up in Birmingham and, despite that fact, had a happy childhood in a loving, middle-class household. My parents gave me everything I could have ever wanted – and in return I drove them crazy with what they labelled my 'ants in pants' syndrome. I just couldn't sit still. I always wanted to be outside, exploring or playing football or going to the park. As soon as I could talk, my catchphrase became 'What are we doing next?'

Mum and Dad, understandably, coped with this by shipping me off at every available opportunity to my grandparents down the road in Handsworth. And it was, bizarrely, in that concrete jungle of north Birmingham in the early 1990s that my love for the great outdoors was forged. Every Saturday, my little brother Tom and I, wearing our matching electric-blue shell suits, would be dropped off at Bush Grove and go for a long walk.

Grandpa, who was as tall as a giant and smelled of roll-up cigarettes, would lead the way. He always looked really smart, in a collared shirt, tie, and boots so impeccably polished you could almost see your reflection in them. Granny, with a fresh perm and bubbly demeanour, would take my arm and sync footsteps as we chanted, 'Left, right, left right, I had a good job and I left' – her Brummie version of a military marching song that, fittingly, suited her penchant for telling bosses where to stick it. As we weaved along the back streets of Handsworth, through urban parks and past allotments, Tom and I would listen carefully for the roar of the West Bromwich Albion faithful, trying to predict whether it was Bob Taylor or Andy Hunt who had put the mighty Baggies ahead.

We'd cross the 'hole in the wall', a gap in the high brick wall along Park Lane leading to Sandwell Country Valley Park. To me, aged ten, that hole was a magical gateway into a land of endless opportunities beyond the city limits; a land where you could jump in puddles, clamber over fallen trees, run through woods, gaze over rolling greenery as far as the eye could see, throw stones into ponds, feed ducks and pat horses, chase your little brother along country paths with reckless abandon, and hike for mile after mile in a haze of childhood happiness. I can vividly remember thinking my life was going to be full of times like this.

Two decades later, I was sitting on the grey corner sofa in the lounge of my semi-detached house in Birmingham, feeling utterly depressed. I was unfit, unmotivated and unhappy; a jaded, cynical shadow of my former self. I'd snapped moodily at a colleague that morning, got absolutely nothing done in the office, and then bailed on the post-work run in favour of stuffing my face full of fried food. I knew I was in a bad place, but I couldn't see a way out. I felt trapped. How had I ended up here? Not by design, that's for sure. Life had just happened. I'd floated along without a pre-planned route map, a victim of not knowing who I was or what I truly wanted from life.

I thought about the long and winding journey I'd been down. After graduating with a degree in modern history, I'd set up Sport 4 Life UK, a charity in Birmingham using sport and outdoor activities to improve the lives of disadvantaged teenagers. It was meant to be my dream job – making a difference, shunning the corporate world, being entrepreneurial and working, at least some of the time, outside. But it didn't pan out like that. The reality of the job, particularly as the organisation grew rapidly, seemed to clash with my personality. I was stressed all the time and couldn't relax. The responsibility of employing a team weighed me down. The uncertainty of our funding made me a nervous wreck. I compensated by working long hours, chaining myself to my desk and attempting to control things I simply couldn't control. It was a great job – but it just wasn't right for me. It was making me unhappy.

But I stayed for several years. Why? Because I didn't want to be labelled a quitter and because I couldn't face admitting I'd spent so long in the wrong job. Moreover, I didn't know what else I could do and I was worried about the financial implications of dropping down the pay scale. These were all valid concerns, but by listening to them rather than my heart, I was living a lie. My mental health deteriorated as a result. I suffered from low-level anxiety and depression, had a fierce temper, and developed a negative way of thinking that drained the joy out of everything.

Eventually I plucked up the courage and willpower to take some baby steps towards improving my lot. I had therapy sessions; I took a sabbatical and temporarily lived in the Lake District; I reduced my hours at Sport 4 Life and pursued my love of writing by studying a part-time journalism course; I made a conscious effort to spend more time hiking, running or wild camping in the great outdoors; and finally I switched careers, quitting my role as a charity manager to become a newspaper reporter. All these changes helped, but my mood was still up and down. I hadn't figured out a way to escape an office-centric existence, and my negativity demons were still haunting me.

I was in one of those pessimistic frames of mind as I shuffled along the corner sofa in my lounge trying to get comfortable. I glanced at the alluring mountains pictured on the cover of the *Trail* magazine lying on the floor. My last escape to the great outdoors – a wild camping and fellwalking weekend in the Lake District – felt like a distant memory. I was dedicating one weekend a month to outdoors adventures, as well as odd days and evenings here and there wherever possible. To many people that might seem like a lot. But for me it was never enough. The more time I spent in the great outdoors, the more convinced I became that I wanted to build my life around it, and the more disillusioned I became with not being able to do so.

Life is shit, I thought, pondering what ten-year-old James would make of this existence I'd carved out for myself. I flicked through the diary on my phone, ignoring the 17 unread work emails that were gnawing away at my brain, and scribbled down some calculations on the back of the magazine.

'This is terrible,' I said to Becky, my wife, prompting her to probe for more information.

'What is?' she obliged, reluctantly lifting her gaze from our expensive 32-inch flat screen.

'I've worked it out. Last year I spent 235 days in an office staring at a computer but only 48 days travelling, climbing mountains and exploring the great outdoors. My life is a ratio of five parts mind-numbing boredom to one part fun.'

'Don't worry about it – you think too much,' replied Becky, attempting to dodge another late-night, relaxation-shattering discussion about our life goals. But I wasn't done.

'Isn't there more to life than all this?' I asked, a monologue brewing. 'Aren't you bored of living in this city, of sitting at the same desk in the same office every day, of abandoning our dreams, of living for the weekend and hating the nine-to-five grind?'

'I guess so, in a way – but it's just what you do, isn't it? That's life.' Becky too had been through a series of career upheavals as she searched for the right path in life. Previously a mental-health nurse, she found the emotional turmoil of that world too great, so she quit and became a manager in primary care. It was well paid and office-based, yet still stressful in a different way.

'But does it have to be?' I countered. 'What if we took a different route? What if we said, "Screw it" to paying gas bills, setting down roots, investing in ISAs and chasing promotions? What if we chose instead to go backpacking, travel the world and pursue our passions? To watch less TV and climb more bloody mountains?'

'We've been talking about this for years, James, but never done anything. What's stopping us?'

I was scared. It was comforting to talk about flipping our lives upside down – but terrifying to genuinely consider doing it. There were so many reasons not to: mortgages, pensions, careers, societal expectations, and fear of the unknown. Would we be ruining our careers and throwing our financial security down the drain? Would we be labelled as work-shy wasters by our high-flying friends? What if it all went horribly wrong?

Or maybe, just maybe, it would be the best decision we ever made. I could feel a dizzying, are-we-really-going-to-do-this? excitement rise in my stomach.

'Perhaps we should go for it then. Better to regret doing something than regret not doing it, right?' I posed tentatively.

'OK,' said Becky, smiling.

And with that simple 'OK' our lives changed for ever. A week later our house was up for sale, two round-the-world plane tickets had been reserved, and eBay was cluttered with our unwanted possessions. Others might tell you about a watershed moment that pushed them into an adventurous lifestyle. Maybe they'd hit rock bottom and had nowhere else to turn, or an epiphany had struck while they were perched triumphantly on a mountain summit – but for Becky and me it wasn't anything saccharine like that. It was simply a conversation on our sofa, surrounded by fish-and-chip wrappers, and the startling realisation that while financially it made sense to stick to our good jobs and secure futures, emotionally it would be self-destructive.

It was a slow and painful process getting things in order. We eventually sold our house, settling for £8,500 less than we'd bought it for in 2006, pre-credit crunch. It was an unwelcome financial hit, but thankfully a decade of working in reasonably well-paid jobs, with no kids and a far-from-flamboyant lifestyle, meant we'd already built up a mini treasure-trove of savings that could fund our gap year.

Once the contracts for the house sale were signed, the situation became real. This crazy idea was actually happening. So we handed in our notices at work. It was a frightening and unsettling thing to do. We almost backed out on several occasions, as 11th-hour doubts crept in. *What are we doing? Have we just condemned ourselves to a lifetime of unemployment and homelessness? Oh God, are we going to regret this?* But we stayed loyal to our convictions and it felt like a weight off our shoulders.

Despite all the obstacles and barriers and dead-ends, which might've tripped and blocked so many, we actually made it out of the maze to the beginning of the rest of our lives. Next, we tied up all the loose ends – closing down accounts, stashing our remaining possessions in my dad's loft, SORN-ing our cars, applying for travel visas, booking our gap-year adventures – and, finally, we were off. The plan? Six months travelling the world followed by six months of living and working on a remote Lake District farm.

Our backpacking adventure was the trip of a lifetime, half a year of wanderlust-soaked, sun-drenched exploration through Australasia and South East Asia. We lived in a van, trekked through snake-infested rainforests, swam with sharks, chilled on tropical beaches, climbed volcanoes, ate fried locusts in the jungle, camped in the wilderness, learned to surf (badly) – and immersed ourselves in an intoxicating state of relaxation that comes only with having no direct debits, no daily routine and no adult responsibilities whatsoever.

Of course, things went awry here and there: we nearly died when the 175mph winds of Cyclone Winston, the most intense tropical cyclone on record in the Southern Hemisphere, smashed into Fiji; in New Zealand we witnessed a campervan crash off the road to Milford Sound, which left the vehicle crumpled in a ditch and two German tourists in critical condition despite our best efforts to help; and on several occasions our wimpy English dispositions left us screaming as we encountered snack-stealing monkeys, bed-invading cockroaches, tent-raiding possums and myriad other scary creatures. But, aside from the odd mishap, it was a fulfilling experience, a time of feeling as if we were truly squeezing every last drop out of life.

Back in Blighty, our hedonistic journey of self-discovery and reinvention showed no sign of slowing. We settled into life at Snittlegarth, the most northerly hill farm in the Lake District National Park, which boasted one eccentric family, innumerable sheep, five dogs, two pigs, a rowdy brood of breakfast-laying chickens and Marco the peacock, who rarely let you sleep past 7am. We'd arranged the placement through Workaway, a scheme that matches travelling volunteers with local hosts. Our role was quite simple: to put in daily shifts of unskilled manual labour in return for our board and lodgings. The landscape was beguiling; under the shadow of Binsey fell, it was all winding dry-stone walls, rolling green fields, tumbling gills and atmospheric woodland. We fed chickens, tended to the Herdwicks, fixed fences, shovelled shit, painted gates and whatever else Rod the farmer entrusted to us, knowing full well we were 'townies' who basically had no clue what we were doing. I loved working outside, with the sun on my back and the wind in my face, and the Lake District scenery tugged at my heartstrings every morning. But it couldn't last for ever. The end of the 12 months arrived and our gap year in our 30s was over.

The downside? We returned to Birmingham with heads full of memories and wallets empty of money – and no real plan for the future. A vague notion that we'd become Instagram famous or that my blog traffic would skyrocket, enabling us to travel the world non-stop on a wave of money-making clicks, hadn't come true. Our approach had proved to be boom and bust: 12 months of 'wahey' followed by the prospect of a rapid demotion back to 'meh'. To put food on our plates and a roof over our heads, we needed cash, but how could we do that without falling back into the trappings of our old lives? How could we navigate this next hurdle in life without getting horribly lost again?

We were temporarily living with our respective parents. It was far from ideal. No one wants to be back in their childhood bedroom aged 33. We were desperate for a more permanent solution, but unsure exactly what that would look like. Where did we want to live? What type of jobs should we apply for? There were lots of questions and not many answers.

'What about this one?' said Becky, trawling the web for job vacancies in a geographically scattergun approach, as she half focused on her iPad and half watched *Emmerdale* on her parents' TV.

'It sounds horrific,' I replied grumpily. 'There's no way I'm going back to work in an office full-time. I can almost feel the dreaded pull of real life sucking us back in and I don't like it. I don't like it one bit.'

'Fair enough – this one?'

'I don't want to work in a café, even if it is in the Lake District. I want to do something at least vaguely intellectual.'

'OK, smartarse – what's the plan, then?' retorted Becky.

I didn't know. Perhaps we were destined to be navigationally challenged for the rest of our lives.

CHAPTER 2

BACK ON TRACK

So I started working on our life plan. And I mean really working on it. I read books, trawled blogs, wrote SWOT-analysis diagrams, scribbled notes, crunched budgets and took long meditative walks. At times it felt like a maths puzzle I couldn't solve or a riddle I couldn't figure out. How could we have more adventures, spend more time outdoors, have the flexibility and freedom to hike off into the sunset if and when we felt like it, while simultaneously earning enough money to get by? How could we turn our gap year into a gap life?

I even found myself, like a deranged version of Russell Crowe from *A Beautiful Mind*, scrawling down algebra-style equations in an attempt to unlock the secret to living adventurously. But clearly I didn't have the genius for it – the solution to the formula always eluded me. Half in jest, I'd scribble down things like: if x is adventure, y is time and z is money, then x requires $y + z$, but y and z are inversely proportional, because you trade y for z at work, so to increase y, you earn less z, or to increase z, you have less y, and therefore in conclusion you should (a) buy a lottery ticket, (b) rob a bank, (c) sell your body, (d) jump off a bridge or (e) bury your dreams deep, deep down and never mention them again.

Geeky maths jokes aside, Becky and I slowly began to make progress. We established that there were several options. We could blitz full-time jobs for six months, save up as much cash as possible, and then ditch it all to travel the world again. But then we'd be stuck in a cyclical world of big highs and desperate lows. Perhaps we could become digital nomads, working remotely from laptops anywhere in the world, combining travel and jobs in perfect harmony. But our backgrounds in charity management, regional journalism and primary care were hardly suited to such an approach. Or maybe we could live in a campervan, or volunteer abroad, or retrain as outdoor instructors, or rent a remote cottage in the mountains, or work part-time and use the extra days off to go on smaller adventures. But which option would be right for us?

We found it helped to focus on the things we hated about our old lives – living in a city, working in an office and being too busy for adventures. We looked for solutions and suddenly everything began to fall neatly into place. We left our parents' homes in Birmingham and rented a small flat in the lovely market town of Cockermouth in Cumbria, putting us within touching distance of the stunning Lake District mountains. Next we found jobs that didn't involve being chained to a desk. I secured a three-day-a-week job as a fundraiser for mountain-path repair scheme Fix the Fells and also launched my fledgling career as a freelance outdoors writer. At the same time Becky snapped up a zero-stress part-time vacancy at a shop in Keswick. The last piece of the puzzle was slashing our expenditure to mitigate our reduced earnings – we shopped in Aldi not Sainsbury's, watched Netflix rather than Sky TV, boiled noodles instead of dining out, and ditched the pub in favour of quiet nights in. We downsized our lives, trading in expensive luxuries that we didn't really need and never really missed, in return for an adventurous existence.

You too can create a more adventurous life for yourself, if you really, genuinely, wholeheartedly want to. If you live in a city and hate it, could you move somewhere more appealing, such as close to the mountains, on the coast or even abroad? Or, if you hate your office job, could you retrain to bag your dream outdoors job, such as climbing instructor, or National Trust ranger, or marine biologist? If you say you can't, your excuse is probably 'It wouldn't work financially'. For some, this may legitimately be true and you will have to settle for living adventurously just at weekends. But, for many, there will be a way to make the finances work by living frugally and prioritising adventure over unnecessary luxuries. Take a minute to consider this: you can buy a two-bedroom house in Frizington in West Cumbria for £40,000. Granted, it might not be in the nicest area, but you could be mortgage-free in a matter of years and, 20 minutes from your door, you could be walking along the shores of Ennerdale Water on your way to climb Pillar. Nothing is impossible.

Another simple but incredibly effective tactic Becky and I used to make our lives more adventurous was working part-time. Perhaps you could too. Fifty extra days of adventure every year are potentially within your grasp. Simply take one extra day off each week, reduce your weekly expenditure by the equivalent of a day's pay and, hey presto, you've broken even and freed up 50 days for outdoor exploits each year. How exciting is that? Becky and I took this exact approach. We both worked four days per week and, as such, were £150 down a week compared with full-time hours. But we managed to save £150 by making lots of small adjustments – cutting back on daily cappuccinos and walking rather than driving – as well as a couple of big changes, such as downsizing our home. Of course, such a strategy might not work for everyone and there are hundreds of factors affecting individual finances. Perhaps your employer won't play ball, or maybe cutting back isn't feasible. But, if you're committed and determined, you might just be able to do it. What epic adventures might you enjoy with your newfound 50 days of freedom?

Things were looking up. Our lives were back on track. Becky and I could drive for 30 minutes in any direction and find adventure: walking around Buttermere, or running through Whinlatter Forest, or standing triumphantly atop Blencathra. Adventure was all around. What's more, we had time to enjoy it, with our extra day off per week on top of weekends and annual leave. We were having our cake and eating it – and no one had handed it to us. We'd made it happen.

But there was still one niggling thought at the back of my mind. I wanted to go on a 'big' adventure. I longed for something grand, something that could rival the superlative heights of the gap year, something that could quench my seemingly insatiable wanderlust. Was that too much to ask? Maybe I should just learn to be grateful and settle for mini adventures. Was it even possible to integrate an epic expedition with a job and an everyday lifestyle?

My internal calculator started crunching numbers. If I worked four days per week on average, then I'd have three free days a week, including weekends. Over half a year, say the window of better weather from approximately April to September, that would be 78 days off. Throw in three weeks or 12 days of annual leave and I'd have a whopping 90 days to play with. *Surely that's enough time for a big adventure*, I thought – but what, exactly?

I went upstairs and pulled a dusty plastic storage container from under the bed – no *Playboy* mags, just my stash of adventure books and travel magazines. I started flicking through old copies of *Wanderlust* and *Adventure Travel* and tossed dog-eared paperbacks on to the mattress. Two small, light blue books caught my eye: *The Mountains of England and Wales* by John and Anne Nuttall. I picked up one volume and read the back cover. 'There are over 400 mountain summits in England and Wales which reach the height of 2,000ft and it is the ambition of many walkers to climb them all.' An idea began to sprout in my mind.

'Is peak-bagging cool?' I asked Becky, as she boiled the kettle and dropped tea bags into two mugs.

'Peak-what-ing?'

'Peak-bagging. It means ticking off, or "bagging", a predefined list of mountain peaks. Kind of like a big challenge.'

'Sounds as if it's for middle-aged men with beards who don't have girlfriends,' she replied.

'But would you class a peak-bagger as an "adventurer"?'

'It's not exactly on-trend. Adventurers climb Everest and trek through the Amazon jungle. Or paddleboard the Thames on a plastic-collecting eco mission. Or complete 100 marathons in 100 days accompanied by all the friends they made through Instagram along the way. Hillwalking is for geeks in anoraks. Don't you fancy sea kayaking?' she added.

'Too scared of sharks,' I countered.

'Cycling?'

'Kills your arse.'

'Running?'

'Couldn't cope with the chafing.'

We continued in that vein. Mountain biking? I look stupid in a helmet. Wild swimming? No one wants to see me in a wetsuit. Trail running? Too unfit. Triathlon? Not cool enough. Arctic expedition? Beard too wispy. Climbing? It's petrifying. Base jumping? I don't want to die.

This banter was all part of our light-hearted adventure rivalry. Becky had chosen not to join me on my peak-bagging challenge, deciding her dodgy knees weren't up to the climbing and that wild camping sounded way too much like slumming it. Instead she signed up for five 100km walking challenges across Britain, which she would use to fundraise for Dementia UK in memory of her grandfather Frank, who sadly had died after living with dementia. Her walks, organised by Action Challenge, would include regular food tents, support crews and hordes of new friends to walk with. Our running joke was that, while I would be slogging up some obscure mountain all alone to go bivvying in a bog, she'd be walking around the sunny Isle of Wight with a posse of hiking comrades, her hands full of free Haribo and Dairy Milk.

I was happy, however, to be going solo and unsupported. This would unashamedly be my challenge and my challenge alone. I was raring to go. With my 90 days off, it was vaguely feasible to attempt to tick off every 2,000ft mountain in England and Wales, known colloquially as the 'Nuttalls' after the authors of the guidebooks. I knew it would be tough. Two hundred and fifty-six mountains in England; 190 mountains in Wales; 1,047 miles to walk; 277,789 feet to ascend; 1,095,250 steps to take – the stats, if you stuck religiously to the books' routes, were daunting. In addition, as a quick bit of research revealed, no one had ever completed the Nuttalls so quickly. I had accidentally set my sights on a peak-bagging record – and it felt right.

The whole idea was up my street. How did I know? Because during my late 20s, despite a phase of self-indulgent depression, peak-bagging had become my favourite hobby. On free weekends, whenever I could muster up the energy, I'd throw my tent and hiking gear into the car and drive up the M6 to Cumbria to switch off from my Birmingham-centric existence and go wild camping in the fells. My mission back then was to climb the 'Wainwrights' – the 214 mountains featured in the seven pictorial guides by iconic writer Alfred Wainwright. Buoyed by nostalgic childhood memories of family pilgrimages to climb Cat Bells and walk around Derwentwater, I was obsessed with Lakeland and ticked off the entire list.

I loved every minute of it. In the city I felt agitated and frustrated, but out walking and camping in the wild places of the Lake District I was happy and free. It was as if I was tapping into something intrinsic, like an ancestral yearning to be connected to landscape and nature. I found the process of putting one foot in front of the other both therapeutic and healing. It cleared my head, helped me de-stress, and put life's little problems into perspective.

Similarly, the unpredictability of the outdoors was life-affirming. It was such a contrast to the routine and control of everyday life. I loved the way that one minute there was beautiful sunshine, the next there was snow; one minute I was on the path, the next I was hopelessly lost; one minute everything was going well, the next I was staring danger in the face. It was exhilarating.

I loved so many other aspects of hiking too. I enjoyed testing myself, going outside my comfort zone and feeling as if I'd really accomplished something. After all, what better sense of achievement could there be than from self-propelling yourself to the top of a mountain? The exercise gave me a real buzz and I relished the opportunity to get fitter and live more healthily, while the simplicity of my only goal for the day being to walk from A to B always gave life a wonderful clarity. And then, of course, there was the fresh air, the wildlife, the escapism, and the way the view from a summit could make my soul sing. To summarise, I was hopelessly, utterly in love with hiking.

My secondary motivation behind taking on the challenge was to deliberately detach myself from the internet, social media and my phone. Don't get the wrong impression, though. I wasn't some iPhone junkie who couldn't go three minutes without uploading a pouting selfie to Instagram, before sobbing uncontrollably because it got only 12 'likes'. And my challenge wasn't a weird version of going technology cold turkey, escaping to the hills beyond the reach of 4G in an attempt to detox from obsessively watching funny-cat videos on YouTube. I didn't even use my phone that much compared with many people. But, even so, I was worried about my creeping tech addiction. I could sense myself getting hooked and I didn't like it. I didn't want to be incapable of going five minutes without checking my apps; to judge my self-worth by how many followers I had; to reduce my social interactions to on-screen 'likes' rather than face-to-face conversations; to constantly waste hour after hour in a black hole of Facebook-feed scrolling; or to become more interested in getting a killer pic 'for the Gram' rather than being mindful and living in the moment.

Instead, I longed to switch off from the stress of never-ending notifications; to wake up on a mountain and look first at a sunrise, not a screen; to relearn how to spend time in quiet self-reflection rather than feeling compelled to stare at a little black box of entertainment. However, I wasn't going to delete my social-media accounts or throw away my iPhone. In fact, I was planning to take my phone with me into the hills for its GPS maps. But, as an experiment in self-improvement, I challenged myself to conquer my phone addiction. I planned to do so with a self-imposed rule for my challenge: all phone use, including calls, texts and internet, was banned while I was in the mountains, except for 30 minutes each evening to send 'All is well' messages and to post photos to Facebook, Twitter and Instagram. That way I felt I could keep my worrying family happy and still document my travels on social media, but in a fashion that would directly tackle my phone addiction. I also reasoned that learning the self-control to limit my phone usage, rather than cut it out completely, would be a more relevant lesson for everyday life. Was less phone time going to lead to more happiness? I was convinced it would.

'So you're definitely going for it then, this mountain challenge of yours?' Becky asked.

'I can't back out now – I've already told so many people about it.'

'You've still got time to change your plans to something cooler.'

I laughed. Who cared if climbing the Nuttalls wasn't cool? It was happening – 446 mountains in six months, the hillwalking odyssey of a lifetime. I was going to be the biggest hiking geek in the whole of Britain.

CHAPTER 3

ORGANISED CHAOS

I found myself wondering whether I should start my adventure in nothing but a pair of Union Jack boxer shorts. And maybe a pair of socks to stuff down the front of them. What can I say? It gets cold in the mountains.

One of my favourite adventure books is *Free Country* by George Mahood, who cycled from Land's End to John O'Groats without spending a single penny. Oh, and he set off wearing only a pair of Union Jack boxer shorts. No other clothes. Without his phone or wallet. Without a bike. With no plans whatsoever – no route, no timescale, no accommodation. But he still made it across the length of Britain courtesy of the generosity and kindness of the public, who clothed him, housed him, fed him, and gifted him a series of rusty, half-broken bikes. It is a hilarious book. In fact, if I were you, I'd stop reading this drivel and buy *Free Country* instead. It is way funnier. Anyway, back to the point, George undertook an adventure of going with the flow and seeing what each day brought. It brought chaos – but in a good way.

That approach appealed to me. Unpredictability was one of the things I loved about adventure. Not knowing what was around the corner was exciting and exhilarating – and, in the past, I'd often found that the best parts of an adventure were when things went wrong, or your plans changed last minute, or you veered off the expected course. I wanted, therefore, to keep my planning to a bare minimum. I wanted to be flexible and adaptable, and free to follow my nose. And I wanted to embrace rather than resist the unpredictability. I wasn't after chaos, though. What I needed was organised chaos.

I sat down at my computer, determined to start planning my adventure. My internet search history progressed like this: 'George Mahood author', '*Free Country* adventure book', 'Union Jack boxer shorts', 'Union Jack underwear' and, somehow, I ended up stuck on a Google images page with photo after photo of hot girls in Union Jack bikinis. It was very easy to get distracted by the internet. I was procrastinating. The thought of going on my big adventure filled me with a buzzing sense of excitement; but the thought of planning said adventure filled me with a mind-numbing sense of boredom. It all felt a bit too much like hard work. But I forced myself to get serious. I needed to stop thinking about quirky adventure gimmicks and instead start planning my expedition properly. There was no way you could climb 446 mountains in six months on your days off from work without a decent level of planning.

An encounter of years gone by popped into my head as I wrote 'Mountain Challenge: Planning' in bold at the top of a Word document. When I walked the GR20 in Corsica with my friend Joe, we met a German hiker in a mountain refuge. He had the most incredibly detailed plan for his walk in his notebook – virtually a minute-by-minute timetable for the route, what to expect, where to get supplies, how many miles to hike and metres of ascent to complete, where to stay for the night and so on and so forth. I half expected it to include timings for when to take a dump. While the safety measures and degree of preparation were to be commended, it seemed to drain the sense of adventure out of the experience. The recollection was a timely reminder that I never wanted to be like that.

After much time-wasting, I decided my first task was to familiarise myself with the two volumes of *The Mountains of England and Wales* by

John and Anne Nuttall, the Cicerone guidebooks that my challenge
was based upon. I studied them carefully, as well as the accompanying
www.nuttalls.com website, and kept notes on my laptop.

There were 446 Nuttalls – defined as 'any summit of 2,000ft or
more which rises above its surroundings on all sides by at least 50ft' –
for me to complete: 256 in England and 190 in Wales, split across 26
distinct mountainous regions categorised by John and Anne (see map
on pages vi–vii). Geographically, the peaks were pretty spread out,
ranging from the Cheviots on the Scottish border to Dartmoor on
the south coast to the Rhinogs on the western coast of Wales. Luckily,
three of the main regions in England were within an hour or so of
my house – the Lake District, the North Pennines and the Yorkshire
Dales – while the Peak District was only three hours away. In Wales
the mountains were focused predominantly in the Snowdonia ranges
of the north, as well as the Brecon Beacons to the south and a few
out-on-a-limb peaks in central Wales.

The books helpfully detailed 107 day-walks, complete with route
descriptions, maps and background information, that would take the
reader to every summit. This was a veritable gold mine of handy
advice for my challenge. But there was one small problem. I had
only 90 days to play with in which to complete the 107 walks – in
addition, for some trips, I needed to factor in time to drive hundreds
of miles.

I wasn't too worried, however. I was confident I could shave off
17 days using a few simple tactics. For starters, a handful of the
guidebook's walks – such as a four-mile route up Flinty Fell in the
North Pennines and a two-mile climb of Foel Cwm Sian Llŵyd in
the Berwyn mountains – could easily be ticked off in half a day.
Next, I intended to save loads of time and mileage through wild
camping and hitchhiking. By sleeping high in the hills, I could
avoid unnecessary descents and long walks out of the mountains;
and, by hitchhiking back to my car, I could potentially walk linear
routes to efficiently bag the most peaks in the quickest time. In the

Brecon Beacons, for example, where the 23 Nuttalls stretch out on a relatively straight east–west axis, I estimated that by sleeping under the stars and blagging a ride I could complete the guidebook's seven suggested routes in just three days. I was anxious, though, not to reduce my challenge to a robotic trudge, treating the mountains like a joyless assault course to be completed as fast as possible. Wild camping and hitchhiking would, I hoped, be an adventurous addition to the mission, while efficient route-planning would simply be a clever approach that didn't ruin the pleasures of being out in the mountains.

My final strategy was to group together my days off from work, meaning I could go on longer expeditions – up to six days in a row – and thus minimise the hours I'd spend driving to and from mountain ranges. Luckily, this was possible with my Fix the Fells fundraising job, which involved a lot of home-working, writing grant applications, and thus proved extremely flexible. I was allowed to set my own timetable, within reason, and could generally work Monday to Wednesday one week and Wednesday to Friday the following week. Meanwhile, my freelance writing could be done in the evenings, on a train, in a motorway service station, on the toilet, or whenever and wherever I wanted. In total, I needed to complete 92 full days of work over the six months, the equivalent of working four days a week for 23 out of 26 weeks, with the remaining three weeks taken as annual leave.

Thankfully, both my jobs had high degrees of flexibility. Nonetheless, sorting out my diary was still an absolute nightmare. It felt like trying to fit a square peg into a round hole. I was juggling so many things – my Fix the Fells job, writing commitments (including a 100-page commission for an NGO in Berlin), family get-togethers such as my dad's 60th-birthday party, weekends away, and all the other paraphernalia that comes with normal life. To complicate matters significantly, we were due to be moving from our tiny flat in Cockermouth to a two-bedroom house down the road. But eventually, after multiple rounds of jiggling things around and attempting to squeeze mountain trips between other commitments, I managed to get my calendar in order. I had a list of 82, not 90, mountain dates booked in: a two-week stint of annual leave for a big trip to Snowdonia in August, plus five blocks of 3 days, one of 4 days, two of 5 days, two of 6 days, and 27 ad hoc spare days. My start date would be Thursday, 16 March, and my end date, presuming I made it that far, would be Saturday, 16 September. I knew it would have to be flexible and that things would almost certainly change over time. But it was a start. A good start.

It wasn't exactly a master plan, though. The dates were generally not matched up to walks – and that was deliberate for two reasons. First, I hadn't actually figured out how I would fit 107 walks into 82 days. Instead, I intended to go with the flow, conscious that so many factors – the weather, my state of mind, the terrain, my physical strength – would affect progress day by day and trip by trip. Second, my plan was to chase the sun. I would decide at the last minute on my destination, selecting the region with the most sunshine – or, more accurately, the least rain – on the Met Office website. There was no point in climbing in storms in Snowdonia if it was tropical in Dartmoor, or vice versa.

This approach would make my challenge somewhat disjointed. A traditional adventure is usually a non-stop journey from A to B – a walk across a desert, a paddleboard down a river, a cycle around the world. My adventure, conversely, would be stop-start; continually starting, then stopping when I returned to work, only to start up again. This on-off approach would also mean I'd constantly dip in and out of different geographical regions. It might take several trips, for example, to complete all of the Nuttalls in the Yorkshire Dales. And, when I had six days off work in a row, I might be forced to take on a somewhat disorderly expedition, completing two days of walking in the Cheviots, followed by three in the North Pennines and one in the Lake District. Naturally, I would try to bulk mountains together in a geographically logical manner. But, by chasing the weather and constantly returning to work, there would inevitably be a random element to my schedule. Or, in other words, a Spirograph would probably be needed to plot my travels throughout England and Wales. Organised chaos.

The amount of planning I needed to do, however, was significantly reduced by locating my challenge in Britain. There were no flights to book, no visas to apply for, no foreign currencies to exchange, no travel vaccinations needed, no bookings required for accommodation, and no problems with my camping gas being mistaken for a bomb by airport security staff. In fact, the only complicated planning issue was trying to complete the Nuttalls so quickly alongside my day job. If I'd opted for a slower approach, it would've been pretty damn simple. After all, it wasn't rocket science. Read guidebook, download map, print out hard copy back-up, drive to location, see mountain, climb up mountain, camp (optional), climb down mountain, tick off summit in guidebook, drive home, repeat. That's all it was. Anyone could do it. In fact, you could buy the books today, start tomorrow, and finish 446 summits later. All the mountains in England and Wales – how cool would that be?

Happy with the progress of my timetabling efforts, I turned my attention to more practical matters: equipment, safety, money and food. Again, my choice of adventure minimised the amount of preparation required in each of these areas. One of the brilliant things about hillwalking in Britain during the summer is that it's a cheap and safe activity, requiring few technical skills and not much equipment. There was no £10,000 carbon road-bike to buy; no expensive sea-kayaking safety course to complete; no support team to recruit and keep happy – it was absolutely ideal for me.

I raided the cupboard under the stairs and laid out all of my camping gear in the hallway outside my flat. I pretty much had everything I needed: a basic tent, a warm sleeping bag, an inflatable sleeping mat, a camping stove, gas canisters, brightly coloured sporks, an 80-litre backpack, several dry bags, and a large water container.

Some of the items of kit were battered and bruised. My 15-year-old veteran Lowe Alpine backpack, for example, had missing buckles, fraying fabric and leaking holes. But I didn't care. I was loyal to that bag. I was used to it and it was used to me. We were a good team. Together we'd reached mountain summits, braved storms and conquered challenges. It wasn't an item of equipment, it was a trusted comrade. And that's why it was coming with me.

The same could have been said for my tent, a Vango Banshee 200 that Becky had nicknamed 'Dennis' years ago for reasons long-forgotten. Maybe it was because, after a few nights inside it, you began to look like a bit of a 'menace'. It was green, though, not red and black. Anyway, I'd bought it for just £99 in 2011 and had used it, without any problems, on several trips. I loved it. Though technically a two-man tent, I found it the perfect size for me and my rucksack to cuddle up alongside each other, and the two-skin set-up had always kept the rain out. At 2.4kg it was heavier than I would've liked but, in the absence of a spare £600 for a 1kg Hilleberg tent, Dennis would have to do. A few improvements were required, however. One of the poles, which I'd snapped accidentally during a moment of rushed tent-erecting, needed replacing, and the tent storage bag was ripped to shreds.

I jotted down what I needed to buy: a tent pole, a tent bag and spare gas canisters. That was it. Oh, and two Anker portable powerpacks to enable me to fully charge my iPhone and thus ensure my OS Maps app was always amply juiced up. After five minutes on my laptop it was all ordered for just £45. Obviously, it was helpful that I already owned most of the kit required, but even if I'd had to buy everything from scratch, I'd still have got change out of £500. My desired status of big-adventure-on-a-shoestring was intact.

Next, I headed indoors and piled all of my hiking clothes on to my bed. Did I have everything I needed? I went through a mental checklist from head to toe: warm hat, cap, sunglasses, neck warmer, base layers, quick-dry T-shirts, micro-fleeces, down jackets, waterproof jacket, gloves, thermal trousers, running leggings, shorts, walking trousers, waterproof trousers and thick socks. I had everything.

Most of the clothing had seen better days, but I did have a few shiny new items that I hoped might give me the air of an adventurer worthy of a peak-bagging record. A few years previously, I'd struck up a friendship with a guy called Chris who did PR work for Berghaus. On the off chance, I tapped him up by email for some freebies and he managed to get me a bright blue Extrem rain jacket to keep me dry, a Reversa jacket to keep me warm, and a red hooded fleece to make me look like Little Red Riding Hood, the red Tellytubby, or a hiking legend, depending on your perspective.

The only thing I was missing was a sturdy pair of walking boots. I had some, of course, but they'd been decimated during my gap year. They were holier than the Bible. I loaded up the Cotswold Outdoor website, browsed through the boots section, and then almost fell off my chair when I saw the prices of the pairs I fancied. I was so shocked, an alternative idea immediately popped into my head.

'What did you do with that pair of Scarpa boots that made you cry?' I asked Becky.

'Dunno – are they in the shed? Or the boot of my car?' she replied.

Becky had worn the expensive boots only a couple of times before giving up on them, her blisters had been so bad.

'Do you still need them for anything?'

'Hell no, you couldn't pay me to put them on my feet again.'

'We're both size nine, aren't we? So can I have them?'

'Go for it – you can climb every mountain in England and Wales in a pair of women's hiking boots. Hee hee.'

I found them, tried them on, they fitted. Job done. So that was boots, clothing and camping equipment all sorted – and I'd spent only £45. That left me £955 for the rest of my challenge. I'd budgeted for £1,000 in total, a nice round figure. It was difficult to predict, but

I estimated I'd spend £750 on petrol, £100 on equipment and £150 on wet-weather accommodation. I excluded food from my calculations as I'd be eating at home anyway if I wasn't doing this challenge, so the net cost was nil. Perhaps £1,000 wouldn't be enough, but I liked it as a target. A big expedition at a small cost was an inspiring message to go with my modus operandi of integrating an epic adventure into an everyday life.

My phone rang, the name 'Dad' flashing up on the screen. I resisted the temptation to ignore it and picked up.

'How's it going?' he said.

'All good – I'm just preparing for my mountain challenge, getting my stuff together,' I answered.

'Have you got all the safety gear you need?'

'I think so – let me see, erm, I've got a compass, maps, safety whistle...'

'Yeah, but out of that list you only know how to use a whistle.'

I managed to convince my dad, who comes from a long line of worriers, that I did in fact know what I was doing. But he still insisted on buying me a personal locator beacon, a life-saving device that transmits your precise location to a global network of search-and-rescue satellites. It doesn't require a mobile signal and is easy to activate if you get into trouble. 'When you fall off a cliff or break your leg, you'll thank me for it' was the way Dad put it.

His worrying was rubbing off on me, too. Was I really prepared for what lay ahead? Were my skills up to scratch? A quick Google search, which revealed such national newspaper headlines as 'Lake District hikers warned as death toll triples to 30 in just a year' and 'Climbing Snowdon can be more dangerous than Everest, warns expert', hardly helped my mindset. But I dismissed it all as negativity and re-engaged the logical side of my brain.

I did know what I was doing. Despite my self-deprecating persona, I was confident I was adequately prepared. I'd already solo climbed the Wainwrights in the Lake District, including numerous wild camping trips, so I was fully aware of what I was getting myself into. I was physically fit and mentally strong; I knew my limits and had a track record of sensible decision-making out in the wild; and I'd previously completed a navigation course at the Plas y Brenin mountain centre. Navigation was my weakest area. I knew how to take a compass bearing and measure 100m by counting steps, but I still found it remarkably easy to get disorientated in mist. Getting horribly lost was definitely going to happen to me at some point. Perhaps I should do a navigation refresher course? But I decided against it because I had an ace up my sleeve. The OS Maps app, which uses GPS to pinpoint your exact location, would be my back-up plan if my compass skills let me down. A subscription cost only £20 per year and gave me access to all the 1:25,000 maps I needed, as well as tools to design routes, print paper back-ups, download map tiles to my phone for offline use, and track my position when out in the mountains. Technology to the rescue.

My final planning task was to stock up on food for my wild camping trips. I already had a set menu in mind that I'd refined over the years, focusing on items that kept well, were lightweight and could cope with being thrown around in a backpack. I never opted for freeze-dried food or camping ready meals – they were way too expensive and way too disgusting. Instead, for my dinners I would alternate between spaghetti and rice, with a variety of sauces for flavour – Dolmio smoked bacon and tomato and Blue Dragon sweet chilli and garlic were my favourites – while a large chorizo sausage was my meaty addition. For lunches, I would have oatmeal crackers or tortilla wraps with peanut butter or Nutella, followed by raisin-nut mix, dried cranberries, dried apricots, banana chips and dates; for breakfasts, I'd rustle up porridge sachets and instant coffee. And every meal would be supplemented with large quantities of flapjacks, chocolates, sweets and cereal bars as sugary, energy-giving snacks.

I went to my local Aldi and loaded a trolley with the various items I needed. Back at home, I filled an empty kitchen cupboard with my adventure supplies, feeling happy with the contents. Now all I needed to do before each trip was select the right amount of food. This was always a tricky task, but achievable if I laid out each meal individually, with portion sizes I knew were right for me. I then planned to add a few extra snacks, a dried-soup sachet and a pack of instant noodles as emergency back-ups.

I closed the cupboard door, resisting the temptation to steal a Snickers bar before I'd walked even one metre, and thought, *I've done it, that's the adventure well and truly planned*. I'd completed all I could – and it felt great. All things considered, it had been remarkably simple. Anyone with half a brain could plan an adventure like this. It was going to cost less than £1,000. No technical skills or expensive equipment were needed. There was no complicated admin or painstaking research to undertake. The only entry requirement was a bit of outdoorsy determination and a willingness to give it a go.

CHAPTER 4

CALAMITY JAMES

Mountains 1–27

DATE	REGION	MOUNTAINS
Thursday 16 March	North Pennines Western Fells	Great Dun Fell 2,782ft (848m)[1] Little Dun Fell 2,762ft (842m) Cross Fell 2,930ft (893m) Bullman Hills 2,001ft (610m) Long Man Hill 2,159ft (658m) Round Hill 2,251ft (686m)
Friday 17 March	North Pennines Western Fells	Melmerby Fell 2,326ft (709m) Fiend's Fell 2,080ft (634m)
Saturday 18 March	North Pennines Western Fells	Backstone Edge 2,293ft (699m) Knock Fell 2,605ft (794m) Meldon Hill 2,516ft (767m)
Sunday 19 March	North Pennines Western Fells	Grey Nag 2,152ft (656m) Tom Smith's Stone Top 2,090ft (637m) Black Fell 2,178ft (664m)
Monday 20 March	North Pennines Western Fells	Thack Moor 2,000ft (610m) Cold Fell 2,037ft (621m) Bellbeaver Rigg 2,034ft (620m) Viewing Hill 2,129ft (649m)

DATE	REGION	MOUNTAINS
Tuesday 21 March	Lake District Western Fells	Grey Knotts 2,287ft (697m) Brandreth 2,346ft (715m) Base Brown 2,119ft (646m) Green Gable 2,628ft (801m) Great Gable 2,949ft (899m) Kirk Fell East Top 2,582ft (787m) Kirk Fell 2,631ft (802m) Fleetwith Pike 2,126ft (648m) Honister Crag 2,067ft (630m)

[1] All mountain heights quoted are taken from the list maintained by John and Anne Nuttall at www.nuttalls.com.

There's a character in *The Beano* called Calamity James who has buck teeth, bad hair and disastrous luck, and gets himself caught up in all manner of calamitous scenarios. Sometimes I think I'm the adventure equivalent of Calamity James. My teeth are relatively straight and my hairstyle isn't too bad, I hasten to add – but I do seem to have an uncanny knack of plunging into self-induced misfortune when at large in the great outdoors.

I've been lost, without food or tent, in the deepest, darkest depths of the Transylvanian mountains, forced to shelter in an eerie, abandoned hut and wait for Dracula to come and finish me off. I've been rumbled by the gamekeeper after accidentally wild camping in the country estate of vacuum billionaire James Dyson, and I've made botched attempts to scale walls and break into a Lake District youth hostel after losing my key card. I've been divebombed by a territorial buzzard and charged by angry cows; fallen head first into muddy quagmires and taken wrong turns into perilous gullies; dropped my car keys in the snow on Cadair Idris; broken my only spork in half on day one of an eight-day wilderness trek; and gone camping without my tent poles or sleeping bag or any food. If it can go wrong, it's happened to me.

And so, in true Calamity James style, my peak-bagging mission started in incongruous fashion. I had six days off work from Thursday to Tuesday and my original plan was to climb all 24 Nuttalls in the North Pennines' western fells. It would be a six-day non-stop expedition, with no returns home and five nights sleeping wild. But I wasn't feeling too confident – the weather, as appeared to be the case across the whole of England and Wales, was looking pretty darn gnarly. After 12 hours and six summits I'd seen only two views: a constant, all-encompassing white-out in front of me, and my drenched boots submerged in a muddy swamp below me. My pre-trip fantasies of clear blue skies, glorious wild camps and long lonely hikes over sun-gilded fells were quickly dashed, replaced instead by the harsh reality of trench foot, zero visibility and damp sandwiches. And I'd managed to forget any spare underwear, so I was stuck with one pair of boxers for almost a week.

It rained constantly for the first day. I felt like a drowned rat: cold, wet and miserable. The mountains dealt me a severe beating. The notoriously fierce Helm Wind was matched in intensity only by the thunderous rain, while the drowning hill fog made it difficult to maintain both accurate navigation and morale. This was about endurance more than enjoyment. But I still managed to tick off six tops.

I'd parked at Knock, a small hamlet east of Penrith at the base of the mountains, and tramped up the winding road to the other-worldly radar dome and masts of Great Dun Fell. Next, I slipped and slid on the Pennine Way's mill flagstones to Little Dun Fell and Cross Fell, the highest mountain in England outside of the Lakes, before concluding my virgin day of Nuttalls-bagging with an uninspiring loop of the minor bumps of Bullman Hills, Long Man Hill and Round Hill.

My saviour on that first rain-battered outing was Greg's Hut, a former miner's house turned rustic mountain bothy. I knew about it from the website of the Mountain Bothies Association, a charity which maintains 'simple shelters in remote country for the use and benefit of all who love wild and lonely places'. These huts or buildings, which number almost 100 across Britain, are unlocked and available for anyone to use free of charge – and they are perfect as a wet-weather alternative to wild camping. At the end of day one in the mountains, after being unceremoniously pounded by the North Pennines' rain and wind for hours on end, I simply couldn't resist the temptation. I wimped out of my original intention to sleep in Dennis and headed for the sanctuary of Greg's Hut.

I joyously entered through the big green door, as if leaping through a porthole into another dimension where swirling winds and driving rain could no longer hurt me. I felt unbelievably grateful for the simple protection of four walls. The communal room was adorned with hanging Nepalese prayer flags and a portrait of John 'Greg' Gregory, who died in a climbing accident in the Alps – a tragedy that inspired his friends to renovate the bothy in his memory. Crumbling white-washed walls turning green with damp and mould, an assortment of old plastic chairs of the type you'd expect to be discarded in a skip behind a school, and a solitary Tasmanian Devil cuddly toy gave the room an odd feel.

But I loved the bedroom, which was cosy and full of character. The centrepiece was a small wood-burner on a raised platform, complete with an assortment of metal contraptions for poking and prodding the fire and an accompanying single blackened glove that looked as if it had been in the bothy since it opened in 1972. I had a blaze going in no time, thanks to the bags of kindling, coal and logs stored to the side, and put into action a massive drying operation – virtually every item I had with me was soon drip-drying from the plastic line. I set water to boil on my camping stove and pulled up a plastic chair.

I leaned back and pointed my toes directly at the roaring fire, as I sipped on a hot chocolate. I looked around the room. The wooden sleeping platform was empty except for my laid-out mat and sleeping bag; candles that had melted into bizarre mangled shapes flickered on the shelf in front of the solitary window, casting shadows over the smoke-stained white walls; and the cooking shelf was cluttered with leftover gas canisters, packs of noodles, matches, lighters, old newspapers, discarded toys and a bottle of long-out-of-date tomato ketchup. It was a heart-warmingly, eccentrically ramshackle scene that was simultaneously homely and basic. The only sounds were the rush of the wind, the pounding of the rain, the crackle of the fire and the faint squeaks of the resident mouse, my companion for the night. I might've been battered by the conditions, but I felt happy to be actually doing this, to be following my dream and to be taking on an epic challenge.

I woke up startled, adrenalin and fear giving me a strange sense of alertness despite it being the middle of the night. What was that noise? A door was creaking and banging eerily in the wind. Is someone trying to get in? Oh God, I'm going to die. It's the ghost of a 19th-century miner; it's a deranged axe-wielding shepherd; it's the abominable Creature of Cross Fell. I turned on my headtorch and, tentatively, went to investigate. Of course, it was nothing alien, just the door slightly off the latch. I sorted it and, shivering, cocooned myself back in my toasty four-season sleeping bag.

The next morning I felt cagey and fearful, like a bruised boxer reluctant to return to the ring for another round of punishment. The weather had not changed one bit. In fact, it was looking even worse. I desperately wanted my kit to be as dry as possible for the day ahead, so I put my boots and walking leggings as close to the fire as I thought safe, and tended to my bubbling golden-syrup porridge. Two minutes later and the smell of burning tingled my nostrils. It wasn't the oats. I turned around to see smoke rising from my boots and leggings. I wanted my peak-bagging game to be 'on fire', just not literally. I couldn't recall the Bothy Code off the top of my head, but I presumed 'Don't burn the bothy down' was central to it. In a flash, I grabbed the Scarpas and leggings away from the fire, spurting water at them out of my bottle. The tongue of the left boot was badly singed, while the leggings had two large burn holes and the seam of the plastic zip was half melted. One night in the wild and I'd almost set the bothy ablaze. I imagined the resident mouse rolling his eyes, saying, 'Who is this incompetent buffoon?' 'I'll tell you exactly who it is,' I replied. 'It's Calamity James.'

With disaster narrowly avoided, I slid my feet into my horribly wet, and now scarred, boots and headed outside, the words 'Once more unto the breach' on my lips. Day two was an instantly forgettable trudge in low cloud over boggy, pathless moorland to Melmerby Fell and Fiend's Fell. The latter's name conjures up connections with an evil spirit – and the conditions were fittingly devilish and apocalyptic as I made it to the top. But there was one moment that broke the monotony and brought a smile to my face. I unexpectedly received a text message from my mum, who is not an avid phone user, saying 'Keep going, you can do it, I'm very proud, love Mum xx'. It gave me a disproportionately huge psychological boost as if a few simple words on an electronic screen could remotely give me the tight, loving, caring hug I needed.

Day three was a real struggle: heavy rain all day, no visibility whatsoever, and strong buffeting winds that almost knocked me off my feet. It was a long old slog through endless boggy moorland to bag the three Nuttalls of Backstone Edge, Knock Fell and Meldon Hill. It felt like battling against a stormy sea, with every peat hag another line of crashing waves to negotiate. Capsizing or drowning seemed like a distinct possibility at times in that muddy, hellish quagmire – and I didn't even get to see High Cup Nick, which my Nuttalls guidebook described as the 'finest' glaciated valley in England.

After a further night of refuge courtesy of Greg and his hut, I woke early and marched out of the rain-battered hills back to my car at Knock. I turned the heating on full blast, stripped off in the back seats and groaned with pleasure as I pulled on a set of fresh, dry clothes. Then I scoffed down three flapjacks, breathed a long sigh of relief, as if to compose myself, and consulted my guidebooks.

I drove to a lay-by on the A689, close to the town of Alston. It was still raining and I was feeling a bit low. I was tired and grumpy and the last thing I felt like doing was plodding through the clag to another muddy, uninspiring mountain. *Am I enjoying this? Is it a terrible, terrible idea, after all?* Part of me just wanted to go home, put on my pyjamas and watch Netflix on the sofa wrapped up in a duvet. But that wasn't an option. So, somewhat reluctantly, I shoved my feet into my horribly damp boots, grabbed my backpack and started plodding wearily over the grouse moors to tick off the summits of Grey Nag, Tom Smith's Stone Top and Black Fell.

I made it to the three summits, benefiting from absolutely no views whatsoever, and began descending gently north-east towards my car as the rain continued to soak me through. As I followed the swollen Gillerdale Burn downhill from Black Fell, dusk was arriving in that lonely, forgotten valley – and I was thinking how utterly boring the North Pennines were. But then, out of the blue, the white-out lifted and the downpours ceased. Birds sang triumphantly, as if celebrating the ending of the rain. The break in the mist suddenly revealed the surrounding mountains. It felt like the unveiling of a secret the North Pennines had chosen to share only with me. I whispered, 'Thank you' under my breath and smiled. And then it started to rain again.

Unable to stomach the prospect of a wet wild camp, I booked myself into Haggs Bank Bunkhouse in Nentsberry for the night and luckily managed to get a five-person room to myself. I had the best shower in the world ever and then had ten hours of glorious, uninterrupted sleep in a real bed. Feeling refreshed and rejuvenated, I spent the following day driving around and climbing four of the random tops in the North Pennines' western fells I had left to complete. It was a stop-start, strange kind of a day. It went like this: drive to Thack Moor, climb up, climb down, back in the car; drive to Cold Fell, climb up, climb down, back in the car; drive to Bellbeaver Rigg/Viewing Hill, climb up, climb down, and job done. It was an unnatural way to go about a day of walking. Only an obsessive peak-bagger like me would find themselves in such a predicament.

But I really enjoyed it. One night of good sleep and I felt like a new man – strong, determined, up for the challenge. I relished the exercise and the flow of happiness endorphins it delivered, while the absence of hill fog meant I was treated to pleasant views of the rolling Pennines greenery. I even spotted a deer on Cold Fell, its outline silhouetted on the skyline as it leaped effortlessly through rough, tussocky grass at a speed I wished I could match; and on Thack Moor I found a set of cartoon reindeer ear-muffs in the middle of nowhere under some heather, a moment that brought a smile to my face. It was a good day in the fells.

The North Pennines weather, however, had the last laugh. As I tramped along an old mine road, returning from Viewing Hill to my car, a horrible sleet storm struck. The wind howled and swirled, my body shivered, and a thousand tiny balls of ice pummelled me from all directions, as if I'd walked into a merciless paintballing ambush. I decided there and then I'd had enough of the bloody North Pennines. I was going home.

✳   ✳   ✳

The Daily Adventure Journal of James
18/03/17: Have you ever found yourself squatting, trousers around your ankles, trying to take a shit on a rain-blasted mountainside while an inquisitive Swaledale sheep stares at you? Trust me, it's not easy. The more you strain, the more the sheep's judging eyes put you off. And the wetter and colder and more wretched you feel. This happened to me in the North Pennines today. It was a brutal way for my hopes of a glamorous adventure to be dashed.

19/03/17: If I ever meet the person at Ordnance Survey who has created the OS Maps app, I'll just have to snog them – even if it's a middle-aged, slightly overweight, male IT worker with bad skin. As in, properly snog them, sloppily with tongues. I won't be able to control my lustful gratitude. The app has got me out of numerous spots of bother already on this challenge, when the clag has descended and I've got woefully disorientated. Mr Ordnance Survey IT worker, I think I love you.

❉   ❉   ❉

I had 24 hours left before my next stint in the office, having cut my Pennines expedition short by a day – but I still needed to bag more Nuttalls. I woke up, opened my bedroom blinds, and was greeted by bright sunshine across the Lake District. I'd struck gold. It was as if my penance had been served in the sodden North Pennines and now the mountain gods were providing a gift from the heavens in recognition of the hardship I'd endured.

I got ready in a rush and jumped in my car, destined for the Honister Pass. Blue skies, broken only by wisps of cloud, were dazzling in comparison with the monotonous grey blanket I'd become accustomed to. A sprinkling of snow clung to the knobbly tops as I drove in excited anticipation along the shores of Crummock Water and Buttermere. It was crisp and cold, with a biting wind. Winter had not yet relinquished its grip on Lakeland.

Similarly, Calamity James's grip on my peak-bagging adventure had not been surrendered. I opened the boot of my car to discover my rucksack was missing. I must've left it at home in the hallway. What an idiot. I weighed up the damage. No packed lunch, no gloves, no hat, no compass, no map, no waterproof jacket and no cash to buy supplies at the slate-mine café. But I did have my warm gear, my boots and a solitary Mars bar. Was it safe to carry on or should I drive back to Cockermouth? The latter seemed totally unpalatable.

I scrabbled together an assortment of gear and supplies from my messy boot: an old, bright pink rain jacket; two long-forgotten gingerbread men; an effeminate camera case, which served as my backpack replacement; and a pair of crusty Slazenger socks for makeshift gloves. So, wearing a garish pink jacket, with socks on my hands and what looked like a handbag over my shoulder, I started climbing steeply towards the summit of Grey Knotts. I was woefully undersupplied and committing heinous crimes against fashion. I could see the headlines: 'Is this man the dumbest fellwalker in Britain?', 'Idiotic hiker lambasted by rescuers after heading into fells without basic supplies' and 'Self-proclaimed adventurer exposed as peak-*blagger*'.

It felt liberating to be in the Lake District. I'd found the North Pennines a tad underwhelming. Naturally, the weather had been a dampener, quite literally, on my experience. Perhaps if the sun had shone I'd have found a desolate charm in those lonely rolling hills. But, as it was, my memories were of never-ending peatland bogs, energy-sapping heather and featureless grouse moors with their lines of shooting butts and strange silences. In comparison, the rocky peaks and shimmering lakes of Lakeland seemed mystical and dramatic – and I was confident the route ahead to Great Gable was not going to disappoint.

The clue is in the name. Great Gable is unquestionably one of the *great* Lakeland fells, a towering mass of rock and crags and cliffs. Captivating to look at – an unbroken, devilish pyramid from the south, the dome of a sleeping, curled-up giant from the north – it is a mountain that captures the imagination and fuels passions; a place that demands respect and admiration, and gets it in spades.

With three tops – Grey Knotts, Brandreth and Base Brown – under my belt, I reached the spur leading to Green Gable. I didn't know where to look. Resplendent scenery surrounded me. I slowly swivelled a full 360 degrees, noticing familiar landmarks – the Langdale Pikes, Ennerdale Forest, Buttermere. Like old friends, they brought a smile to my face, triggering happy memories of Lakeland expeditions of years gone by. Snapping out of my daydreams, I ascended gently to the 2,628ft top of Green Gable before descending red scree to Windy Gap and then snaking up a steep, boulder-strewn path to the Great Gable war memorial.

After a scramble along a line of cairns heading north-west, I emerged at Beck Head, where I found a rock to stand on and ogle the scenery. I still had four Nuttalls to climb – Kirk Fell East Top, Kirk Fell, Fleetwith Pike and Honister Crag – but there was no way I was going to tramp speedily past this sight. You couldn't Photoshop it any better. Wastwater was spread out majestically in the valley below, its surface dancing in the sunlight. Cloud shadows rolled over the heathery slopes of Illgill Head and Yewbarrow, framing the lake perfectly. A gap opened in the sky and God beams, like spotlights from above, illuminated the intricate puzzle of dry-stone walls and fields in Wasdale Head. They glowed an exquisite bright green and I laughed at the sheer awesomeness of where I was and what I was doing. Lingering thoughts of wind and rain and wet feet and white-outs quickly dissipated. 'This is what I came for,' I said to myself. 'I think I'm going to enjoy this challenge.'

CHAPTER 5

A DOUBLE-EDGED SWORD

Mountains 28–46

DATE	REGION	MOUNTAINS
Friday 31 March	Cheviots	The Cheviot 2,674ft (815m) Comb Fell 2,139ft (652m) Hedgehope Hill 2,342ft (714m)
Saturday 1 April	Cheviots	Bloodybush Edge 2,001ft (610m) Cushat Law 2,018ft (615m) Windy Gyle 2,031ft (619m)
Sunday 2 April	North Pennines Eastern Fells	Middlehope Moor 2,008ft (612m) Killhope Law 2,208ft (673m) The Dodd 2,014ft (614m) Flinty Fell 2,014ft (614m) Dead Stones 2,329ft (710m)
Monday 3 April	North Pennines Eastern Fells	Burnhope Seat 2,447ft (746m) Harwood Common 2,356ft (718m) Great Stony Hill 2,323ft (708m) Three Pikes 2,136ft (651m) Chapelfell Top 2,306ft (703m) Fendrith Hill 2,283ft (696m) Westernhope Moor 2,215ft (675m)
Tuesday 4 April	North Pennines Western Fells	Bink Moss 2,031ft (619m)

Peak-bagging is a strange subculture, an underground world that seems to simultaneously bemuse, fascinate, amuse and inspire others. Consider for a minute: who are these people who spend their precious spare time ticking off obscure lists of mountains? What drives them to do what they do? Is their approach adventurous and admirable, or does it suck the romance and heart out of mountain-climbing?

My stance is that peak-bagging is a double-edged sword. The positives are that it gives you purpose, an overarching mission to bring structure and meaning to your hillwalking; it encourages you to explore new places and have new experiences; and it offers a wonderful sense of achievement when you reach a milestone, or indeed the finish. But the negatives are that you can easily become a slave to the list, an unhinged fanatic slogging up a boring mountain in a loveless box-ticking exercise. It is a fine line between intrepid mountain-lover and deranged oddball.

I've met numerous peak-baggers who could fit into both categories, depending on how you look at it. In the intrepid class, I've had the pleasure of meeting Alan Hinkes, the only Briton to have 'bagged' the eight-thousanders, a list of the world's 14 mountains over 8,000m; and Steve Birkinshaw, a Cumbrian fellrunner who miraculously completed all 214 Wainwrights in six days and 13 hours. They are far from the only inspiring peak-baggers out there. Rambler Rob Woodall visited all 6,190 trig points in the UK in a marathon 14-year hiking mission; Myrddyn Phillips climbed every Nuttall in Wales 12 times, once in each month of the year; in 2016 Jenny Hatfield became the first woman to complete all 1,556 Marilyns across the UK; and between 2014 and 2017 Karen Forster, 52, of County Durham not only completed the Wainwrights but did a headstand on all 214 summits. In Scotland, meanwhile, Steven Fallon completed an incredible 15 rounds of the Munros; Lisa Trollope and Libby Kerr ran up all 282 Munros in 77 days, cycling between them for good measure; and Richard Lyon played his fiddle on top of 150 Munros and Corbetts, with a different tune for each summit. I love peak-bagging, so I admire and respect such endeavours, no matter how maverick. But I can also easily comprehend why some outsiders might see these eccentric and obsessive exploits as akin to nerdy train-spotting or dorky stamp-collecting.

Firmly in the oddball camp of peak-bagging was a hiker I once met ticking off Wainwrights near Scoat Fell in Ennerdale. He was the perfect stereotype of a geeky peak-bagger: male, middle-aged, white, bearded, anorak-wearing and socially awkward. I said, 'Hi' and he proceeded to launch, unprompted, into a monologue about how he was taking photos of all 214 Wainwright cairns. He showed me a handful of images on his camera. They were literally zoomed-in shots of piles of stones, no views or backgrounds whatsoever. When he spoke about the cairns a subtle, but noticeable, excitement seemed to descend upon him.

Not all peak-baggers are aroused by cairns, however – or, at least, I don't think they are. I've never asked them directly, but let's presume not. Most peak-baggers are perfectly 'normal'. They don't wear anoraks on Saturday nights, or only talk about GPS devices, or salivate over contour lines. Over recent months I've met a number of peak-baggers who don't fit the traditional mould: cool and hip experience-chasing millennials, young and intrepid solo female hikers, and fascinating people from ethnic minorities. It has been refreshing and exciting to meet a new wave of enthusiasts.

I haven't been able to find any official data on whether the profile of peak-baggers is changing, nor establish whether peak-bagging in general is increasing or decreasing in popularity. No such evidence exists, as far as I can tell. Are more young people, women and ethnic minorities taking part in peak-bagging than ever before? Or are they just more visible because of blogs and social media? And is peak-bagging genuinely a growing movement or has Instagram just made it look that way? My impression and hope is that peak-bagging is growing in popularity, especially among new demographics. In my eyes, that would be a fantastic thing – but I can't say for sure that it really is happening.

Anecdotally, however, it seems to be true. In the Lake District, for example, I have conducted some ludicrously non-scientific and unofficial research into the topic – and it appears to back up my impressions. I ran a poll in a Wainwright-bagging Facebook group with 12,500 members. The results overwhelmingly supported the notion that walking the Wainwrights was both increasing in popularity and attracting new types of walkers such as young women, while the group's statistics showed that 40 per cent of members were female and 20 per cent were aged 13–34. As one witty group member commented on my post: 'It's not all MAWMWBs (middle-aged white men with beards) these days.'

On the flip side, other prominent Lake District experts expressed concerns that social media might give a distorted impression, with one suggesting the fells were still populated by 98 per cent white people and 65 per cent older men. In the absence of any official data, no one really knows, I'm afraid.

Peak-bagging as a discipline was born in Scotland in the 1890s with the publication of Sir Hugh Munro's iconic list of Scottish mountains. Since then, peak-bagging has been popularised around the world, spawning myriad different challenges and a dedicated army of enthusiasts. The most intrepid tick off a challenge like the Seven Summits, the highest peak in every continent. The geekiest do something eccentric, like climb all the English tops in alphabetical order. On a spectrum from totally weird to totally epic, I felt my challenge was somewhere in the middle.

In Britain there are a number of rival logs of hills and mountains. The Nuttalls, my chosen tick-list, is based on *The Mountains of England and Wales* books by husband-and-wife duo John and Anne Nuttall. They define a mountain as 'any summit of 2,000ft or more which rises above its surroundings on all sides by at least 50ft' or, in metric terms, 610m and 15m. I felt grateful to John and Anne for that 50ft-rise criterion, which they used to avoid 'including an excessive number of un-named minor bumps which were unworthy of elevation to mountain status'. That saved my legs a hell of a lot of effort. But if I'd chosen a different list, I'd have saved even more.

There is, in fact, no universally accepted definition of a mountain in Britain. Two thousand feet is often cited as the required height, but not always – and there is little consensus about anything else. To be considered a separate mountain, distinct from its surroundings, does a summit need to have a drop of 15m on all sides, or 30m, or some other arbitrary figure? And is 2,000ft the correct qualifying height, or should it be 600m, or is relative height far more important than absolute height? Many questions, few definitive answers.

Different authors have taken different stances on mountain lists over the years. Alfred Wainwright used a poetic, rather than mathematical, classification system for the Lakeland fells. No one knows exactly why he included some mountains and not others – and some of his choices do seem rather odd. But it seems to me that he wrote about the 214 fells he thought worthy of inclusion by virtue of their beauty, drama and significance, regardless of their height. Conversely, the Scottish mountains are classified specifically on height. The Munros are simply over 3,000ft, the Corbetts are 2,500ft to 3,000ft with a 500ft drop on all sides, and the Grahams are 2,000ft to 2,500ft with a 150m drop on all sides. It's getting a tad confusing, right? We're only getting started.

Across England and Wales, the Marilyns and Hewitts are the main rivals to the Nuttalls list. Compiled by Alan Dawson in his book *The Relative Hills of Britain*, the Marilyns are hills and mountains of *any height* with a drop of 150m or more on all sides, thus prioritising relative height over absolute height. There are 333 across England and Wales, with some interesting results – the great Bowfell in the Lake District is not included, but the high points of the Cotswolds and Chilterns are. The name Marilyn is a pun designed to coincide with the Scottish term Munro. (Marilyn Monroe – get it?) This is slightly ironic, considering the hobby is taken up by people (me excluded, obviously) who have never in their wildest dreams spoken to an attractive blonde. But, as implied by the joke, Marilyn certainly did have notable 'prominences', so it does work.

As a concession, however, Dawson also compiled a list of the so-called Hewitts (an acronym for a Hill in England, Wales or Ireland over Two Thousand feet), which defines a mountain as 2,000ft high with a drop on all sides of 30m. Dawson claimed such an approach avoided 'a large number of relatively boring tops' included in the Nuttalls. The 316 Hewitts in England and Wales, therefore, are a subset of the Nuttalls. A slight expansion of the Hewitts are the Simms, which are 600m or 1,968.5ft in height with a 30m drop.

I chose the Nuttalls list over all others mainly because, well, I already owned the guidebooks. So, in true penny-pinching adventurer style, that was £26 in Amazon purchases saved. But John and Anne's register of mountains also seemed the most comprehensive, with the smallest drop criterion at 50ft and thus the highest number of tops. If I could complete all of the Nuttalls, I could truly say I'd climbed *every* mountain in England and Wales.

To complicate matters further, mountains can – believe or not – have their heights revised up or down. Over time the original Nuttalls list, pulled together using official Ordnance Survey data, has changed as enthusiasts have resurveyed marginal tops using highly accurate modern GPS devices. A few unlucky peaks have been stripped of their mountain titles, demoted from the elite like a football team dumped out of the Premiership into the obscurity of the Championship. Others have secured an improbable upgrade, like a team winning the crucial last game of the season. Bram Rigg Top in the Howgills, for example, fell an agonising 32cm short of the necessary 50ft rise – relegated on goal difference. Conversely, Thack Moor in the North

Pennines edged into the top tier by a mere 2cm – promoted by an injury-time winner.

In fact, the number of Nuttalls actually changed halfway through my challenge. When I started there were 446, but by the time I had finished there were 445. In May 2017, Carnedd y Ddelw in the Carneddau range was demoted from the elite, after a new surveying expedition proved a rise of only 14m. But I still climbed it. I'd committed to climb 446 mountains. That number was seared into my brain. I was going to climb 446 mountains if it killed me – and I certainly wasn't going to let a bunch of technology-wielding geography geeks stop me.

'How many mountains is it in total?' asked Joe, my partner-in-crime on various adventures across Britain.

'In total, 446 – I've got my work cut out,' I replied. 'The books list 441 mountains, but there have been various summits added and deleted over time.'

'Imagine if you got to the very end, thought you'd finished, and then realised you'd miscalculated and missed one obscure top.'

'I'd just have to lie if that happened,' I joked. 'It doesn't quite have the same ring to it – I climbed every mountain in England and Wales, except one.'

'Actually, that's an interesting concept. Adventure is about the journey, not the destination, right? Your challenge should not be about box-ticking, it should be about authentically indulging yourself in the mountain life. So you should get to within 20ft of the final summit and stop, take a quiet moment of self-contemplation, and then turn around and head back down. That would be the legendary thing to do.'

'Get lost,' I laughed as I put the phone down and continued driving towards Northumberland National Park. I had five days off work in a row but my timetable was a little disjointed. I planned first to climb all six Nuttalls in the Cheviots over two days, followed by 12 Nuttalls in the North Pennines' eastern fells plus Bink Moss from the western fells over the following three days.

Ten hours after speaking to Joe I was sitting outside my tent on the banks of Harthope Burn. It was Friday night with no pints of lager or cheesy nightclubs in sight; no take-away boxes or DVD box-sets at the ready. Instead, I was perched on a mossy, lichened log, boiling up chorizo and tomato pasta and listening to the birdsong and the therapeutic rush of the stream.

I'd spent the day hiking in the Cheviots, a range of high-rounded, grassy hills that form the most northerly cluster of England's mountains. When I started from Langleeford and took the ridge up Scald Hill I was not in the zone. I was feeling ill, with a sore throat, a blocked nose and a distinct lack of energy. My mind was elsewhere too, buzzing with to-do lists of tasks at work and chores at home I had failed to complete now that every spare minute of my life was dedicated to peak-bagging. I tried to shake the worries out of my head, but I couldn't.

A long day of uncomplicated walking in sunny climes did the trick. I first climbed to the summit of The Cheviot, Northumberland's highest point at 2,674ft, before looping via the Pennine Way and a rough, pathless section over heather and groughs to pick up the ridge to the tops of Comb Fell and Hedgehope Hill. By the time I'd descended via the tors at Long Crags and Housey Crags, knobbly intrusions of rock that broke the grassy repetitiveness, I was feeling relaxed and happy. The de-stressing qualities of a long hike had unscrambled my brain and obliterated any nagging anxieties.

I slurped up soupy spaghetti and watched two birds swooping, diving and weaving effortlessly through the sky, their strange reverberating calls and whooshing dives shattering the silence. I sat still, letting the isolation and tranquillity roll over me. Then, out of nowhere, the narrator's introduction to *Bananaman* – a childhood cartoon favourite of mine – popped into my head.

'This is Eric, the schoolboy who leads an amazing double life. For when Eric eats a banana, an amazing transformation occurs. Eric is Bananaman. Ever alert for the call to action.'

I came up with my own version.

'This is James, the everyday man who leads an amazing double life. For when James goes on a hike, an amazing transformation occurs. James is Mountain Man. Ever alert for the call to adventure.'

It felt awesome that tense Home James had, once again, metamorphosed into high-spirited Mountain Man.

I hadn't turned my phone on all day and it felt great. No annoying PPI phone calls; no emails to respond to; no voicemails requiring action; no inane, time-wasting, irrelevant banter from WhatsApp groups; no social-media notifications from negative trolls slamming my latest blog post as 'nonsense' or 'irresponsibly inaccurate'. I'd always found my phone to be an incessant provider of stress – a little machine that forever added chores to my to-do list. But it couldn't have an adverse impact on my mental health when it was switched off. I was convinced that I had de-stressed so positively during my hike because my phone was off. It felt like a victory. James one, technology nil.

At 8am I decamped, returned to my car and drove south-west to the Wedder Leap picnic site in Upper Coquet Dale, delayed slightly by a road block of Highland cows. I climbed along quiet valleys and through moody forest to Uswayford Farm, before completing an out-and-back in rain to the two Nuttalls of Bloodybush Edge and Cushat Law. Next was a boot-squelching, boggy tramp to Windy Gyle, which lies on the border between Scotland and England, followed by a swift descent back to my car featuring lots of childish puddle-jumping. I camped on a patch of grass next to the car park, wondering whether I was being adventurous or just an irresponsible illegal camper.

I woke early, in order to avoid being spotted, and bade farewell to the Cheviots. I drove to Cowshill, a village at the top of Weardale, slap bang in the middle of the North Pennines Area of Outstanding Natural Beauty. My plan was to climb all 12 Nuttalls in the North Pennines' eastern fells in just two days, despite the guidebook suggesting four day-routes to tick them off. I already had a feasible

A DOUBLE-EDGED SWORD ❋

35-mile route planned, with one night of wild camping in the middle. I packed supplies into my large backpack and headed off, intently studying the paper copy of the map I'd printed off.

It was a long day of mindless, enjoyable plodding over windswept moorland, listening to the grouse I disturbed and daydreaming about the food I had to eat. It was cloudy but dry as I climbed Middlehope Moor, Killhope Law and The Dodd, before dropping into Nenthead to boil up a cup of tea with my camping stove at a tourist picnic spot. I almost certainly looked like a vagrant. From Nenthead's historic mining centre, I ascended good tracks to Flinty Fell and then battled on over pathless slopes to arrive at the summit of Dead Stones. It had turned into a glorious evening as I erected Dennis (that sounds wrong) next to the tall summit cairn. I boiled up tomato soup for dinner and listened to the staccato gargling calls of the ever-present grouse, as the setting sun created a striking sky over the distant, graceful trio of Cross Fell, Little Dun Fell and Great Dun Fell. I felt happy and privileged.

I woke before 6 the following morning, unzipped Dennis (that also sounds wrong) and poked my head out. I was greeted by a scene that filled my soul with joy. A big ball of fire, perfectly round, was rising slowly over gentle rolling hills, painting an ever-changing masterpiece of yellow, orange and red brushstrokes in the sky. I sat and watched, mesmerised. My time on Dead Stones had, ironically, made me feel anything but dead. I felt more alive than I had for years.

Perhaps energised by the sunrise, as if the sheer beauty had recharged my batteries, I smashed out six Nuttalls – Burnhope Seat, Harwood Common, Great Stony Hill, Three Pikes, Chapelfell Top and Fendrith Hill – in a super-efficient morning. It was far from spectacular walking, but the sense of escapism and isolation in the Pennines was charming. After a massive lunch, I marched up Westernhope Moor, my final Nuttall for the day, and then plodded for miles and miles north down the minor road from Swinhope Head before hitching west along the A689 back to my car. I had dinner

in a National Trust car park, drove to the High Force Hotel and, as dusk descended, tramped towards Holwick Scars to wild camp on the lower slopes of Bink Moss, tomorrow's target.

✳ ✳ ✳

The Daily Adventure Journal of James

01/04/17: Geese are evil. Pure evil. Avoid at all costs. I did see the 'Beware of Geese' sign at the farm in Uswayford but I thought it was a joke. I didn't expect to be chased out of the farmyard by a gaggle of hissing psychopaths. I felt like the weak little kid being hounded down the street by a gang of hooded bullies. Except these yobs had white feathers and orange beaks.

02/04/17: Cows are evil. Pure evil. Avoid at all costs. Back doing battle with my arch nemesis, the North Pennines, a herd of stubborn bovines blocked my way through fields. Perhaps it was paranoia but I swear they were giving me looks that said, 'One false move, buddy, and we're going to trample the shit out of you.' Or maybe it was, 'We know what you order in McDonald's – revenge is going to be sweet.' I gave them a very wide berth and tried to project an air that said, 'I've never eaten a burger in my life, honest.'

✳ ✳ ✳

I felt like a slave to the Nuttalls list as I trudged up dull Bink Moss, my final summit of this five-day expedition to the Cheviots and North Pennines. It was a bore, a 10½-mile slog over boggy grouse moors with absolutely no redeeming features. I was there only because of this challenge, doing it just to tick a box. Perhaps I was feeling negative as a result of the exertions of the previous days, or because I'd got precious little sleep the night before, wild camping above the grey crags of Holwick Scars in strong winds, or because a local farmer had given me dodgy looks after I spectacularly failed to tune in to his accent and consequently couldn't understand a single word he was saying.

I forded streams, crossed gates, hand-railed a ridge wall, battled against pathless swampy ground, negotiated peat hags and, finally, after what felt like hours of hard toil, arrived close to the top. Where was the cairn? I'd emerged on to a flat expanse of heather and knoutberry with no obvious summit. I checked my OS Maps app, realised I was slightly off and bee-lined for the marked spot height. Then I saw it. Not a cairn, not a trig point, but two wooden posts, each adorned with an upturned Muck Boot Company designer welly. From some angles, with the poles obscured by the foreground, it looked as if an aristocratic landowner with a predilection for £200-a-pair posh wellies was actually turned upside down head-first in the Pennines peat. It was so ludicrous I started laughing. And I remembered why I love peak-bagging, even on the most boring of mountains.

CHAPTER 6

DAY TRIPPER

Mountains 47–93

DATE	REGION	MOUNTAINS
Thursday 6 April	Lake District Far Eastern Fells	Hartsop Dodd 2,028ft (618m) Stony Cove Pike 2,503ft (763m) Thornthwaite Crag 2,572ft (784m) Gray Crag 2,293ft (699m)
Friday 7 April	Lake District Central Fells	Ullscarf 2,382ft (726m) Low Saddle 2,152ft (656m)
Saturday 8 April	Lake District Western Fells	Great Borne 2,021ft (616m) Starling Dodd 2,077ft (633m)
Monday 10 April	Lake District Western Fells	High Crag 2,441ft (744m) High Stile 2,648ft (807m) Red Pike 2,477ft (755m) Dodd 2,103ft (641m)
Friday 14 April	Lake District North-Western Fells	Hobcarton End 2,080ft (634m) Grisedale Pike 2,595ft (791m) Hobcarton Crag 2,425ft (739m) Crag Hill 2,753ft (839m) Sail 2,536ft (773m) Scar Crags 2,205ft (672m) Causey Pike 2,090ft (637m)

DATE	REGION	MOUNTAINS
Monday 17 April	Lake District Southern Fells	Pike of Blisco 2,313ft (705m) Great Knott 2,283ft (696m) Cold Pike 2,300ft (701m) Cold Pike West Top 2,241ft (683m) Cold Pike Far West Top 2,198ft (670m) Little Stand 2,428ft (740m) Crinkle Crags South Top 2,736ft (834m) Crinkle Crags 2,818ft (859m) Shelter Crags 2,674ft (815m) Shelter Crags North Top 2,543ft (775m)
Thursday 20 April	Lake District North-Western Fells	Robinson 2,418ft (737m) Hindscarth 2,385ft (727m) Dale Head 2,470ft (753m) High Spy 2,142ft (653m) High Spy North Top 2,080ft (634m)
Tuesday 25 April	Lake District North-Western Fells	Whiteside 2,320ft (707m) Whiteside East Top 2,359ft (719m) Hopegill Head 2,526ft (770m) Ladyside Pike 2,306ft (703m) Sand Hill 2,480ft (756m) Grasmoor 2,795ft (852m) Wandope 2,533ft (772m) Whiteless Pike 2,165ft (660m)
Friday 28 April	Lake District Northern Fells	Blencathra 2,848ft (868m) Gategill Fell Top 2,792ft (851m) Atkinson Pike 2,772ft (845m) Bowscale Fell 2,303ft (702m) Bannerdale Crags 2,241ft (683m)

'Day Tripper' by the Beatles was a criticism of 'weekend hippies', half-hearted enthusiasts who were unwilling to become 'full-time trippers' and only hardcore enough to get off their tits on acid on Fridays and Saturdays. Absolute pansies. I mean, what sort of namby-pamby can't hack a daily dose of LSD? I've never done drugs, I hasten to add, but when it comes to mountains I definitely have an addictive personality. I'm no 'weekend peak-bagger'. I'm all in, fully committed, utterly hooked. I'm a mountain junkie with a full-time habit.

Take me away from the mountains for long enough and I reckon I'd end up like Ewan McGregor when he goes cold turkey in *Trainspotting*, lying in a single bed, fidgeting, sweating, and screaming to my parents, 'Just one more score of Helvellyn, one more hit of Crib Goch, plllleeeeaase.' Mountains are my drug. I can't live without them. They give me a dizzying high and I'm addicted. I need them almost every day. But, thankfully, it is an addiction that doesn't have the usual side effects of forcing me to steal handbags off grandmas or live in a cardboard box. Sadly, however, I had to limit my mountain-drug use in April. I couldn't be a 'full-time tripper'. I'd have to settle for being a 'day tripper'. An absolute pansy.

I had a hectic month ahead of me, involving family gatherings, work events and an impending house move, so I could commit to only day trips of Nuttalls-bagging in the Lake District rather than longer expeditions further afield. It was a tad disappointing but such was life. And at least I was excited about exploring Lakeland.

After my adventures in the Cheviots and the North Pennines, I returned almost immediately to everyday life: going to work, doing the 'big shop', sleeping in my own bed, popping to town for coffee, putting the bins out, dealing with household admin, watching the football with my mates – all the usual stuff. The normality was soothing and it was also really useful to have some spare time to dedicate to adventure-planning.

I set myself a target of completing nine day-walks in the Lakes over the next four weeks. I'd do the hikes at the weekends or on odd days off work, generally on non-consecutive days and always returning home each night. I was to become a Lakeland day tripper. Such an approach meant I could better balance April's everyday duties with my Nuttalls mission. However, I was still really looking forward to getting on to the fells.

The Lake District has a special place in my heart, somewhere nostalgic and sentimental, linked to my family's annual pilgrimages to Borrowdale in the early 1990s. Those hazy days of jumping over dry-stone walls, running through fields, exploring becks, walking lofty ridges and climbing gnarly fells must've left an indelible imprint on my spirit. I was inextricably drawn to the Lakes. It always felt like my spiritual home.

I had a whopping 171 mountains to climb in the Lake District. That amounted to exactly two-thirds of all the Nuttalls in England and over a third of the peaks in my entire challenge. It was clear I'd be getting to know my beloved Lakeland even better. John and Anne, mirroring the geographical classifications used by Alfred Wainwright in his collection of guidebooks, detailed the 171 Lake District Nuttalls in 28 day-walks split across seven chapters: the northern fells, the north-western fells, the western fells, the central fells, the southern fells, the eastern fells and the far eastern fells. As they were all within close proximity of my home, I didn't need a complicated plan to tackle them. I would just go with the flow and head north, east, south or west depending on how the mood took me. William Wordsworth famously 'wandered lonely as a cloud' in the Lake District – I couldn't wait to do the same.

Unsurprisingly, I relished those spring days Nuttalls-bagging in the Lakes. From the blue slate cottages of Hartsop, where a farmer's marking spray had left a group of Herdwicks looking like fluffy balls of pink candyfloss, I climbed to the beacon of Thornthwaite Crag and feasted on intoxicating views to Brothers Water and Ullswater. From the immaculately pretty Watendlath, I savoured the tranquillity of gentle walking over Ullscarf and Low Saddle; from Bowness Knott, on the hottest day of the year, I treated myself to a summery nap on an outcrop overlooking Ennerdale Water, before finally mustering the energy to tick off Great Borne and Starling Dodd; and from Gatesgarth, I walked the classic Buttermere Edge ridge over High Crag, High Stile, Red Pike and Dodd in intermittent mist, astounded by the fells' ability to look beautiful even when the sun didn't shine.

The weather turned on my next outing. Battling howling wind and heavy rain, I climbed the faint path to Grisedale Pike via Hobcarton End, and then continued through dense hill fog to Hobcarton Crag and Crag Hill, frantically wiggling my fingers in my gloves in an attempt to ward off the impending creep of an ache resembling frostbite. I cursed my luck as I pressed on over the undulating ridge to Sail, Scar Crags and Causey Pike, knowing full well that the views would be spectacular if only I could see them. Instead I plodded without eye candy along the ridge's succession of humps and bumps that culminate in the rocky swelling of Causey Pike's summit, a prominent excrescence at the crest of the fell I usually referred to as 'the nipple'. To extend the metaphor, I scrambled over the knobbly areola and stood proudly atop the mamilla cairn. That was seven more Nuttalls bagged. Job done.

Or was it? Dusk was descending as I returned to my car parked at the top of Whinlatter Pass, a remote road that winds through Thornthwaite Forest, linking Braithwaite and Lorton and rising to a height of 1,043ft. I turned the key in the ignition. Nothing. I tried again. Still nothing. Oh shit. My car was well and truly conked. I presumed the battery was dead. I turned on my phone to call the AA, but there was no reception. I wandered around this way and that, holding my phone up to the skies, hoping for at least one bar to kick in – but to no avail. This was going well. There was no one around. The Forestry Commission visitor centre was closed. There was no traffic. I was stumped. So I started walking towards Lorton.

'Erm, hi there, I'm sorry about this, but...' I stumbled.

The poor woman who answered the door of the solitary white cottage looked like she'd seen a ghost. Any knock on the door after dark out there in the creepy blackness of the mountains must've felt like the beginning of a horror movie.

'Can I help you?' she said nervously, tentatively peering around the crack in the part-opened door.

'Don't worry, I'm not some sort of weirdo visiting isolated rural houses after dark...' Poor choice of words. 'I'm really sorry,' I continued, trying to salvage the situation. 'My car has broken down just up the road and I've got no reception to call the AA. Could I borrow your phone?'

I could tell the woman's brain was racing, frantically analysing the strange scenario in front of her. I was dressed all in black: black woolly hat pulled down low over my face, tight black fleece, black waterproof trousers, thin black gloves. I was just a balaclava away from looking like a psychotic criminal.

But she wasn't bothered at all. I'd obviously overestimated her anxiety. She happily helped me out and, two hours later, with a fully charged car battery courtesy of the AA, I was finally on my way home for a belated dinner in Cockermouth.

My next outing, three days later, saw me tick off ten mountains in a single walk. One of the quirks of the Nuttalls' definition of a mountain is that sometimes fells have two or more tops that meet the criteria. I loved those places – it was like a buy-one-get-one-free deal. In fact, this day-walk in the southern fells included a seven-for-the-price-of-three offer: the rock-strewn summits of Cold Pike served up three Nuttalls, while Crinkle Crags and Shelter Crags provided two each.

I started from the Old Dungeon Ghyll Hotel in the Great Langdale valley and climbed steeply via the Wrynose Fell shoulder to the beautifully pointed summit of Pike of Blisco (or Pike o'Blisco, if you prefer), my first Nuttall of the day. I lingered at the top for five minutes, breathing in the landscape and scenery. The serrated skyline of rocky tops around Langdale was a source of excitement and inspiration – and I was reminded that sometimes the best part of a walk is when you stand still and take a few moments to truly appreciate your surroundings.

I dropped west to the col at Red Tarn and then climbed easily to the 2,283ft top of Great Knott, which lay just off the main path, before detouring south to bag the trio of the often-ignored rocky pillars of Cold Pike. Next, I looped to the 2,428ft summit of Little Stand, an unwelcome delay to the thrills ahead, and finally began the ascent north to Crinkle Crags.

If you prefer rough, wild mountains, as I do, then the Crinkles are a dream: the ridgeline is a 'crinkly' succession of towers and depressions that creates a wild scene of both splendour and starkness. It didn't disappoint. The drama was amplified by the weather, with clouds intermittently rolling over, masking the views one minute, only to reveal eye-watering panoramas the next. I ticked off the twin tops of Crinkle Crags and Shelter Crags and then descended east back to the valley via the Buscoe Sike path, feeling elated about a brilliant day in the hills.

I returned to work for the next three days. I spent Tuesday in the office at Kendal, on Wednesday I attended a couple of meetings and hot-desked in the Threlkeld office, and on Thursday I worked from home. I had originally planned a day-walk on Friday, but Becky's grandfather, Frank, had sadly passed away and we were attending his funeral in Birmingham. I was worried about falling behind on my schedule. So I worked bizarre hours on Thursday, writing my Fix the Fells funding bids from 7.30am to 10.30am and 5pm to 9.30pm, thus freeing up the middle of the day for a swift shift of Nuttalls-bagging in the Newlands Valley.

Instead of my boots I donned my running trainers and climbed the tops of Robinson, Hindscarth, Dale Head, High Spy and High Spy North Top as fast as I could. My fellrunning technique was far from professional. Bent over double and panting for breath, I struggled uphill in what was more of a quick walk than a full-throttle run, and then flew downhill with flailing arms, feeling completely out of control. The time pressure made me stressed too. I didn't enjoy the outing. It felt more like an errand I had to get done, rather than a pleasure. It was strange and unsettling to find myself thinking about the mountains in that way.

✳　　✳　　✳

The Daily Adventure Journal of James

20/04/17: Mountains will transform you into a thin person, but make you think like a fat one. When I'm out peak-bagging, I become totally obsessed with food. I can't stop thinking about it. I hallucinate about flapjacks constantly, salivating at the mouth, and have filthy daydreams about what I'm going to do to my jar of Nutella when I finally get my hands on it. I spend all morning fantasising about lunch, then all afternoon fantasising about a mid-afternoon snack, and then all evening fantasising about dinner. But I'm allowed to, because I'm burning so many calories. It's guilt-free gluttony – and if that's not a reason to start peak-bagging then I don't know what is.

25/04/17: Is there anything more indecisive in this world than the weather in Britain's mountains? It makes more U-turns than a Tory government. Today in the Lake District, the weather went from glorious sunshine to snow to hail to rain and then back to glorious sunshine. One minute I felt as if I wanted to be inside one of those Michelin Man-style, all-in-one mountaineering suits you see people wearing up Everest, the next I was ruing the absence of a pair of Speedos and a bottle of Hawaiian Tropic tanning oil in my rucksack. Utter madness.

✳　　✳　　✳

After a weekend in Birmingham devoid of any outdoors activities, Becky and I returned by train to the Lakes on Sunday evening. I had two days off over the next week – Tuesday and Friday. On the Tuesday I experienced four seasons all at once in the north-western fells near my home, as I aimed to tick off the eight Nuttalls of Whiteside, Whiteside East Top, Hopegill Head, Ladyside Pike, Sand Hill, Grasmoor, Wandope and Whiteless Pike. One minute hailstones were pounding into my face horizontally, like an extreme exfoliation treatment, on the ascent of Whiteside from Lanthwaite Green; the next it was all blue skies, bright sunrays and uplifting views from the summit of Hopegill Head. Bizarre.

Conversely, it was one-dimensional weather during my hike on Friday: sunshine and only sunshine. It was a beautiful day in the northern fells, climbing the mighty Blencathra from Threlkeld before zig-zagging home via Gategill Fell Top, Atkinson Pike, Bowscale Fell and Bannerdale Crags. I scrambled up Hall's Fell – an ascent praised by some as the finest ridge in the Lakes. That's certainly how it felt. I bounced along rocky arêtes and craggy towers with a spring in my step, feeling as fit as I'd been for years, as confident as I'd been for decades, and as content as a man with a life-affirming clarity of purpose. This whole challenge was playing havoc with my mood, as if I'd contracted a case of mountain bipolar disorder. One day I was desperately low, the next I was on a crazy high. But, atop Blencathra in the sunshine, I felt as if I was living the dream. Maybe this was my destiny?

CHAPTER 7

SLEEPING WILD

Mountains 94–105

DATE	REGION	MOUNTAINS
Saturday 29 April	Black Mountains	Black Mountain South Top 2,090ft (637m) Black Mountain 2,306ft (703m) Twmpa 2,231ft (680m) Rhos Dirion 2,339ft (713m) Waun Fach 2,661ft (811m) Mynydd Llysiau 2,175ft (663m) Pen Twyn Glas 2,119ft (646m) Pen Allt-mawr 2,359ft (719m) Pen Cerrig-calch 2,300ft (701m)
Sunday 30 April	Black Mountains	Pen Twyn Mawr 2,159ft (658m) Pen y Gadair Fawr 2,625ft (800m) Chwarel y Fan 2,228ft (679m)

Wild camping is sleeping under the stars in the great outdoors, but not in an official campsite. It is pitching your tent on a mountain summit, cuddling into your sleeping bag on a remote beach, sheltering under your tarp in an atmospheric forest, or laying out your bivvy bag on a sweeping ridgeline. It is a magical pursuit – an easy, inexpensive activity that will revive your verve for life and open your eyes once more to the wonders of the world. It is escapism in its purest form; it is losing yourself in nature; it is feeling vulnerable and exposed – and surviving; it is returning to a primal simplicity; it is getting far away from roads, cities, shops and mobile-phone reception; it is resetting your equilibrium; and it is good, old-fashioned adventurous fun.

'But is it legal?' I hear you ask. 'And where can you do it?' The law is somewhat convoluted but, in layman's terms, wild camping is legal in some places, such as Scotland and Dartmoor. In others it is technically illegal, unless you have the landowner's permission (which is highly unlikely), but generally tolerated as long as you follow a few simple rules. These include: not leaving any trace, setting up late, leaving early, being discreet, not lighting fires, carrying away all litter, performing toilet duties away from water sources, burying human waste, and minimising your impact on the environment.

I got into wild camping about a decade ago. It is one of my favourite things to do – the only activity that sends me into a child-like state of excitement and anticipation – and I've been lucky enough to sleep wild on numerous occasions, in Britain and abroad. I've never once been berated by a landowner, or told to move on, or handcuffed and thrown in jail.

Having waxed lyrical about wild camping, however, I should make it clear that it can often be a perverse kind of pleasure – the sort of activity that you enjoy *after* rather than *during*. In particular, this applies if your tent is being slammed by torrential rain and thrown around by gusting winds; or if the 'flat' spot you selected turns out to feel distinctly lumpy when you're lying on top of it; or when you're shivering in sub-zero temperatures, wondering why on earth you traded in a comfy mattress for a glorified plastic bag on an icy mountain top. After one especially bracing wild camp a few years ago, I wrote a journal entry entitled 'The 16 stages of a wild camping adventure'. It went like this:

1. Arrive at your destination, full of energy and zest for life. 'We're off on an epic adventure!'

2. Spread all of the outdoors gear you own around the car, before stuffing it randomly into your selection of 13 differently coloured dry bags.

3. Test the weight of your backpack. 'Oh my God. There is no way I'm carrying that up a mountain.'

4. Recklessly ditch gear that you later end up needing. 'Can I get away with no poles for my tent?'

5. Set off with initial enthusiasm. 'This is actually not too bad.'

6. Five minutes later, chronic back pain kicks in.

7. Get absolutely destroyed by the driving rain, howling winds and freezing temperatures.

8. Spend hours searching for the perfect camping spot, only to run out of sunlight and settle for somewhere totally average. 'Right, it's a choice between that swamp, this sheep toilet or that boulder field.'

9. Set up tent (usually in the rain). Everything you own is wet.

10. Boil up a 'dinner' you probably wouldn't feed to your dog under normal circumstances.

11. Have a horrendous night's sleep, during which you continually slide down your sleeping mat.

12. Wake up, drink four Nescafé 3in1 coffees, eat porridge (any other type of breakfast is strictly banned on wild camping trips) and then decamp.

13. Daydream continually about a hot shower, a warm bed and a hearty meal.

14. Eventually arrive back at your car, looking dishevelled and weather-beaten, a shadow of your former self. 'I look, and feel, like a hobo.'

15. Head off, feeling more than ready to return to civilisation.

16. Spend two minutes at home. All memory of the hardships disappears instantly and you're already romanticising the wild camping life – the wilderness, the fresh air, the freedom. 'When can I get out again?'

Many of my wild camping trips over the years have adhered to this timetable, but some have gone down an even more bizarre and calamitous path. Once, in Tasmania, I spent half the night wielding my hiking poles as weapons in an attempt to chase away a ludicrously persistent brushtail possum, who seemed desperate to join me in my tent (how come that happens only with annoying marsupials rather than long-legged Swedish backpackers?). In the Sierra Nevada mountains of southern Spain, Joe and I found ourselves doing star jumps on a mountainside at 3am, having woefully underestimated how cold it would be. And in the Lake District, as I slept in a sheepfold in the middle of nowhere, I almost died of shock when I was woken in the depths of the night by the sound of a mysterious voice chanting rhythmically, 'Is anybody there?' It turned out to be a mountain rescue member searching for a missing rambler.

But perhaps my most memorable wild camping mishap came in the quintessentially English countryside of the Cotswold Way, a 102-mile trail from Bath to Chipping Campden. At dusk, Joe and I set up camp in a small copse just outside Tormarton, oblivious to the fact that we were about to sleep rough in the grounds of vacuum-billionaire James Dyson's country mansion, Dodington Park. All was well, until two beaming 4x4 headlights sliced through the darkness and aimed straight for us.

'Oh shit,' I said, glancing nervously at Joe. He looked and smelled like a vagrant – glazed eyes, dishevelled hair, clothes covered in muddy splatters. I looked the same, if not worse.

A short man wearing a dark green shooting jacket and with a rifle slung over his shoulder stepped out of the car.

'Please don't shoot us,' I whispered, half in jest, half in fear. We approached him tentatively, attempting to look like respectable middle-class ramblers rather than liberty-taking tramps.

'We're just walking the South Downs Way,' stuttered Joe. Clearly the situation had muddled his brain. We were 175 miles from that trail.

The gamekeeper ignored that slip of the tongue and looked us up and down inquisitively, as if mentally calculating our worth. Was he going to march us off the land at gunpoint? Was he angry, or bemused, or pitiful? Where was this all going?

'Look, lads – just don't disturb the pheasants, all right? They are more important than you.'

And that was that. Our place in the hierarchy of life had been set – less significant than a pheasant. Only three days on the trail and we'd fallen so far down the food chain, we'd have to give up our sleeping bags to long-tailed gamebirds if they wanted them. We were now the pheasants' bitches. But we didn't care. It felt strangely indulgent to be spending the night at the leisure of one of Britain's foremost business gurus.

On most of these wild camping trips I took my tent, but on some I slept in a bivvy bag – a thin, lightweight, weatherproof sack that slides over your sleeping bag, making a dry night's sleep possible without a tent. Such an approach, with your head open to the elements, offers an even more intimate interaction with the wild. The sounds of night creatures are unmuffled, the stars dazzle above you, and your senses are highly attuned to every raindrop and every gust of wind.

As Alastair Humphreys, inventor of the microadventure and champion-in-chief of the bivvy, puts it: 'In a bivvy bag you are not cocooned from the environment as you are in a tent. When inside a tent, you are basically in a rubbish version of indoors. If you want to be sheltered from the outdoors, hidden from the sky and the world, then you might as well stay at home rather than swapping your nice house for a cramped, damp, flappy, lumpy version of home. In a bivvy bag you really are outside. You feel the breeze on your face, look up at the stars and sit up to a brilliant view in the morning.'

I was looking forward to putting my bivvy bag to the test once again as I prepared for a trip to the Black Mountains – my first peak-bagging foray into Wales of this Nuttalls challenge. I split the journey to South Wales by driving down to Birmingham on the Friday night so I could also grab a cheeky curry with my parents and brothers.

'What if a squirrel crawls over your head?' said my dad, spooning chicken dhansak with pineapple on to his plate.

I instantly regretted mentioning my plan to go bivvying. This was going to be a banter free-for-all.

'A badger might do a shit on your face when you're asleep,' added Adam, my youngest brother, leaning over the table to rip off some naan.

'You might get humped by a horny fox,' piped up Tom, my other brother. 'Or wake up with a hedgehog's arse in front of your eyes.'

'More importantly, what about all the insects and creepy-crawlies – couldn't they just crawl inside your sleeping bag?' questioned Mum, looking a tad concerned. 'And what if it rains?'

'Won't it be freezing cold?' added Cath, Adam's girlfriend. 'And uncomfortable? Have you heard of B&Bs? They have beds and electricity and everything. Why don't you just book a room?'

'All alone in the dark, won't you be scared of psychopathic, pitchfork-wielding farmers who wander the hillsides at night?' asked Dad, delivering a finishing blow in the wisecracking frenzy.

'There's one way to find out. I'll let you know after my trip,' was the only reply I could think of.

And so, the following evening, I found myself snuggled into my bivvy bag, staring up at the forest canopy. Was I hallucinating? The night sky was an ethereal blur of swirling shapes and light, ever-changing and mesmerising. Moonlight danced through gaps in the trees and celestial stars seemed to glimmer wondrously through the foliage. It was life from a different perspective. The air was musty and filled with the sounds of the forest – a scurrying insect, the rush of the wind in the leaves, the distant hoot of an owl. I felt alive, as if existing back-to-nature had reinvigorated my soul and heightened my senses. I heard every sound, breathed in every smell, savoured every view. And I hadn't once been molested by an amorous fox or defecated on by a loose-bowelled badger.

Twelve hours earlier I'd parked up at Capel-y-ffin (the chapel on the boundary) and read in my Nuttalls guidebook that Victorian diarist Francis Kilvert had written about a 'buxom comely wholesome girl with fair hair, rosy face, blue eyes, and fair clear skin' washing at a tub next to the village brook. I set off, hoping I might have a similar experience.

I crossed the Afon Honddu, tramped through green fields and hopped over wooden stiles, before meeting a group of ramblers on the steep ascent over open hillside to the Hatterrall Ridge.

'Stand aside, here comes a fit person,' shouted one of the walkers to his friends.

'What have you got in the backpack?' joked another, chuckling at the size of my overflowing 65-litre bag compared with their dinky day-bags.

'Mainly Snickers bars,' I replied, wishing it was true.

Located at the north-eastern tip of the Brecon Beacons, the Black Mountains are a group of grass-and-heather-cloaked hills on the England–Wales border. Steep escarpment edges make the ascents tough, but the flat ridges offer seemingly endless miles of easy walking – much of it on the historic Offa's Dyke Path, a 177-mile national trail.

I hit the famous path and turned left to tick off the dual tops of Black Mountain, before continuing on the well-maintained track towards Hay Bluff that – despite not qualifying as a Nuttall – rises proudly from the gentle rural land to the north. A ginger horse posed on the steep escarpment edge, its blond tail and mane flowing in the breeze. It gazed longingly down to Hay-on-Wye, as if daydreaming about exploring the quaint 'town of books'.

Making good time, I descended to Gospel Pass and climbed to the grassy summit of Twmpa, which is also known as Lord Hereford's Knob. It immediately reminded me of the time Tom and I, aged 11 and 13, climbed it with Dad and our cousin Mark. It was a free-for-all of childish jokes that went a bit like this:

'Look, I'm bouncing up and down on Lord Hereford's Knob,' said Tom, as he literally bounced around the summit between fits of giggles.

'I never thought I'd see the day I was sitting on an aristocratic knob,' said Dad.

'Check this out – I'm sucking on Lord Hereford's Knob,' I added, throwing a boiled sweet into my mouth and feeling very proud of my witty remark.

With no one around to jest with this time, I didn't make any knob jokes and instead pressed on to Rhos Dirion. I then skirted around the Grwyne Fawr stream before climbing the gentle north ridge to the 2,661ft summit of Waun Fach, the highest point of the Black Mountains.

Away from the crowds of the Offa's Dyke Path, I was relishing the lonely ridge-walking. The sky was filled with white cloud, but the sun broke through intermittently and my views of distant peaks, forests and rolling countryside were unobstructed. Feeling energetic, I pressed on and visited the summits of Mynydd Llysiau, Pen Twyn Glas, Pen Allt-mawr and Pen Cerrig-calch. I contemplated camping on the ridge but it felt exposed and windy, so I dropped down into the valley and set up my bivvy in a small forest on a flat patch of ground next to a mossy, half-derelict dry-stone wall.

I'd spent all day with my phone in airplane mode. Once again, detaching myself from the constant buzz of technology and the chatter of the internet had chilled me out. I was happy and relaxed, and didn't feel at all compelled to switch on my iPhone. Nothing was that urgent. I could reply to emails later in the week and check my WhatsApp messages when I got home. It was joyous to be escaping the stressful immediacy of the internet. I felt as if I had been freed from the shackles of my phone and was no longer constrained and stressed by its constant flow of notifications. And I wasn't bored either. I was surrounded by natural, wholesome entertainment: the songs of the birds, the vistas of the rolling hills and the enchanting atmosphere of the forest.

✻　　✻　　✻

The Daily Adventure Journal of James
29/04/17: Volvic have their 'Touch of Fruit' range of waters, with exotic flavours like watermelon and strawberry. But you can't imagine them bringing out a new 'Touch of Sheep' collection, with flavours including rotting Herdwick intestines and decaying Swaledale guts. And that is why I really should start filtering my water. So far I've just been filling my bottles straight from fast-flowing becks and I haven't had any stomach problems. The untreated water tastes incredible, icy cold and gloriously refreshing. But today I almost filled up before, at the last minute, spotting a dead sheep upstream. Mmm, yummy, stream water infused with particles of deceased sheep innards. Probably best avoided.

✻　　✻　　✻

I woke early and – with the insignificant tops of Pen Twyn Mawr, Pen y Gadair Fawr and Chwarel y Fan ahead of me – climbed briefly towards Mynydd Du Forest. I stopped at a solitary tree on the hillside, threw my backpack down and set about preparing breakfast. One night in the forest and I was drunk on a nature-induced state of relaxation. I sipped on my strong, sugary coffee and thought about Ronald Turnbull's words on the lottery of bivvying in his excellent *The Book of the Bivvy*: 'They are the best of nights: they are the worst of nights.' I felt so grateful I'd experienced the former.

CHAPTER 8

SPIES, ELEPHANTS AND A PORSCHE

Mountains 106–156

DATE	REGION	MOUNTAINS
Friday 12 May	Lake District Northern Fells	Carrock Fell 2,165ft (660m) High Pike 2,159ft (658m) Hare Stones 2,057ft (627m) Great Lingy Hill 2,021ft (616m) Knott 2,329ft (710m) Little Calva 2,106ft (642m) Great Calva 2,264ft (690m)
Saturday 13 May	Yorkshire Dales Northern Fells	Yarlside 2,096ft (639m) Randygill Top 2,051ft (625m) Fell Head 2,100ft (640m) Bush Howe 2,044ft (623m) The Calf 2,218ft (676m) Calders 2,211ft (674m) Nine Standards Rigg 2,172ft (662m)
Sunday 14 May	Lake District Western Fells	Steeple 2,687ft (819m) Scoat Fell 2,759ft (841m) Black Crag 2,717ft (828m) Pillar 2,926ft (892m) Looking Stead 2,057ft (627m) Red Pike 2,710ft (826m) Seatallan 2,274ft (693m) Haycock 2,615ft (797m)

DATE	REGION	MOUNTAINS
		Little Gowder Crag 2,405ft (733m) Caw Fell 2,264ft (690m) Iron Crag 2,100ft (640m)
Tuesday 16 May	Lake District Northern Fells	Long Side 2,408ft (734m) Carl Side 2,447ft (746m) Skiddaw 3,054ft (931m) Skiddaw Little Man 2,838ft (865m) Sale How 2,185ft (666m) Lonscale Fell 2,346ft (715m)
Wednesday 17 May	Lake District Western Fells	Yewbarrow 2,060ft (628m) Yewbarrow North Top 2,021ft (616m)
Friday 19 May	Lake District Central Fells	Codale Head 2,395ft (730m) High Raise 2,500ft (762m) Thunacar Knott 2,372ft (723m) Pavey Ark 2,297ft (700m) Harrison Stickle 2,415ft (736m) Pike of Stickle 2,362ft (709m) Loft Crag 2,231ft (680m)
Thursday 25 May	Lake District Southern Fells	Seathwaite Fell 2,073ft (632m) Seathwaite Fell South Top 2,070ft (631m) Allen Crags 2,575ft (785m) High House Tarn Top 2,244ft (684m) Red Beck Top 2,365ft (721m) Looking Steads 2,543ft (775m) Glaramara 2,569ft (783m) Combe Head 2,411ft (735m) Combe Door Top 2,218ft (676m) Dovenest Top 2,073ft (632m) Rosthwaite Fell 2,008ft (612m)

I was now exactly two months into my challenge. That felt scary. One third of my target time had gone in a flash. I'd completed 22 days of walking and climbed just over 100 peaks, which equated to nearly a quarter of the Nuttalls – I was making decent progress. My body was generally coping well and I was feeling strong and single-minded. I was a little behind schedule, but it was nothing to worry about and I was determined to retain a positive outlook. There was plenty of time to catch up. And it felt great to see my Nuttalls total edge upwards. The Cheviots and Black Mountains ranges were done and dusted; I'd climbed 31 out of the 36 tops in the North Pennines; and 56 of 171 Lakeland fells were now ticked off. But there was a long way to go and I couldn't rest on my laurels. I needed to speed up.

The past 11 days in particular had slowed me down. Since my Black Mountains expedition I hadn't climbed a single Nuttall. I'd worked for eight days and spent every other waking minute moving to our new house: packing up boxes, shuttling to and from our old flat, emptying boxes, transferring energy and council tax contracts, sorting out broadband, liaising with carpet contractors, driving to Birmingham to collect stuff from my dad's loft, trying to ensure our landlord would repay our deposit, and doing a hundred-and-one other menial tasks. It was an unwelcome distraction and a big stress. We had originally intended to move the previous autumn but the purchase had fallen through and now, after numerous delays, our move was finally taking place at the worst possible time for me. It was a massive hassle. But I consciously forced myself to stay positive. This was the way it was, I couldn't control events, and my Nuttalls-bagging would soon resume.

And so, with the house move superficially dealt with, I was determined to boost my summit stats over the next fortnight. I was working as normal but had set aside seven days in my diary. My aim was to complete seven long day-walks, all in the Lake District, and to return home each night to eat proper food, sleep in a proper bed and – if I could face it – unpack a few more boxes.

My first destination was Back O'Skiddaw, the rounded, grassy hills to the north of (or 'back of') Skiddaw. 'Boring', 'featureless' and 'downright average' – these are the criticisms regularly thrown at the much-maligned Back O'Skiddaw fells. Exhilarating knife-edge arêtes, I'm-on-top-of-the-world summits, precipitous crags and naked cliffs – you won't find any of those. But if you want to escape the crowds, switch off and be alone, it's the place to be.

That's exactly what I experienced as I climbed, all alone, from the minor road towards Carrock Mine, with the rush of Grainsgill Beck and singing larks overhead providing a soothing soundtrack. The woody smell of heather tingled my nostrils and my eyes were drawn down the charming Mosedale valley. It was a peaceful, serene setting.

But, as my pre-walk research revealed, this place hadn't always been so tranquil. On and off for 130 years this fellside had been alive with the mining of valuable metals, including lead, copper, arsenic and tungsten. This industry provided the backdrop to perhaps one of the most bizarre moments in the history of the Lake District's fells.

In 1917, amid the grip of German-spy mania, a government geologist was sent by the Geological Survey to explore Carrock Mine for further tungsten, which was highly valued in armaments manufacture. Because of the secret nature of his mission, he refused to explain to the locals what he was doing. They smelt a rat – or, more accurately, a German spy – and decided to take the law into their own hands. So a posse of angry Cumbrians sneaked up on the innocent rock expert and, in the words of a local report, 'roughed him up a bit', which I presume meant he was beaten to within an inch of his life by a lynch mob of burly Lakeland sheep farmers. The act of self-administered justice ended with the poor geologist locked in a school overnight. Police eventually cleared up the confusion the following morning – and so ended the Lake District's one and only James Bond–style moment of espionage theatre.

There were no spy mix-ups unfolding as I climbed to Carrock Fell's delightful summit, the collapsed wall of an ancient fort crowned by a cone-shaped cairn. I looked north-east, where a patchwork quilt of misshapen fields, a puzzle of yellows, light browns and greens, was punctured only by the odd farmhouse or towering church spire. It was a charming English countryside scene that I found more enticing than the surrounding mountains. I walked west towards High Pike, my boots squelching in the boggy ground, as white cotton-grass swayed hypnotically in the wind.

Half an hour later I was perching on the slate bench of the 2,159ft summit, indulging in another of Back O'Skiddaw's hidden treasures – not the view into Lakeland, but the one out of it. I could see Scotland. The Solway Firth shimmered in the afternoon sun and distant Scottish hills, especially Criffel, glowed enticingly, as if begging to be explored. There was no one else present, bar a single hiker on the Cumbria Way path to my left. I felt quiet and contemplative.

I walked south-west to tick off the minor bumps of Hare Stones and Great Lingy Hill, which hardly seemed worthy of mountain status, and headed off-piste over wet, pathless slopes towards Knott. I dropped down steeply to an obvious col before ascending Little Calva and then followed a wall to the summit cairn of Great Calva, a fusion of piled stones and a mangled metal gate. I'd smashed out seven Nuttalls in great time, pounding through the miles and ascents like a man with a century of mountains already under his belt. I felt intrepid and adventurous. *I'm a hiking legend*, I thought. And then, right on cue, two tiny lambs walked past the Great Calva cairn, as if to deliberately quash my delusions of adventure grandeur. If Bambi-legged baby sheep could potter around these tops with ease, maybe I wasn't that heroic after all? As they tend to do, the mountains were keeping me grounded – and I was thankful for that.

The following day, a Saturday, I headed south from Cockermouth towards Sedbergh and the grassy, domed hills of the Howgills. If you were driving north on the M6, bound for the Lake District or Scotland, you may well have had your eyes drawn east near Kendal to the rolling fells of the Howgills. You may well have wondered what it'd be like to go walking there – but it's unlikely you ever have. The quiet, no-frills tops are barely frequented, overlooked because their rounded, grassy nature, devoid of crag and cliff, isn't exciting enough to attract the time-poor hiking enthusiast.

But a peak-bagger can't be picky. And so, despite the heavy rain and blustery wind, I parked up at the Cross Keys Hotel on the A683 with six Nuttalls in my sights. The Howgills are a bit like a no man's land, wedged between the Lake District and Yorkshire, part of Cumbria but located within the expanded Yorkshire Dales National Park. As I struggled towards Cautley Spout, England's highest waterfall, I was struck by the parallels between the Howgills' identity crisis and my own strange double life. I was wedged between adventure and normality, part of the intrepid elite but located within the everyday world of jobs and routine.

Alfred Wainwright famously described the Howgill Fells as looking like a herd of sleeping elephants. As I tramped towards the waterfall, I contemplated the image for a second and let my mind play games with the simile. Maybe the smooth, rounded body lines of a family of dozing elephants were exactly what I needed for a decent day in the fells in bad weather. No technical navigation skills would be required to climb the gentle slopes of an elephant's trunk. And there'd be no chance of falling to my death down a precipice when descending the curved mound of an elephant's bottom. Unless I plummeted into an elephant's ass crack. That would definitely be one ravine to avoid.

I snapped out of my daydreams about elephant bottoms and continued slowly towards Cautley Spout. Before reaching the foot of the falls I veered north to Bowderdale Head and climbed steep, grassy slopes to the 2,096ft summit of Yarlside. The rest of the day was a series of ridges and cols, pathless ups and downs, and then more ups and downs, as I ticked off Randygill Top, Fell Head, Bush Howe and The Calf. From Calders, my final top, I bent double in the wind, pulled my hood down tight over my face to shield it from the lashing rain, and strained my eyes through the shifting cloud in an attempt to get a view across the fells and a glimpse of the herd of sleeping elephants. I couldn't see it.

The Howgills were complete, but my day was not over. With a relentless schedule ahead of me, I decided to take the opportunity to tick off one more summit – the solitary 2,172ft top of Nine Standards Rigg, near Kirkby Stephen. The clouds were long gone and the evening sun made a welcome appearance as I plodded across moorland towards my final goal. Nine Standards Rigg's summit is adorned with a line of ancient 'stone men', a series of huge, column-like cairns up to ten feet high. Were they built by miners? Or designed as boundary markers? Or constructed to deceive the Scots that a fearsome army was waiting on the ridge? No one really knows. And I didn't give it much thought, blinkered by my desire to get up and down and back home again with minimal fuss and maximum efficiency.

Twelve hours later I parked up at Bowness Knott, which was busy with Sunday-morning day trippers, threw my backpack over my shoulder and trudged down the gravel road along the shores of Ennerdale towards a skyline of enthralling peaks. My plan was to double up, completing two day-walks from the Nuttalls guidebook in a single day. Pillar, Steeple, Red Pike and ten other tops were on the schedule. The night before I'd designed a route on my laptop using my OS Maps subscription – it came out at almost 25 miles with 10,000ft of ascent. I wasn't feeling too confident of making it as I crossed the River Liza, tiptoed in fear around a herd of cows and then climbed through lichen-rich forest next to the deep gorge of Low Beck.

I emerged from the trees to the open fellside, next to a half-collapsed dry-stone wall, and picked a path through the heather to ascend the Long Crag ridge towards Steeple. I negotiated a boulder-strewn section and scrambled up a small gully through a stony barrier, before the ridge sharpened and rose magnificently over a succession of rocky towers to climax at an exposed summit. Surrounded by precipitous drops, I stood proudly atop Steeple, like the King of Wild Ennerdale. No one else was on the summit. I had the mountain all to myself. I surveyed my realm: the lake, a striking deep blue in colour, stretched out towards the flat plains of the west coast; dense forest lined the valley bottom in a coat of multi-coloured green; the wide bed of the River Liza meandered gracefully; grassy ridges dazzled in the hazy morning sunshine; and shattered crags, scree chutes and knotted cliffs painted a rocky work of art.

I lingered on the summit, understanding what Wainwright meant when he described Steeple as 'one of the best', a 'fine pointed peak' that 'commands the eye and quickens the pulse'. Finally I dragged myself away and descended to a mini col before rising again to the main ridge. I turned left and followed a wall to the bulky summit of Scoat Fell, which sadly dominates over Steeple to the south, and on to Black Crag. Next I descended a boulder field to Wind Gap and then climbed north-east to the broad plateau summit of Pillar.

After long, slow out-and-backs to both Looking Stead and Red Pike, I eventually arrived back at Scoat Fell, having bailed on my idea to also visit Yewbarrow. My 13 Nuttalls mission had been a failure, falling victim to illogical route-planning. I should have climbed Looking Stead first and then headed west, sticking to the ridges, but my burning desire to experience the Steeple ridge had created an inefficient mess of a plan. But I didn't care – it had been worth it.

I chatted to a few other hikers as I visited the remaining tops of Seatallan, Haycock, Little Gowder Crag, Caw Fell and Iron Crag. Stories, and sometimes sweets, were exchanged and – feeling sociable – I enjoyed the friendly, supportive camaraderie of the outdoors community. But, with dusk descending, I was all alone as I dropped over pathless ground from Iron Crag towards the valley. The walking, over boulders and dense heather, was rough but the atmosphere was almost jubilant. Ennerdale felt alive at dusk: the dipping sun gilded the fells in a celebratory twilight, birdsong increased in volume, and gangs of energetic lambs charged around the fields, leaping with joy. I was almost tempted to nestle down for the night.

✳   ✳   ✳

The Daily Adventure Journal of James
13/05/17: Alfred Wainwright once wrote, 'There's no such thing as bad weather, just inappropriate clothing.' I'm not entirely sure, but I think he may have been referring to the use of plastic Aldi sandwich

bags as makeshift 'waterproof' socks when your sodden boots are leaking. I tried this technique today, tying the bags over my feet in a desperate bid to halt the impending creep of trench foot. And I can officially confirm that it didn't work: the plastic made my feet sweat, the bags were difficult to tie properly around my ankles and, ultimately, the material proved porous. But every cloud... With that technical analysis in print, fingers crossed, that's a lucrative gear-reviewing contract secured with *Trail* magazine.

14/05/17: If I ever met the insipid pillock flying that peace-shattering, escapism-ruining, buzzing drone around Ennerdale today I'd kick him in the balls and smash the drone over a boulder. Or, at least, that's what I fantasise I'd do if I wasn't actually (a) utterly petrified by confrontation, and (b) a polite middle-class boy more likely to compliment the man on his 'excellent flying technique' than to express my internal rage.

✳   ✳   ✳

Fast forward two days, and I was wagging my thumb on the A591 near Keswick, trying to get a ride back to my car at Ravestone Lodge. I'd spent the day in mist, rain and wind, climbing the Long Side and Carl Side route to Skiddaw, before detouring briefly to the grassy mound of Sale How and then descending over Lonscale Fell to the Latrigg car park. Feeling exhausted and sodden, I'd decided on a whim to bail on a long return loop via Skiddaw House and Dash Falls and instead opted to try and hitchhike back to my car.

Several clapped-out campervans and empty farmers' 4x4s whizzed by, ignoring my best please-pick-me-up smiles – and then, to my utter disbelief, a flash sports car pulled over.

'Any chance of a ride up the road?' I said, wide-eyed at the sight of a gold, red and black Porsche emblem on the shiny bonnet. It was a humdinger of a car: metallic grey paint job, glimmering alloys, go-faster spoiler, tinted windows, low-to-the-ground aerodynamic shape and a roar that sounded more akin to a spaceship than a road-going vehicle. In short, it was slightly better than my 15-year-old rusty VW Golf.

'Jump in, dude,' replied the Lake District's answer to Lewis Hamilton. He looked suave and stylish, with his hair fashionably messed up and a Ralph Lauren logo on his polo shirt. As if it was nothing, he calmly shifted a crate of expensive-looking wine off the passenger seat, adding, 'Having a little soirée tonight.' I felt like a fish out of water; a geeky rambler who had accidentally taken a wrong turn and ended up at a high-society champagne party.

'Nice ride – what car is this?' I asked, hiding the fact that I know absolutely nothing about cars.

'Porsche Cayman GT4 – my pride and joy,' said Lewis happily, as he put pedal to the metal and sped around the sharp twists and turns of the rural road like a pro.

'How much is it worth?'

'A hundred thousand pounds.'

I glanced guiltily down at my feet. My boots had deposited a few kilograms of wet, sticky, brown Skiddaw mud on his bespoke interior. If the car was worth £100,000, that was five grand's worth of damage at least. This nice guy had offered me a lift out of the kindness of his heart and, in return, I'd made the footwell of his Porsche look like the bowl of an unflushed toilet in a dodgy late-night curry house.

The following day I was back working for Fix the Fells but, rather than a day in the office, I had meetings in Wasdale discussing the issues of erosion on Scafell Pike and the disturbances in the valley caused by National Three Peaks participants. By 3pm we were finished and I was in exactly the right place to visit Yewbarrow and Yewbarrow North Top, the twin Nuttalls I'd run out of time to climb during my epic route from Ennerdale three days earlier.

I doubt there has ever been, in the history of man, a better post-work excursion than climbing Yewbarrow in the sun. It was special. The skies were a brilliant blue, complemented by streaks of high, wispy clouds and the glaring orange sun. The fell looked beguiling – a triangular pyramid with gentle lower slopes topped by craggy protrusions and rocky clefts. It was simultaneously graceful and rugged. Gazing up at it from the car park, I felt as if I was falling in love – or was it lust? – with Yewbarrow.

Caked in sun cream, I climbed from Overbeck Bridge to the gateway between Dropping Crag and Bell Rib before scrambling to Great Door and then over the ridge to the top. It was a thrilling climb – so much better than ticking it off from the Red Pike ridge, which had been my original plan. From the summit, the views down to Wastwater and across to the Scafells were vast and immaculate. I wanted to stay in that moment for eternity.

Two days later I crashed back down to earth with my next walk. Running short on time, this was another outing wedged between a split shift of Fix the Fells home-working. I drove to Great Langdale, which was misty and overcast – the distinctive skyline losing some of its allure as a result. From Dungeon Ghyll I marched up Stickle Ghyll to the tarn and the domineering cliffs of Pavey Ark, before veering north-east and north away from the main path. I passed the striking cone of Sergeant Man, a delightful knoll that doesn't qualify as a Nuttall, and instead visited the dull top of Codale Head. I was struck by the futility of a mathematical approach to defining mountains. It led to anomalies like this – but, I figured, that was the nature of the beast and I didn't have a better solution.

Feeling somewhat fatigued, I pressed on to High Raise and Thunacar Knott before returning to the more popular tops of the Langdale Pikes, including Pavey Ark, Harrison Stickle, Pike of Stickle and Loft Crag, and then descending south-east by the Dungeon Ghyll path. There I felt the first sign of injury, a twinge of pain in my left knee every time I took a step downhill. Was my body finally starting to crack under this relentless schedule?

Four out of the next five days were spent working, with the spare day booked in as a much-needed 24 hours of rest and relaxation.

But on the Thursday, as dictated by my strict calendar of peak-bagging commitments, I had to refocus on the Nuttalls. My task was a nine-and-a-half-mile circular route of the Glaramara group of fells in Borrowdale, with over 3,000ft of ascent to contend with and 11 tops to visit: Seathwaite Fell, Seathwaite Fell South Top, Allen Crags, High House Tarn Top, Red Beck Top, Looking Steads, Glaramara, Combe Head, Combe Door Top, Dovenest Top and Rosthwaite Fell.

Seathwaite is famously the wettest place in England but, miraculously, the quaint hamlet was transformed into Costa Del Seathwaite on the day I visited. It was baking hot, the sky was cloudless and the aroma of Ambre Solaire sun cream lingered on my skin, reminding me of childhood holidays to Tenerife. Wearing only shorts, a light T-shirt and trainers, I headed south along Grains Gill to Stockley Bridge, and climbed steeply to Seathwaite Fell. It was a perfect day, an absolute joy to be out in the fresh air enjoying the mountains rather than stuck behind a desk in a stuffy office. I looped around Sprinkling Tarn and then ticked off a never-ending succession of minor tops heading north-east on the bare, rocky Glaramara ridge. It ended with Rosthwaite Fell, a sublime exposed summit with a rocky turret. I stood on top of the highest point and gazed over Borrowdale. The sun was shining. The skies were blue. The animals of Lakeland were celebrating life; the Herdwicks were grazing happily, the birds were singing joyously and the insects were buzzing busily. 'Circle of Life' from *The Lion King* played in my mind and I felt like a victorious Simba, perching atop Pride Rock and rejoicing with the creatures of his kingdom.

CHAPTER 9

HITCH'N'HIKING

Mountains 157–175

DATE	REGION	MOUNTAINS
Friday 26 May	Yorkshire Dales Southern Fells	Ingleborough 2,375ft (724m) Simon Fell 2,133ft (650m) Whernside 2,415ft (736m)
Saturday 27 May	Yorkshire Dales Southern Fells	Gragareth 2,057ft (627m) Green Hill 2,060ft (628m) Great Coum 2,254ft (687m) Calf Top 2,000ft (610m) Great Knoutberry Hill 2,205ft (672m) Dodd Fell Hill 2,192ft (668m)
Sunday 28 May	Yorkshire Dales Southern Fells	Drumaldrace 2,014ft (614m) Yockenthwaite Moor 2,110ft (643m) Birks Fell 2,001ft (610m) Buckden Pike 2,303ft (702m)
Monday 29 May	Yorkshire Dales Southern Fells	Great Whernside 2,310ft (704m) Darnbrook Fell 2,047ft (624m) Fountains Fell 2,192ft (668m) Fountains Fell South Top 2,172ft (662m) Pen-y-ghent 2,277ft (694m) Plover Hill 2,231ft (680m)

I descended steeply from the 2,000ft top of Calf Top, crossed Barkin Beck and threw my ludicrously heavy backpack down next to the Barbondale road. I sat wearily, gulped on my stream-filled water bottle, and waited for a car to pass. Five minutes later, a silver Vauxhall Corsa came chugging up the minor road, labouring somewhat. I stood, smiled, ran my fingers through my hair, and waved my hitchhiker's thumb. I could consciously feel myself trying not to look like a murderer or rapist.

The driver, a kindly looking woman perhaps in her 60s, caught my eye momentarily. In that instant, I could tell I was being judged. She drove by hastily, speeding up if anything – was that a look of fear or panic on her face? Perhaps I looked like a hitchhiking lunatic? Three more cars passed by in a similar vein. It felt like a series of drive-by character assassinations.

The next to ignore my thumb-wagging pleas was an old red hatchback, with a young girl in a car seat on the passenger's side and a middle-aged woman driver with curly, messy hair. She whizzed by, almost oblivious to my existence. And then, to my immense surprise, slammed on the brakes 30ft down the road and stopped in front of a cattle grid. Had something unrelated caused the sudden stop? Or had the driver had a change of heart? I swung my backpack over my shoulder and went to find out.

As I approached the car, a green Land Rover pulling a trailer appeared from the other direction. My hitchhiking had inadvertently caused a road blockage.

'Any chance of a lift towards Dent?' I asked calmly, leaning in towards the driver's window.

'Yes, yes, get in, hurry up, c'mon, quickly,' barked the woman, clearly flustered by the farmer's presence.

I opened the door, feeling a bit like a naughty kid who had been berated by the headteacher. But there was no space to sit – a pile of possessions was in the way.

'Wrong side, wrong side,' shouted the stress-head in an exasperated tone. So I frantically jumped in through the other door, cradling my backpack on my lap, as the red hatchback reversed with a roar of over-revving to allow the 4x4 to pass. I felt apprehensive. Maybe she was the lunatic, not me? Maybe I was going to spend the next decade as a sex-slave imprisoned in the basement of a remote Yorkshire cottage? Had I just got in a car with a deranged Dales death-monger?

I need not have worried. The woman turned out to be kind and amiable – and simply maternal, rather than bossy. 'Seat belt on please, James' was a heart-warming concern for my safety, not a desire to have me tied up. We chatted jovially about my challenge, her life and the joys of the Dales, as we tootled along the narrow lane towards Gawthrop. She was interested in me, while I felt grateful for her selfless generosity. Hitchhiking is often synonymous with danger and fear, but I've always found it to be an activity that restores my faith in humanity. Kindness and serendipity in action.

We turned right and followed the River Dee towards Dent, her home village. It took twice as long as it should have. At almost every corner she stopped to talk to a neighbour through her wound-down window, like Harry Redknapp on deadline day, or wave to a friend, or chit-chat with a pensioner walking along cobbled lanes to the local shop. When she wasn't socialising, she gave me a running commentary on the village: 'That campsite there, that belongs to Bill, who lives in that cottage we passed, and I'm friends with his daughter Anne, whose kids Lisa and Josh are at the same school as my children.' Or words to that effect. I was struck by this charming sense of community, as if the Dales were one big happy family. I was looking forward to being a small part of that family over the next few days.

My plan was to hitchhike at various stages, whenever a long section of road-walking lay between me and the next peaks on my list. It would always be on rural roads, so I was reasonably confident of getting a lift. Hitchhiking is a dying trend in Britain. Gone is the

1970s heyday of motorway junctions lined with thumb-wagging travellers. Cheap coach travel and high levels of car ownership are partly to blame, coupled with a miasma of fear. The 1986 film *The Hitcher*, about a hitchhiking serial killer, can't exactly have helped, nor can a number of high-profile hitchhiking-related murders. An AA poll in 2012 declared hitchhiking a dead art in Britain, with 91 per cent of drivers unwilling to stop and fewer than one in 100 very likely to offer a ride. But, without wanting to belittle the obvious risks, I was excited about hitchhiking in Yorkshire. It was my chance to meet some locals and get an insight into life in the Dales – and, as a peak-bagger, it would save my legs a series of long roadside slogs.

Two days earlier, I started my mini Yorkshire Dales expedition in Ingleton at 1pm, after a minor mishap involving putting the wrong Ingleton into my sat nav. I parked up in a lay-by just to the east of the town and flicked through my numerous map print-outs. I had an ambitious route planned, almost 100 miles in total, with the equivalent in ascent of Mt Kilimanjaro from sea level to summit. My intention was to climb all of the Yorkshire Dales' southern fells – a group of 19 mountains located, approximately, in a rectangle of land bounded by the towns of Ingleton, Dent, Hawes and Kettlewell. It would take four nights of wild camping and include climbs of Yorkshire's trio of famous peaks: Ingleborough, Whernside and Pen-y-ghent.

I set off – weighed down by four days' worth of food in my backpack – and climbed north-east on the treadmill of a track towards Ingleborough. Summer had come early. It was 25°C and I was soaked in sweat in no time. Thankfully, the Help for Heroes cap I found discarded next to a gate was shielding my eyes from the sun's glare, while a series of springs to the right of the path were ideal for a spot of refreshing head-dunking.

Ingleborough is Yorkshire's second-highest mountain but is arguably number one in its affections. Enthusiastic locals have been known to label it 'the finest mountain in the world'. That is an exaggeration, but it certainly is a magnificent peak. Unfortunately I'd taken the boring way up, missing out on the high-sided gorge of Trow Gill and the deep chasm of Gaping Gill. But, atop the 2,375ft summit in glorious sunshine, it still felt like a great start to my foray into the Dales.

A couple of athletic guys, probably in their early 20s, marched speedily to join me at the summit, as if the Dales were an assault course to be conquered. They were taking on the Yorkshire Three Peaks Challenge – a 24½-mile hike over Pen-y-ghent, Whernside and Ingleborough that must be completed in less than 12 hours. They'd reached their final peak ahead of schedule, leaving only a descent to Horton-in-Ribblesdale.

'What are you up to?' asked one of the guys, who sported a hipster beard and a cap worn backwards.

'Erm, I'm climbing 19 mountains around the Dales,' I replied, feeling somewhat guilty about possibly raining on their adventure parade.

'Where are you camping?' asked the other.

'Wherever I can find a spot,' I answered, unsure whether they saw me as a rambler oddball or an adventure guru.

'Epic. Have a good one, bro' – and, with that, they strode off purposefully, as if a PB was at stake.

I nipped to the easy top of Simon Fell and then took the main path north, descending to Chapel-le-Dale. The views back to Ingleborough were breathtaking. From a yellow field alive with radiant buttercups, I gazed at the distinctive profile of the mountain – a stepped ridge leading to a table-like top, backed by a dazzling blue sky. This was hiking at its very best.

Whernside was my next target. I picked my way through a series of ramshackle farmyards, wondering why farms were always so messy. One alone had four derelict tractors, seemingly abandoned here and there, as well as giant jumbled piles of wooden posts, discarded sheep-feed plastic tubs, old bicycles and toys, warped metal gates, rusting agricultural contraptions, and all manner of other trash and tat. The barns had smashed windows and caved-in roofs; the hedges were adorned with hundreds of shreds of the black plastic used to wrap hay bales; and the entire place was coated in a soggy mix of mud and cow shit. It was the foul-smelling opposite of the buttercup paradise I'd just left.

I continued down a lane to an idyllic-looking cottage. A mother and her baby were enjoying the sunshine in their garden, which was raised on a platform above the path. As I passed by, I must have accidentally surprised a dozing canine because, in an instant, an angry dog – I think it was a Dobermann – was baring its teeth and barking aggressively at me at face level. I nearly jumped out of my skin and, letting out a pathetic yelp, dived forward, seeking safety beyond a gate.

Fuelled by Jaffa Cakes, I climbed steeply via a path labelled on my map as 'A Pennine Journey' to the unexpectedly windy Whernside ridge, and then pressed on to the 2,415ft summit. I was feeling tired and ready for dinner, so I dropped briefly west and found a flat, grassy, sheltered spot. Perfect. I went through my wild-camping routine. Pitch tent. Check. Blow up sleeping mat. Check. Lay out sleeping bag. Check. Boil up rice. Check. Collect water from nearby beck. Check. Watch in bewilderment as the sun sets over Green Hill, painting the sky with a swirling veneer of pinks, oranges and yellows, and shading the surrounding mountains with an intense blue. Check.

The following morning, feeling stress-free after a night under the stars and almost 24 hours without using my phone, I descended steep, pathless slopes into Kingsdale, only to climb straight away to the next ridge. I headed south on an out-and-back to the trig point of Gragareth, that left me contemplating the irony of going to such extremes to escape the concrete jungle of urban life only to be greeted by an ugly concrete plinth on the top of a mountain. Next, I took the ridge to the knoll of Green Hill and beyond to Great Coum, before dropping north-west over a mogul field of grassy, bouncy mounds to Barbondale. Cursing the officious bureaucrat who had resurveyed Calf Top, thus elevating it to mountain status and adding it to my to-do list, I laboured up steep slopes to the summit, turned straight back down, and then broke my Dales hitchhiking virginity with the aforementioned ride in a red hatchback.

In Dent, I dived straight into the George & Dragon pub for the three Cs: a Coke (Diet), a crap (more civilised than squatting on the mountainside) and a charge (of my iPhone, to ensure the OS Maps app was amply juiced up). I salivated over the food menu but, remembering my status as a cash-poor peak-bagger, opted instead to eat my oatmeal crackers with peanut butter on a bench in the churchyard. I happily watched the slow hustle and bustle of the village: tourists passing through, locals chatting with their neighbours, an old lady gardening, barrels being delivered to the pub. It didn't have the ruggedness of other mountainous areas, but Yorkshire was winning me over with its quaint rural charm.

I walked towards the river, intent on hitching another ride five miles down the road to the Arten Gill Viaduct. A few cars passed me by before a woman in her 50s, wearing hippyish clothes and glistening in sweat, appeared from an allotment on the other side of the road.

'Where are you going?' she asked, smiling warmly.

'Just down the road,' I replied vaguely, checking the map on my phone for a more accurate answer.

'No worries, jump in,' she offered, as her partner – a man in his 60s with rough stubble but a kindly face – pulled up in their estate car.

'How do you like the Dales?' the man asked.

'I can't believe how good the weather has been. I've been so lucky.'

'Not luck, my friend, the sun always shines in Yorkshire.'

I laughed – and we continued to exchange pleasantries. The couple were getting married in a week. They seemed really happy and I wished them all the best with their big day. They asked what I was up to and were intrigued by my peak-bagging antics – although my hardcore status was shattered when they recited an anecdote about an old friend, a retiree with a big pension and no wife, who walked a non-stop round of all 1,556 Marilyns, only to immediately complete a second round in reverse order.

We pulled off the road and I jumped out of the back seat, thanking the couple profusely. And then the man dropped a bombshell – 'Be careful. A big storm is coming.' That was news to me, as I wasn't routinely checking the forecast. I preferred to be at the mercy of Mother Nature and vulnerable to whatever the mountains threw at me, rather than over-informed by Met Office updates that might, if inaccurate, spark unfounded fears or unrealistic hopes. After all, the unpredictability of the wild was something I relished. But, as I glanced up at dark, brooding clouds in the distance, it didn't take a genius to foresee what was coming.

I spent ten minutes putting on my waterproofs and stuffing all of my gear into dry sacks, before tentatively climbing up to Arten Gill Viaduct, part of the much-loved Carlisle–Settle railway. The skies were getting moodier by the second and I half wondered whether I'd be wiser to shelter under the towering arches. But I dismissed the thought and continued along a good track to a gate, keeping an anxious eye on the menacing sky, and veered north over grassy slopes, aiming for the top of Great Knoutberry Hill. As I neared the summit, the storm finally hit. Sheet rain pounded down, soaking everything, and thunderclaps roared with an intense ferocity. I was 70 per cent petrified for my safety and 30 per cent awe-inspired by the sheer power of nature. But I ignored my doubts and dashed for the trig point, hoping desperately that I wasn't about to be struck by lightning. Anxieties raced around my head: *have I become so obsessed with peak-bagging that I'm risking my life to bag another top? Is the visor of my hood strengthened with metal wire? Are my reactions fast enough to dodge a bolt from the heavens if one does strike?* I placed my hand fleetingly on the concrete pillar, turned around immediately, and ran full-pelt back down to the gate.

The rest of the afternoon and evening was a soggy slog, as waves of heavy rain rolled over. I took the Pennine Bridleway south and the Ribble Way east, passing disused barns of varying degrees of squalor that I seriously considered sleeping in. But I soldiered on through strong winds and misty white-outs to the uninspiring top of Dodd Fell Hill and then descended, feeling genuinely despondent, towards Rock Edge Cottage, which I'd spotted on the map and hoped might prove my saviour from this stormy hell. I found the building – but, alas, it didn't have a roof. Plan B it was.

I walked north-east on a minor mountain road, daydreaming of hitching a ride to a warm, dry B&B in Hawes. No cars passed, however, so I leaped over a stile and reluctantly set up my tent at the right-angle join of two walls, which I hoped would provide the maximum possible shelter. The rain lashed and the wind whipped, as I hastily pegged down the flapping sheets of Dennis. I contemplated skipping dinner, feeling eager to dive under cover at the earliest opportunity, but decided a proper meal was needed. I boiled up rice with sweet chilli sauce, using fingers that were turning decidedly wrinkly, as if I'd soaked for too long in a bath, and thought about Ronald Turnbull's quip – 'They are the best of nights: they are the worst of nights.' This was definitely the latter. I was cold, wet, tired and miserable, desperate to be anywhere other than on an inhospitable, rain-blasted hillside. But, by comparison with being outdoors, my slightly damp sleeping bag felt like a luxury hotel's finest king-size bed. I slept like a log.

At lunchtime the following day, I found myself lying on my back on the village green in Buckden with my hands cupped behind my head, like a sun-worshipping tourist on a swimming-pool lilo in Marbella. The sun was blazing in a blue sky and the entire contents of my bag were laid out around me in a major drying operation. The conditions had slowly improved throughout the morning, which I'd spent plodding over Drumaldrace, Yockenthwaite Moor, Yorkshire's boggiest hill, and Birks Fell, and by midday the weather was unquestionably glorious.

I lingered in Buckden waiting patiently for my kit to dry out, making numerous trips to the village store for fizzy drinks, flapjacks and sausage rolls, and people-watching as Bank Holiday tourists pottered around the pretty Wharfedale village. It felt healthy and wholesome to entertain myself for a lazy couple of hours without needing my iPhone. Eventually, I mustered the energy to pack up and headed north out of the village on the Buckden Rake, before turning right on the main path to the 2,303ft summit of Buckden Pike, carefully looping around a herd of cows in the process. I reached the tall cone-shaped cairn that marked my final Nuttall of the day and briefly continued south along the ridge in search of a wild-camping spot. After the horror show of the previous night, it seemed I was now in for a treat.

The bright red head of a grouse bobbed up and down among the long grass in front of my tent, its yellow-brown feathery ball of a chick not far behind. A gentle breeze swirled and two inquisitive sheep looked my way, as if utterly puzzled by my presence. Thousands of fluffy white cotton-grass heads hovered above the greenery, as if a giant bag of cotton-wool balls had been dispersed over the landscape. I gazed down over rolling hills and cottage-flecked valleys. Rays of sunshine broke through dramatic white clouds, sending beams of light from above to illuminate the Dales. My soup, whose can I'd been forced to smash open with a rock in a rage of caveman-like desperation due to its lack of a ring-pull and my lack of a tin-opener, was bubbling loudly on my stove. I felt in high spirits: relaxed, worry-free and totally content with life. It was the best of nights.

❋　　❋　　❋

The Daily Adventure Journal of James
28/05/17: Imagine for a second that you wake up at 3am in your tent and need a wee. Outside on the bleak mountainside it is pitch black, blowing a gale, freezing cold, and raining cats and dogs.

What do you do? There are three options: (a) hold it in and hope the urge passes (it won't and you'll spend the next five sleepless hours thinking, *Why the hell didn't I just go at 3am?*); (b) risk it and wee into an old Diet Coke bottle you have lying around (unless you're very careful, this generally leads to your £500 Rab four-season sleeping bag being sprayed with yellowy splashback); or (c) bite the bullet and head outside to do your business (which may leave you so cold and wet that sleeping becomes an impossibility). Option (b) should not be attempted, under any circumstances, when you need a number two.

29/05/17: I wonder if a wild-camping peak-bagger has ever been arrested for possession of Class A drugs? I very much doubt it – but I reckon I came pretty close today. I have a very sweet tooth and, when I go on adventures, I carry around a small plastic Ziploc bag full of white sweetener tablets for my hot drinks. The little white 'pills' could easily resemble a stash of hardcore narcotics. Add in my dishevelled appearance and drifter status and the look is complete. At any rate, it definitely shocks middle-class parents in a quaint Dales lunch-spot when you accidentally leave the Ziploc bag on a picnic bench.

✻   ✻   ✻

I woke at 5am to the sound of heavy rain. I snoozed till 8am and then, unwilling to venture outside to boil up porridge, chomped through dry crackers for breakfast. Feeling more awake, I decamped with military efficiency and took the misty ridge south to a prominent war memorial. The cross commemorates five Polish RAF airmen who fatally crashed on the mountain during a snowstorm in 1942 – one crew member survived, crawling to safety through a brutal blizzard by following the snowy footprints of a fox that led into the valley.

I marched with purpose to the Park Rash Pass road, via Tor Mere Top, and climbed steeply to the 2,310ft top of Great Whernside.

Then I headed briefly south-west to the exposed Scout centre at Hag Dyke, before descending in mizzle to a campsite full of unhappy-looking families packing wet fold-away chairs, soaked barbecue grills and drenched tents. Several mums had eyes that said, 'Why the hell didn't Dave book a hotel like I told him to – I might just divorce him over this.'

My jaw nearly hit the floor as I arrived in Kettlewell. Crowds of pint-swilling, bacon-sarnie-scoffing tourists were crammed outside a pub, watching a bizarre festival. Troupes of Morris dancers pranced and waved white handkerchiefs; a middle-aged lady in a skirt skipped around a pair of swords on the floor, while a man in a flat cap played the accordion; and groups of 'entertainers' milled about, their faces painted half-white, half-black, their top hats adorned with flowers, feathers and badges. It was rural England at its most eccentric.

The fat, aristocratic-looking man who picked me up in his Range Rover an hour later didn't put it so diplomatically.

'I just stumbled across a strange festival in Kettlewell,' I said, trying to make conversation. He was kindly giving me a lift into Littondale, so the least I could do was be friendly.

'Ah, the Morris dancers who come over here every year from Leeds,' he said. 'Or, as us locals refer to them, "the sad fuckers".'

His potty mouth showed no sign of abating as we squeezed past an oncoming caravan on the narrow lane.

'Fucking timewasters these caravanners – clogging up the roads but not spending a penny in the local community. Bloody freeloaders.'

I was enjoying his mini rants so much, I had half a mind to get out some popcorn and settle in for the entertainment.

'Lovely place to live, though, Littondale – right?' I prompted.

'No one really likes where they're from – I fucking hate it.'

And with that last expletive, I disembarked and strolled past ivy-cloaked, dreamy cottages towards Litton Hall. I crossed the River Skirfare and skirted the northern slopes of Darnbrook Fell on a good track, before following a dry-stone wall that climbed over grassy slopes towards the summit. I was beginning to struggle. My back was aching under the weight of my backpack, my energy levels were dipping, and the drizzly rain and low cloud were testing my patience.

I pressed on, hoping for a second wind or at least a break in the precipitation. My boots squelched in muddy ground as I dropped south-west past a forest towards a tarn. I veered south and reached the undistinguished knoll of Fountains Fell South Top. Visibility was slim to non-existent. I retraced my steps carefully, critically aware that getting lost in this white-out would be pretty damn easy, and weaved over land pockmarked with old coal pits and fenced-off shafts to the 2,192ft top of Fountains Fell. 'Grand views of Pen-y-ghent' were promised in my Nuttalls guidebook. I could barely see my hand in front of my face.

Unsure of my plans, I descended west on the Pennine Way to Silverdale Road and tramped along the tarmac for about a mile to Dale Head Farm at the base of Pen-y-ghent. I presumed the mountain was there, but I couldn't see it. I was torn – should I embrace my tiredness, batten down the hatches, and set up camp for the night in the hope that a new day would bring kinder weather? Or, with only two Nuttalls left to complete my 19-peak pilgrimage to the Yorkshire Dales' southern fells, should I just crack on and get it done?

Lured by the prospect of a 'proper' meal if I could make it to Horton-in-Ribblesdale, I opted for the latter and continued down the track through the farmyard. Taking zero pleasure from the experience, I climbed the steep southern ridge of Pen-y-ghent, passing through twin cliffs as the wind and rain dealt me a severe thrashing. The only silver lining was being freed from my backpack, which I dumped for later collection at a path junction. I reached the trig point at the 2,277ft summit and, entering a fatigue-fuelled, trance-like state of mindless walking, somehow managed to complete an out-and-back to Plover Hill, a descent back to my rucksack, and a final laborious stomp west into the town.

Ignoring the penny-pinching voice in my head telling me to wild camp in the school playing fields, I stumbled into The Golden Lion which, according to Google, offered beds in a bunk room for £12 per night. Dripping with rain, coated in mud, and smelling like a man who hadn't showered or used deodorant for four days, I tiptoed to the bar, trying not to knock over a table full of pints with my unwieldy backpack. Perhaps I was being paranoid, but I swear some of the locals smirked at each other, a knowing look that said, 'Check this guy out – freak alert.'

I booked a bed in the 15-person bunk room, which I was informed was entirely empty except for me, and set about making myself look vaguely respectable. This stay was impromptu, so I was far from adequately equipped – no towel, no toiletries, no clean clothes. But I just about managed to de-smell, implementing an improvised and unorthodox shower routine. I washed with a small bottle of mint Original Source shower gel I discovered discarded in a cubicle and then dried myself with repeated dabs of paper from a spare toilet roll (hoping, with all my heart, that a fellow guest wasn't about to burst in to the sight of me, stark naked, gently prodding my pasty skin with Andrex like a pervert with a toilet-tissue fetish). Feeling refreshed, back in the bar I wolfed down pie-and-mash and a pint of Diet Coke, and then crawled into my wooden bunk-bed feeling ecstatically happy about the protection of a roof and four walls.

The following day I was left with the sole task of hitching back to my car in Ingleton. But in which direction? Ingleborough, the inconsiderate mountain, was in the way. So I had a choice of hitchhiking south to Settle and then north-west on the A65, or north to Ribblehead and then south-west on the B6255. Experience had taught me that hitching was easier on minor roads, so I opted for the latter – and it didn't take long. A young chap, an engineer from Liverpool working for Mouchel, picked me up in his dinky, logo-emblazoned company car. He was heading to the Hanson Aggregates quarry just north of Ingleton, so could take me almost all the way to my car. He loved hiking and outdoors activities, so we chatted about adventures of days gone by and laughed and joked as Radio 1 played in the background. I hadn't known the guy two minutes ago, but now we were chatting away like old friends on a road trip. Hitchhiking had added a touch of humanity to my Yorkshire Dales expedition, generosity, friendship and big-heartedness combining to remind a lonesome peak-bagger of the joys of social interaction.

CHAPTER 10

A STRANGE DOUBLE LIFE

Mountains 176–188

DATE	REGION	MOUNTAINS
Sunday 4 June	Lake District Southern Fells	Bowfell 2,959ft (902m) Bowfell North Top 2,841ft (866m) Esk Pike 2,904ft (885m) Rossett Pike 2,136ft (651m)
Friday 9 June	Lake District Southern Fells	Harter Fell 2,142ft (653m)
Sunday 11 June	Lake District Eastern Fells	Heron Pike 2,008ft (612m) Heron Pike North Top 2,037ft (621m) Great Rigg 2,513ft (766m) Fairfield 2,864ft (873m) Hart Crag 2,697ft (822m) Dove Crag 2,598ft (792m) Little Hart Crag 2,090ft (637m) Red Screes 2,546ft (776m)

I returned home from my 19-peak wild-camping adventure in Yorkshire on Tuesday at 4pm. By 7.15 the following morning, I was driving to Kendal for a day in the office. In the blink of an eye I'd swapped my muddy hiking outfit for smart trousers and collared shirt; exchanged my map and compass for a laptop and ring binder of files; and traded friendly hitchhiking for a boring commute. One minute I was standing atop an exposed summit, watching the sunset and feeling like the king of the world, the next I was in a dingy printer room photocopying 50 copies of a 100-page funding bid.

It felt like I had a split personality: half intrepid, footloose mountain addict, and half regular guy with a regular nine-to-five routine. This strange double life was a constant feature of my challenge and it was difficult to get my head around. Sometimes I utterly despised returning to reality – I wanted more than anything to be back out on the trail, in the fresh air and open spaces, focusing on my Nuttalls goal rather than being distracted by work. At other times I craved the normality, relishing the chance of a hot shower, a warm bed, an evening on the sofa, and a comforting dose of ordinariness, familiarity and routine. But most of the time I just felt overwhelmingly busy, as if I was constantly trying to fit two hours of stuff into every hour available. It was stressful.

I coped with it in a simple way. I didn't do anything radical, like catching up on sleep in the office stationery cupboard, surviving on an exclusive diet of Pot Noodles, or showering only once a month. I simply lived a ruthlessly efficient existence. I stopped watching crappy TV; resisted the urge to faff around on social media or get lost in a YouTube black hole; banned myself from using the snooze button; and never had a day of bumming around the shops or lazing about the house. It was remarkable how much time you could free up if you cut out the mindless time-wasting. It felt life-affirming to be blinkered by a single goal. My priority was the Nuttalls and nothing else mattered. For the first time in my life, I had a crystal-clear clarity of purpose – and it felt great.

It would be wrong to suggest, however, that it was possible to climb so many mountains and still keep on top of everything else. I was forced to let other parts of my life slide. My room looked like a bomb had hit it; mounds of unwashed clothes filled corners; stacks of unread letters piled up on my desk; and ever-growing to-do lists remained uncrossed off. I neglected other parts of my life too: I stopped playing five-a-side football; I didn't catch up with friends or family; I never had a night out; and my performance at work was almost certainly below par.

Inevitably, I also spent less time with Becky. Whenever anyone asked me 'How does your wife feel about you doing this challenge?', which happened a lot, I always joked that she was enjoying the time away from me. But in reality it put a bit of a strain on the relationship. I couldn't give Becky the care or time she deserved and I felt guilty as a result. Becky, meanwhile, worried a lot about my safety, missed me when she was home alone in the evenings, and felt aggrieved that she was working hard while I was out enjoying the mountains. At times a cloud loomed over us.

But, overall, we coped reasonably well. Becky was understanding and considerate. She knew how much this challenge meant to me and backed me the whole way, even when it was difficult for her. She cut me some slack, baked me flapjacks, took on household jobs that I was neglecting, and sent me encouraging texts when I was struggling. In return, I tried to find space for a bit of quality time here and there – a coffee in town, a pub meal, a day out, a trip to the cinema. I can't sugar-coat it: spending that much time apart is not recommended for a healthy relationship. But we found a way to fudge through it.

It helped, too, that Becky is a strong, independent woman. She wasn't daunted by the prospect of time alone – in fact, she filled her days with planning and completing her own 500km walking challenge. Another big help was the wonder of mobile-phone technology. We were often able to stay in contact by text. On occasion I was beyond signal for hours or days, but most of the time I would stumble into patches of coverage and could send a message saying I was safe and well or inform her of my plans. A quick text went a long way to put our minds at rest and help us cope with the distance between us.

At times, however, it felt as if I couldn't stop everything – my relationship, my job, my home life – from spiralling out of control. My routine was utterly manic. I was spinning plates, trying to avoid a seemingly inevitable catastrophe of shattered porcelain. On a daily basis I cursed myself for not figuring out a way to take three months off work and climb all the mountains in one big trip. But this was the nature of the beast. I wanted to keep my job and I needed a monthly income – and the whole point was to see if an epic adventure could be integrated into an everyday lifestyle.

That thought was reassuring as I struggled through Wednesday, Thursday and Friday at the office, still feeling weary from my Yorkshire Dales expedition. I wrote funding bids, de-clogged my email inbox and attended meetings – and then filled my evenings with updating my journal and planning routes for future trips. I spent Saturday catching up with a couple of freelance writing jobs and chilling out at home, and then on Sunday I had a day set aside for more Nuttalls-bagging.

I drove to the Langdale Valley, having planned a nine-mile route up Bowfell, Bowfell North Top, Esk Pike and Rossett Pike. Ten hours later, I sat on my couch, my adventure journal on my lap and a pencil behind my ear, and tried to recall the day's events. I honestly could not remember a thing. Was I becoming blind to the beauty of the mountains? Had I regressed to a brain-dead peak-bagging robot? Could I be suffering from too-much-of-a-good-thing syndrome?

Where was it I had started from? What did the Great Slab of Flat Crags look like? Had I met anyone or had anything out of the ordinary happened? After 175 mountains and 33 hikes over the past 12 weeks, everything was blurring into one amorphous memory, with each hike indistinguishable from the next. For most hillwalkers, especially those based in big cities away from the mountains, a climb of magnificent Bowfell would be something to excitedly anticipate beforehand, relish during the event, and then relive after. For me, it felt more like a burden, part of the daily grind of my Nuttalls challenge. Perhaps it was the cloud, rain and limited visibility that had caused my brain to switch off? Or maybe I'd reached some sort of subconscious limit, a watershed point at which mountain apathy had set in? I desperately hoped not.

❋ ❋ ❋

The Daily Adventure Journal of James
04/06/17: Is it possible to use a plastic spork without breaking it in half? Today I snapped yet another one, trying to scoop Nutella out of a jar to go on my tortilla wraps. That takes my collection of split-in-half sporks to at least 18. I really should buy a titanium one.

❋ ❋ ❋

The following week I felt as if I was leapfrogging constantly between my two lives, shifting between alter egos with schizophrenic regularity. Everyday James was Dr Jekyll and Adventure James was Mr Hyde; water from a mountain stream was my transformative serum; and my lustful after-dark exploits were peak-bagging and wild camping.

Everyday James drowned in emails and admin at the office from Monday to Wednesday, before spending all day Thursday setting up and coordinating the Fix the Fells stand at the Keswick Mountain Festival. But Friday was a spare day, with 'Mountain Challenge' highlighted in red on my Google Calendar, so I switched hats and became Adventure James for another fleeting stint.

I drove to Hardknott Pass, delayed by a succession of tootling tourists and slow tractors, and set about climbing Harter Fell, an isolated mountain between Eskdale and the Duddon Valley. Yet again the clag was down, with visibility poor to non-existent. As if to torment me, the Nuttalls guidebook described 'a fine steep cone of a mountain rising to a rocky top with one of the best summits in England'. I marched to the top, unable to appreciate the full grandeur of the mountain, and then plodded down to my car and metamorphosed back into Everyday James.

Saturday was spent manning the stand at the Keswick Mountain Festival – and I was meant to be doing the same on Sunday. However, on arriving at Crow Park on the shores of Derwentwater at 9am, I was greeted by the sight of a gazebo graveyard. A brutal wind was whipping down the lake and had wreaked havoc throughout the exposed site of the festival village. A steward in a high-vis jacket told me the festival was cancelled. I dilly-dallied for 15 minutes, genuinely tempted by a duvet day, but I felt obliged to take the opportunity to up my Nuttalls total. After consulting the guidebook, I eventually decided to head for the Fairfield Horseshoe.

I parked up at Rydal Mount, hiked past a busload of Japanese tourists, and emerged on to open hillside. The weather was as gnarly as hell, with gusting winds and heavy rain. A couple, looking psychologically beaten, had bailed on their attempt and were heading back down. As we chatted briefly, they questioned the sanity of my continuing – but I ignored the doubts. I pressed on against my better judgement and tramped over Heron Pike, Heron Pike North Top and Great Rigg to Fairfield, before turning right along the ridge to complete the famous looped walk via Hart Crag, Dove Crag, Little Hart Crag and Red Screes.

The wind was ferocious, lashing over the ridge with an end-of-the-world intensity. On less exposed sections, it would hold your weight, empowering you to pull off the Michael Jackson anti-gravity lean as if you were starring in the 'Smooth Criminal' video. At other times, the wind was so powerful it would knock you off your feet, or force you to lie down and hold on to a boulder for stability. When I wasn't panicking with fear, I was laughing deliriously at the sheer awesomeness of Mother Nature's might.

It was a brutal, testing day in the fells, but I never felt as if the end was nigh. I made it down safely and felt ecstatic that I'd unexpectedly bagged a bonus eight Nuttalls. That might just make the difference between completing this challenge on time or not.

CHAPTER 11

THE MIND OF A PEAK-BAGGER

Mountains 189–200

DATE	REGION	MOUNTAINS
Monday 12 June	Yorkshire Dales Northern Fells	Wild Boar Fell 2,323ft (708m) Swarth Fell 2,234ft (681m) Baugh Fell 2,224ft (678m) Knoutberry Haw 2,218ft (676m)
Tuesday 13 June	Yorkshire Dales Northern Fells	Lovely Seat 2,215ft (675m) Great Shunner Fell 2,349ft (716m) Little Fell 2,188ft (667m) Hugh Seat 2,260ft (689m) Archy Styrigg 2,280ft (695m) High Seat 2,326ft (709m)
Wednesday 14 June	Yorkshire Dales Northern Fells	Rogan's Seat 2,205ft (672m) Water Crag 2,192ft (668m)

I had the next three days off work and I wanted to complete the Yorkshire Dales' northern fells, a list of 19 mountains located in a triangular wedge of land between Sedbergh, Kirkby Stephen and Hawes. I'd already ticked off the six tops in the Howgills, as well as Nine Standards Rigg, so I had 12 Nuttalls left in my sights. I would complete them, I hoped, in a three-day expedition, with two nights away from home.

Originally I had intended to drive to Wild Boar Fell first thing, but yesterday's storm meant I had to spend the morning packing up the Fix the Fells stand at the Keswick Mountain Festival. It took much longer than anticipated and so, feeling annoyed that real life was again getting in the way, I was running late as I sped down the M6 towards Sedbergh. I didn't arrive at Uldale, the start of my walk, until 3.30pm.

The sky was grey and light rain was falling as I plodded over rough moorland grass to Sand Tarn, following the stone wall flanking Needlehouse Gill. I looped around the tarn and scrambled on gritstone boulders to the 2,323ft top of Wild Boar Fell, my first Nuttall of this trip. With hill fog obscuring the views, I descended south to a col with a small tarn, wondering exactly how many mountains I'd stood atop in a white-out – maybe it had already reached 100?

I gently ascended to the 2,234ft summit of my next peak, Swarth Fell, and then followed a wall first south-east and then south-west as it dropped steeply towards Holmes Moss Hill. The flat ground was saturated. I stepped carefully, trying to place my boots on patches of grass that looked firm, and kept one hand on the metal rail of a rickety fence for stability. I veered away from the fence, sensing I was less likely to be ensnared by the quagmire over to my left. I misjudged it, took a hesitant step and my right leg disappeared into the muddy swamp to well above the knee.

Shit. I tried to pull it free. Nothing. I tugged again. Nothing bar squelching and gurgling sounds. The more I struggled, the more it felt as if I was being sucked deeper into the bog. To make matters worse, just as I was trying to stay calm, I spotted the half-submerged carcass of a dead sheep about five feet to my left. *Oh God, am I destined for a similar fate? Is this how it all ends? What did Bear Grylls do when I saw him escape from quicksand on one of his action-man TV shows?*

Needless to say, I wasn't really that close to death. After a couple of attempts at shuffling and squirming in different directions, I finally freed my cold, wet, soiled leg and continued through the swamp, which mercifully became easier to negotiate, towards Rawthey Gill Foot. The drama of Holmes Moss Hill was, however, not quite over. I spotted a number of large birds perched in a row along a rusting metal fence. My first thought was that they were birds of prey, and as I got closer I realised it was indeed a parliament of short-eared owls. Disturbed by my presence, they flew off, squawking loudly and angrily, and one circled over my head. I'd never seen anything like it before.

I climbed alongside Rawthey Gill on a faint sheep trod. The browny-red stream cascaded over rocky ledges in a series of mini waterfalls, while thick moss gave the green banks a bouncy, soft feel. The only sounds were the tumble of the water and the rustle of a sheep or two in the overgrowth. It was an enchanting little valley that felt remote and secret. Hundreds of black slugs looked imperturbable, relaxing on the wet grass, and every now and then a flash of rodent fur would dash into a hole. What were they? They were so lightning quick, I couldn't tell.

I veered south to Gill Head and emerged at a flat plateau with a collection of small tarns. The climb had drained me of energy and I suddenly felt ravenously hungry. Stupidly, I'd thrown only a couple of snacks into my backpack during the afternoon rush to get my walk started. I wolfed them down and pressed on to Tarn Rigg Hill, the 2,224ft top of Baugh Fell. It was 7pm and I still had about two hours to go. By the time I'd nipped west to the nearby Nuttall of Knoutberry Haw and taken the flat ridge to West Baugh Fell Tarn, I was feeling light-headed and empty-stomached. Adequate sustenance is vital in the mountains – and I was used to chomping on all manner of unhealthy snacks in the joyous knowledge that my calorie-burning stats were through the roof. This was my first experience of mountain hunger and I hated it.

By 9pm I had stumbled back down to my car. I was too hungry to bother with cooking anything, so I stuffed my face with a peculiar dinner of chorizo wraps, and peanut butter on Hobnobs. An added oddity was that I couldn't find a knife, so I found myself plastering the crunchy spread on to the nobbly biscuits using my fingers, like a famished toddler let loose in the kitchen. When my hunger was well and truly satisfied, I turned the key in the ignition and drove east as heavy rain began to fall. The forecast had predicted as much and, consequently, I'd booked myself into Hardraw Old School Bunkhouse, an independent hostel in the village of Hardraw, just to the north of Hawes.

I checked my phone during my self-imposed 30-minute evening window for internet use and a WhatsApp message from my friend Ed popped up. Our conversation went like this:

Ed: 'How's it going?'

Me: 'All good, buddy. I'm currently in a 30-person bunkhouse in the Yorkshire Dales and I'm the only person here – creepy.'

Ed: 'That's basically the start of every good horror movie – I'll send a search party for you.'

Me: 'Oh God, I think the front door might've just creaked open.'

Ed: 'It was nice knowing you.'

After a fitful night of sleep broken by horror-filmesque nightmares set in a Dales bunkhouse, I woke at 7.30am, ate a breakfast of granola, and prepared for another battle with the fells. My plan was to climb six Nuttalls, combining two of the guidebook's day-walks into one linear route heading roughly north-west from Hardraw to Outhgill, followed by a hitchhike back to the bunkhouse. It was a misty, drizzly day, but it could've been worse. I donned waterproofs and my spare pair of walking boots, opting not to brave yesterday's still-damp pair, and headed through the village to cross Hardraw Beck. I chuckled as I passed a pub with a sign stating 'Hippies Use Backdoor: No Exceptions', weaved my way through fields to the open hillside, and then plodded over pathless moorland to Lovely Seat, my first Nuttall of the day.

As I descended north-west to a minor mountain road on the way to Great Shunner Fell, I contemplated the way my mind worked while out on my own in the mountains. What did I think about all day? Did I substitute internal conversations for human interaction? Was my brain active and alert, solving problems, realigning, de-stressing? Or was I slipping into a state of brain inactivity, like a computer in sleep mode?

It was all of these things and more, I concluded. During my first day of walking after a period of work, my mind would invariably be plagued with worries. *Damn, I forgot to post that letter. I must remember to email Richard. I'd better phone Joanne when I'm home.* But over time these would dissipate as the therapeutic process of being out in the mountains worked its magic. Work problems no longer seemed so insurmountable; solutions presented themselves; a sense of perspective materialised; and a deeper sense of relaxation kicked in.

This effortless self-reflection went beyond the work arena, too. When out in the mountains, I often found myself thinking about my life in general – my family and friends, my relationships, my hopes and dreams, my mental health – and always seemed to gain a clarity and decisiveness that eluded me in the concrete jungle. Time alone in the mountains was the 'kicking leaves' time I needed to make good life decisions.

Once I'd overcome the tense mindset of real life, my internal world could go in a number of directions while solo hiking. Sometimes I'd think quite practically, calculating how many Nuttalls or miles or wild camps there were left to complete during a trip; or mentally storing information about the walk and the day's experiences, ready to transfer them to my adventure journal that evening. At other times I'd become incredibly inquisitive about something random, wondering about a hiker in the distance (Who is he? Where's he from? Why is he here?) or maybe contemplating the history of the dry-stone wall next to me (When was it built? Who were the men who built it? How did they manage such back-breaking work?). On other occasions my internal dialogue would be entirely haphazard – a long-forgotten memory would surface from my subconscious, or a funny moment from years gone by would pop into my head and make me smile.

When things got monotonous, I might count steps or fence posts, or try to recite the starting eleven of West Bromwich Albion's 2002 promotion-winning team. When I stood atop a clear summit, I tried to identify the mountains I'd already visited and those that lay ahead, envisaging what the rest of my hike would entail. And when I was feeling lonely or tired or fed up, I thought fondly about my loved ones and looked forward to the time when we would be reunited. Sometimes, when I'd spent too long alone in the mountains, I'd do strange and disinhibited things, such as loudly mimicking the gargling calls of the ever-present grouse; rapping verses of my favourite hip-hop songs, gesticulating with my hands like a strange fusion of a geeky rambler and Kanye West; or descending into bizarre daydreams about discovering a dead hiker or being attacked by a stag. But, thankfully, I never fully regressed into a state of wilderness-induced insanity. I never once got down on all fours to graze the lush grass with a herd of cows, nor did I ever start talking to the Herdwicks in an attempt to woo the prettiest ewe with my best chat-up lines.

However, more often than any of the thought processes above kicking in, I'd simply get into a mindless rhythm of putting one foot in front of the other. I would walk for hours on end thinking about absolutely nothing at all. I'd get to lunchtime and wonder what on earth I'd thought about for the last four hours – I couldn't recollect a thing. My brain was empty. And in a world where we are all so busy, so preoccupied and so stressed, it was liberating and joyous to feel so vacant.

Even when I was at my most unoccupied, however, the subject of food would always infiltrate my mind. From about 10am I'd obsess about what I was going to have for lunch, where I'd eat it, when I'd eat it and what order I'd eat it in. Two wraps to start with, then raisin-nut mix, then cranberries, then banana chips, and then four – no five – rows of white chocolate. It was a great motivator, a reward to inspire me to complete one last ascent or smash out one more mile. And the food wasn't just about providing sugars and nutrients for my muscles – a good meal always gave me a huge morale boost out in the mountains.

So, after a slap-up lunch on top of Great Shunner Fell, I felt ready for the afternoon ahead. I'd already ticked off two Nuttalls in the morning, but I had four more to go. I followed a zig-zagging wall west over a wide ridge which felt like a lonely no man's land of high moors, to reach Little Fell. I turned north and ascended easily to the 2,260ft top of Hugh Seat, where a 17th-century monument known as Lady's Pillar commemorates the life of Sir Hugh de Morville, one of the knights who murdered Thomas Beckett in Canterbury Cathedral in 1170. I continued north over the Mallerstang Edge escarpment to my final two Nuttalls, Archy Styrigg and High Seat, enjoying the odd glance back to the cragged lip of Hangingstone Scar. Then I completed my day's walk by dropping down to the picturesque hamlet of Outhgill.

The only problem was where I'd ended up. I was 11 miles from the bunkhouse in Hardraw and, to avoid a long, energy-sapping tramp home, I'd need to get a ride. I started ambling south on the wall-lined road, turning green with envy at the Dales cottages I passed, and put my thumb out whenever a car appeared. It didn't take long. A retired couple, who'd moved to Yorkshire from London and also ran a B&B on the Isle of Skye, kindly took me all the way back to Hardraw. Two hours later, after a giant pasta dinner, I curled up in my bunk, feeling utterly drained from the day's exertions.

❋   ❋   ❋

The Daily Adventure Journal of James

12/06/17: Consider for a minute – would you walk for five hours, uphill, alone, through torrential rain and raging wind, to visit a cinema with a screen that you knew didn't work? Obviously, you wouldn't. I wouldn't either. No one would. It would be idiocy. So why do I climb mountains in such objectionable weather when I know full well clouds will obscure any and all views? You can't even get popcorn or pick'n'mix on top of a mountain.

13/06/17: I need to improve my small-talk technique in the fells. Today I realised I have exactly the same conversation with everyone I meet in the mountains, as if it's scripted. It goes like this. Me: 'Lovely/terrible day, isn't it?' Hiker: 'Beautiful/awful, we're so lucky/ unlucky.' Me: 'Where are you heading?' Hiker: 'Oh, just to X – and you?' Me: 'I came up from Y and I'm heading to Z. Well, have a good day, nice to meet you.' Hiker: 'You, too – bye.' I'd much prefer it went like this. Me: 'Hi there.' Hiker: 'Oh my God, are you James Forrest, the legendary peak-bagger? I've seen you on Instagram. You're my adventure hero. Can I get a selfie with you?' This has never happened. Ever. I think I want it to happen.

✳ ✳ ✳

As I prepared my breakfast in the hostel kitchen the following morning, a thrush flew straight into the window with a loud thud, knocking itself out, like a kamikaze pilot on a suicide mission. A fellow guest, a woman, let out a yelp of anguish and rushed to aid the short-sighted bird, giving it water and placing it in a shoebox lined with paper towels.

Half an hour later, two coast-to-coast cyclists appeared, freshly showered, and began brewing coffee and preparing their lunches. They were oblivious to the navigationally challenged bird incident earlier. We all started chatting and the woman suddenly remembered the drama and started to recount the tale.

'Did I tell you about my thrush?'

For a split second the two cyclists glanced at each other, as if to say, 'Jesus, too much information.'

Clearly brainwashed by some very effective advertising, I almost blurted out in parrot fashion: 'Vagisil medicated cream gives you the fast thrush relief you need as part of an intimate daily care range.'

But before I could, the woman swiftly shifted the thought-train from personal hygiene to the real story. 'I mean, a thrush flew into the kitchen window this morning and I saved it.'

I packed up my stuff, loaded the car and drove towards Muker in Swaledale, as the sun shone brightly in a blue sky. I had one walk and two Nuttalls left to complete on this mini trip – and it looked like it would end on a high. I walked past the village's attractive cottages, which glowed almost golden in the sun, and arrived at a swinging wooden gate providing passage through a dry-stone wall. Beyond were a series of riverside meadows alive with wild flowers: seas of green bursting with flashes of yellow, orange, pink and purple. After two days of grey weather and dreary green scenery, it was a dazzling Technicolor tapestry. I almost felt as if I needed sunglasses to cope with the brightness.

I crossed the River Swale at Ramps Holme Bridge and took the old Corpse Way north, before climbing the delightful gorge of Swinner Gill. I stopped to snack on four gingernut biscuits and made a mental note that this was my favourite section of walking in the Yorkshire Dales so far. But, regrettably, the rest of the hike couldn't live up to that standard. From the head of the waterfall it was a dull trudge along a bulldozed shooting-track to the summit of Rogan's Seat. I mulled over the strange situation that many of our mountains are managed not for hikers but, as grouse moors, for a minority of tweed-wearing, shotgun-wielding hunters. Then I continued north for a mile along a fence to the 2,192ft top of Water Crag.

By a quirk of timing I reached two milestones simultaneously as I placed my hand purposefully on the concrete trig pillar of Water

Crag. That was my double century up: I'd climbed 200 Nuttalls. I was tempted to raise my hands aloft in triumph like a cricketer who has just reached a milestone score. It was also exactly three months since I'd started. I was halfway through my epic challenge, with 50 per cent of my target time elapsed. But I'd ticked off only 45 per cent of the mountains. I basked in the glory of my double century but also felt a pang of nerves. After all I'd been through already, did I really have enough energy and determination left in the tank to climb 246 mountains over the next three months?

CHAPTER 12

A CLOUD IN THE HEAVENS

Mountains 201–218

DATE	REGION	MOUNTAINS
Monday 19 June	Lake District Eastern Fells	Birkhouse Moor 2,356ft (718m) Striding Edge 2,821ft (860m) Helvellyn 3,117ft (950m) Nethermost Pike 2,923ft (891m) Dollywaggon Pike 2,815ft (858m) Seat Sandal 2,415ft (736m) St Sunday Crag 2,759ft (841m) Birks 2,041ft (622m)
Tuesday 20 June	Lake District Eastern Fells	Catstye Cam 2,920ft (890m) Helvellyn Lower Man 3,035ft (925m) White Side 2,831ft (863m) Raise 2,897ft (883m) Sheffield Pike 2,215ft (675m)
Wednesday 21 June	Lake District Eastern Fells	Hart Side 2,480ft (756m) Green Side 2,608ft (795m) Stybarrow Dodd 2,766ft (843m) Great Dodd 2,812ft (857m) Clough Head 2,382ft (726m)

I only ever got one detention at secondary school. It wasn't for fighting, or swearing, or truancy, or smoking weed, or punching the history teacher everyone hated. Nothing badass like that. It was for 'sheep worrying'. Basically, one step away from 'sheep shagging'.

Let me explain. On a geography field trip to Snowdonia in 1996, a group of about seven of us, aged 12, were messing around in our spare time and getting into mischief: throwing boulders into a stream, climbing on top of hay bales, exploring empty barns, and playing tag in a field. The latter at some point morphed into running around and chasing sheep. It wasn't kiss chase, though. I promise.

In our eyes, we were just city boys having a laugh in the countryside – and we didn't realise how many monstrous rural *faux pas* we were committing. We were left in no doubt, though, when a shotgun-wielding farmer, so irate he was frothing at the mouth, turned up and marched us off his land, spitting insults in a thick Welsh accent.

Inevitably, our teachers berated us fiercely, saying we had brought the school into disrepute, and dished out Saturday-morning detentions to us all. I was distraught. What would my parents think? I was a goody-two-shoes and a straight-A student. Things like this didn't happen to me. I felt guilty when I got an A-minus, let alone going home with a detention card with the words 'sheep worrying' written next to 'reason for detention'.

I need not have worried about my parents, however. The real trauma was encountering Mr Lambie, the tall, bearded teacher who had slapped us with the detention. For the next five years, the remainder of my school career, he would immediately launch into a high-pitched 'Baaaaaaa' whenever he saw me in the corridor, much to the amusement of everyone present. Looking back now, it was excellent banter but at the time I wanted him to die a slow and painful death. Preferably by having his guts ripped out by some sort of demonic ram, while the rest of the sheep flock 'Baaaaaaa-ed' ironically.

Those embarrassing school memories suddenly flooded into my mind as I plodded through the fields outside Patterdale, near Ullswater in the Lake District. A high-pitched bleat from a sheep teleported me instantly back to my school in 1996 – and I turned around in panic, half expecting to see Mr Lambie surrounded by legions of my friends, laughing at my misfortune. Of course, it was only an innocent Herdwick, but the memory still made me cringe and turn a shade of red. I laughed it off. I certainly wouldn't be chasing any sheep on this occasion. I had enough mileage to get through as it was.

After my mini expedition to the Yorkshire Dales' northern fells, I'd spent the next three days working, followed by a relaxed Sunday hanging out with Becky. I then had Monday, Tuesday and Wednesday free for Nuttalls-bagging. My plan was to complete three day-walks in the Lake District's eastern fells, including some of the national park's iconic routes. I was really looking forward to it, particularly with the Met Office website displaying that rare sight – big, round, bright suns pretty much constantly for the next few days.

On the Monday I drove to Patterdale at the south-western end of Ullswater, which has a reputation as one of Britain's most beautiful lakes. I walked down the lane alongside Grisedale Beck before veering north-west uphill for the top of Birkhouse Moor. It was an anti-climax of a Nuttall, but I didn't care. Ahead lay Striding Edge, the razor-sharp ridge that leads to the summit of Helvellyn – one of the Lake District's most spectacular walks.

I continued briefly south-west along a dry-stone wall and bumped into a Polish hiker, who was frowning over his map. He asked for help with directions. Red Tarn, the mountain lake that sits majestically in a hollow surrounded by the curved auditorium of Helvellyn's cliffs and crags, was temporarily hidden from view, leading to the confusion. The quality of his map hardly helped. He was navigating off a ludicrously basic plan, printed out from Google on a single sheet of A4 paper. It had a dire lack of detail – no contours, no footpaths, almost no features and no scale. He might just as well have written the word 'Helvellyn' in biro on his hand and used that. But I didn't judge or condescend. I put the hiker's mind at rest and we chatted jovially, walking together to the Hole-in-the-Wall and beyond that to the beginning of the ridge.

Striding Edge is a knife-edge arête: a sharp, narrow spine of rock with precipitous drops on either side and a tightrope of a path edging along the top. It is a rip-roaring route with high levels of exposure. One slip could be fatal. However, it is not technically difficult. Classed as a Grade 1 scramble, the easiest rating, it is well within the grasp of most competent hillwalkers, given the right conditions.

And that is certainly what my new friend and I had. The sky was light blue and filled with fluffy, marshmallow-like clouds; the air was still and calm; and the stony trod below our feet was bone dry. Beams of sunlight burst through the cloud canopy and warmed our necks. The grassy valleys radiated green, the yellow tracks of exposed subsoil far below us transported hikers the size of ants, and Red Tarn and distant Ullswater turned a majestic purple-blue. It was a Lakeland scene of such beauty that it felt like your heart was doing somersaults and your head was spinning.

We detoured slightly off the path to visit High Spying How, a rocky spot at the beginning of the ridge that marks the Nuttall top of Striding Edge. But the real excitement lay ahead. We tiptoed carefully along the gnarly ridge, as if travelling along the spiny backbone of a sleeping dinosaur we dared not wake. Our hands gripped bare rock as we negotiated little steps and ledges, and our legs turned to jelly as we gazed wide-eyed 1,000ft down to Nethermost Cove. There was the tantalising taste of danger in our mouths and the tingling sensation of adrenalin in our bodies – but it never felt as if we were recklessly flirting with death.

Our confidence grew and, feeling invincible, we strode speedily along the airy ridge, nimbly hopping over boulders and dancing along the spiky crest like Alpine ibex. We were mountain legends, expertly dealing with a feared razorback ridge as if it were a walk in

Above: As a child, I (second from right) make it to a mountain summit with my grandpa, granny, dad and brother Tom.

Below: Aged eight, hiking with my brother Tom (right) in the Lake District.

Above: Enjoying the Lake District with little brother Tom (left).

Below: On a family holiday in the Lake District, 1991 (I'm on the right).

Above: Greg's Hut bothy in the North Pennines.
Below left: Wet feet in the North Pennines. Below right: Finding a pair of ear-muffs.

Above: Mesmerised by the Langdale Pikes outline, Lake District.
Below: Looking down to Wastwater, Lake District.

Above: Sunset while wild camping at Dead Stones, North Pennines.
Below left: Trying (and failing) to keep my feet dry in the Yorkshire Dales. Below right: Wild camping at Dead Stone

Above: Upwards to the Whiteside summit, Lake District.
Below: Standing atop Steeple, Lake District.

Above: Blue skies over Ingleborough, Yorkshire Dales.

Below: Hitchhiking in the Yorkshire Dales.

Above: Dinnertime while wild camping on Buckden Pike, Yorkshire Dales.
Below: Stumbling across an eccentric festival in Kettlewell, Yorkshire Dales.

Above: Gazing over Ullswater in the Lake District.
Below: Enjoying the views near Yes Tor in Dartmoor.

Above: A chilled-out morning in the Berwyn mountains, Wales.
Below: A glorious evening on the Aran ridge, Snowdonia. Bottom: Hiking in front of Aran Fawddwy, Snowdonia.

Left: Collapsed tent in the Brecon Beacons, Wales.

Below left: Muddy feet near Branstree in the Lake District.

Bottom: Feeling cold, wet and miserable on ascent of Moel yr Oge Snowdonia.

Above: Looking to Crib Goch, Snowdonia.
Below: Walking in the Glyders, Snowdonia.

Above: Wild camping at Elidir Fawr, Snowdonia.
Below: Gazing out over Arenig Fawr, Snowdonia.

Above: Breakfast while wild camping in the Arenigs, Snowdonia.
Below: Relaxing on the summit of Arenig Fach, Snowdonia.

Above: My adventure buddy Joe Moreton, who joined me hiking in the Cadair Idris range, Snowdonia.

Below: Adventuring with Joe on the Cotswold Way back in 2016.

Above: Reaching the summit of Craig-y-llyn, my last Nuttall in Wales.
Below: The old pair of women's hiking boots I wore to complete the challenge.

Above: My final summit: Scafell Pike, England's highest peak.

Below: Meeting John and Anne Nuttall when it was all over.

the park. I'd completed Striding Edge several times before, but never in such pristine conditions. In the hazy, aureate hue of early summer, we stood in silence atop our sawtooth pedestal, and gazed in awe across Lakeland. It was one of those rare and intimate moments when you just felt at peace with the world.

We scrambled awkwardly down The Chimney, a rocky chute that we navigated with a few far-from-graceful bum shuffles, and then scrambled up the daunting-looking but manageable final rock face to the summit plateau. Greeted by crowds of other hikers, my scrambling partner and I sat by the OS trig column and had a well-deserved drinks break. He told me of his love for the wilderness of Scotland, about his life in York, and of his plans to soon return to Poland to start a family. After 15 minutes, we bade each other farewell. He was turning north and east to complete the classic Helvellyn horseshoe, a high-level loop of Red Tarn featuring a scramble up Striding Edge and a scramble down the similarly precipitous Swirral Edge ridge. My Nuttalls-bagging mission, however, was drawing me south.

I descended gently towards the col at Swallow Scarth, keeping the steep cliffs of Lad Crag a safe distance to my left, and then climbed easily to the 2,923ft top of Nethermost Pike. I continued south to the next Nuttall of Dollywaggon Pike and then veered off-piste to descend briefly towards the western edge of Grisedale Tarn. As I did so, my eyes traced the route ahead of me: a steep but short climb south along a fence to Seat Sandal, before descending east to Grisedale Hause, ascending again almost to the summit of Fairfield, and then returning north-east back to Patterdale via the sweeping ridgeline of St Sunday Crag and Birks, the final two Nuttalls on my radar.

I threw my daypack on the ground, lay down in the thick grass and stretched out. The sun was hot and I could feel my exposed arms and legs burning slightly. But I didn't mind. After all the days of horrendous weather, this was indulgent and hedonistic. The softness of the grass on my skin connected me to the fells. I was all alone, except for a raven soaring in the thermals and a herd of sheep grazing in the col below. I watched closely as insects crawled through the maze of grassy blades; Grisedale Tarn winked at me as rays of sunlight twinkled off its deep blue surface; and the bulky mound of Seat Sandal called to me, imploring me to visit its summit. But I ignored its voice – and indulged in a few more minutes of bliss, lying on a hillside and feeling blessed.

✳　　✳　　✳

The Daily Adventure Journal of James
20/06/17: I'd never wish for a hiker to fall down a precipitous ravine and snap their leg in half, break three ribs and mangle their face. Except perhaps that fellwalker near Raise today who brutally blanked me after I loudly and cheerfully said, 'Good morning.' I've always found that 99 per cent of walkers are super friendly, supportive and sociable. The outdoors community is amazing. But then, as with anything, there are the 1 per cent. Who are those people? If you encounter one, trip them up for me, please. Cheers.

✳　　✳　　✳

The following morning I wolfed down a bowl of mixed-berry granola and prepared for the day ahead. I made a sandwich, filled my water bottle, downloaded a map to my iPhone, consulted the Nuttalls guidebook and, in good time, jumped into my car, once again destined for Ullswater. My plan was to complete what I'd started yesterday by climbing the fells on the other side of Red Tarn: Catstye Cam, Helvellyn Lower Man, White Side, Raise and Sheffield Pike.

A dense blanket of white cloud filled the sky as I tramped west along the path high above Glenridding Beck. But intermittent gaps in the sky's white veil revealed patches of blue and flashes of sunlight, like glimmers of hope for a fine day in the fells. And I was confident it would be. I was on an optimistic high. I felt great: well-rested, fit, motivated and content – and utterly mesmerised by the scene ahead.

Catstye Cam is beautiful to look at: an elegant, almost perfect, pyramid, like a child's drawing of a symmetrical mountain. It is the kind of peak that has an irresistible allure for fellwalkers – once seen, it has to be climbed. Its only fault is its proximity to Helvellyn, Britain's favourite walk according to a 2018 poll by ITV. Catstye Cam will for ever live in the shadow of its higher neighbour, all too often relegated to 'side-trip' status for hikers taking on the Striding Edge–Swirral Edge horseshoe.

However, it felt right to be giving Catstye Cam my undivided attention, as I veered south following Red Tarn Beck towards the base of the fell. I turned off the main path before the tarn and climbed steep grassy slopes, awash with white cotton-grass, up the eastern ridge to the 2,920ft summit. My first Nuttall of the day was in the bag. A light wind blew and I felt a tad chilly as I sat on a rock to drink in the scenery.

It was a superb viewpoint from which to look across to Striding Edge. Minuscule figures, silhouetted cinematically by the white-sky backdrop, crept along the jagged arête. Below them, near-vertical grassy slopes, scarred with rough crags, scree chutes and boulder fields, plunged precipitously down to Red Tarn, which looked almost black. From this angle, I felt fretful about the tiny hikers teetering on the razor edge. They were one mistake away from disaster.

I could hardly believe that I'd hiked Striding Edge in winter one year, with a light dusting of snow on the ridge. It was an event that I remembered because it seemed symbolic of risk management in the mountains. I'd done it in micro-spikes – a set of chains and spikes that attach to your boots to provide extra grip, like a cheaper and simpler version of crampons – and, for me, that felt within my limits. I completed the scramble without difficulty. But I saw another couple fully kitted out in helmets and crampons who were roped together. The sight made me wonder whether I was being reckless with my own safety. And then, as if to answer to my question, three young and intrepid-looking fell-runners sped past us in shorts and trail shoes. They agilely progressed along the ridge, always in control. It made me think that safety in the mountains is different for each individual, depending on your confidence and skill set.

Reluctantly I turned my eyes from Striding Edge and focused on the scramble ahead up Swirral Edge. It didn't look as daunting as its partner across the tarn. It was a less exposed, shorter scramble, without such a prominent knife-edge profile. But, naturally, it still had the air of an adrenalin-inducing, nerve-jangling scramble. I was salivating at the prospect. I dropped gently south-west to the col and composed myself before taking the obvious trod eroded by thousands of booted feet before me. I meandered along the ridge, picking my way over stony barriers, overhanging boulders and loose scree, and perched atop a bouldered turret like a mountain goat. I looked out over Lakeland, my heart rejoicing in exultation, and was reminded of one of my favourite Alfred Wainwright turns of phrase: 'One's feet are on the ground, but one's eyes see as from a cloud in the heavens.'

I pressed on and easily gained the summit plateau of Helvellyn. I'd already ticked off the main summit yesterday, so I turned right along the broad ridge to visit the 3,035ft top of Helvellyn Lower Man, my second Nuttall of the day. I continued north downhill towards the saddle, glancing at a fellow hiker toiling uphill. I did a double take. I blinked and shook my head, looking back at the man I'd just passed. He was an old-school gent: brown leather walking boots, thick cream socks pulled over his beige trousers, white collared shirt, black tie, tweed jacket, and navy umbrella as a makeshift walking stick. His face was worn and wrinkled, but warm, and grey wispy hair masked his baldness with a comb-over. The look wasn't a carbon copy, but I did for a second think I was witnessing a reincarnation of Mr Wainwright.

I climbed easily up gentle slopes to the summit of White Side and gazed back at Helvellyn Lower Man, as three daredevil mountain-bikers whizzed down the ridge towards me. I veered north-east to easily gain the summit of Raise, wondering what it would be like to ski the slopes to my right, the home of the Lake District Ski Club, and then descended with a spring in my step to Sticks Pass. Turning right, I followed Sticks Gill east to an area of quarry tips and, feeling surprisingly energetic, climbed straight ahead to quickly reach the summit of Sheffield Pike.

My final Nuttall of the day had been bagged. I counted on my fingers – 13 summits ticked off in the past two days. Not bad going. I deserved a break. I found a lone rock, its grey colour complemented with patches of bright yellow lichens, and sat quietly. It was an ideal platform from which to gaze at Ullswater. The lake stretched out sumptuously into the horizon, its still, blue surface glazed like a sheet of glass. A solitary steamer chugged along the water, breaking the stillness with a rippling V-shaped wake. The undulating humps of Place Fell and Hallin Fell framed the lake perfectly to the south; the gentle mass of Gowbarrow and clusters of dark green woodland, like florets of broccoli, did the same to the north. Fleecy clouds floated in the light blue sky, their shadows rolling over the landscape, while swathes of fellside were bathed golden by shafts of sunlight from above. Britain's most beautiful lake? It was difficult to disagree.

Sixteen hours later I parked up close to the hamlet of Dockray, east of Keswick, ready to climb the five Nuttalls I had left to visit in the Lake District's eastern fells. It was another glorious day. I packed light, carrying a small daypack and wearing trainers, shorts and a T-shirt. I jogged slowly down the minor road to Dowthwaitehead where a sign at a farm, reading 'Due to recent cutbacks the light at the end of the tunnel has been switched off', made me chuckle. I climbed over boggy, pathless ground and then followed a ruined wall to the summit of Hart Side.

I glanced down at the map on my phone and noticed a text message from my wife. I had forgotten to put my device on airplane mode. 'Did you remember to cancel that wardrobe-fitter appointment?' Crap. I hadn't. The rep was meant to be visiting us this afternoon. Luckily, I had two bars of reception, so I crouched down next to the 2,480ft summit cairn, pressed call, and cupped my hands around the phone to try and block out the howl of the strong wind.

'Hello? Hello? Can you hear me?'

'It's a bad line, sir. How can I help?'

'Sorry. I'm on top of a windy mountain. I'm out peak-bagging.'

'Excuse me?'

'Never mind. Can I cancel an appointment, please?'

If ever there was a moment that symbolised the strange double life I was living, it was then. It was so ridiculous it made me laugh aloud. Maybe in a month I'd find myself filing my tax return from a wild-camping spot in remote Snowdonia, or sending work emails while teetering on the perilous Crib Goch ridge. It was also a classic example of why I'd pledged to always switch my phone to airplane mode when in the mountains. One minute I was wallowing in the worry-free joy of walking a sun-drenched Lakeland ridge, the next my mind was consumed with the stresses of my chaotic house move. It was shocking how one simple text could shatter the escapism of the wild and teleport me back into the world of everyday hassles. I needed to be more disciplined with my rules on mobile-phone use in the fells, but I could tell I was beginning to struggle with it.

The next hour or so was enjoyable, easy walking over grassy ridges to the tops of Green Side, Stybarrow Dodd and Great Dodd. I stopped for lunch at Great Dodd's shelter cairn and found myself biting chunks out of a red pepper as if it was a juicy apple. My obsession with peak-bagging was not proving compatible with regular trips to the supermarket, hence that morning I'd grabbed the pepper from my almost-empty fridge. I was actually enjoying its sweet, crunchy taste – but again it seemed symbolic of my eccentric existence. I was reminded of Christopher McCandless talking to his apple in the film *Into the Wild*. I was half tempted to begin a conversation with the capsicum, but just about resisted.

I looped north-west and descended to the prominent knoll of Calfhow Pike before climbing north to the 2,382ft summit of Clough Head, my final Nuttall of the day. The sky was marbled with a swirling mix of blue and white. Low cloud hung down to distant fells, eddying over ridges and threatening to create a spectacular cloud inversion in the valleys. Beams of sunlight pierced the clouds and illuminated patches of hillside, as if they had been purposely selected for the honour. I stopped and stared, swivelling 360 degrees. My feet were on the ground, but my eyes saw as from a cloud in the heavens.

CHAPTER 13

THE BOG OF ETERNAL STENCH

Mountains 219–223

DATE	REGION	MOUNTAINS
Thursday 29 June	Peak District	Bleaklow Head 2,077ft (633m) Higher Shelf Stones 2,037ft (621m)
Friday 30 June	Peak District	Kinder Scout 2,087ft (636m)
Saturday 1 July	Dartmoor	Yes Tor 2,031ft (619m) High Willhays 2,037ft (621m)

'I can't take it any more – this is doing my nut in,' I said, spiralling into a Tuesday-night tantrum of negativity.

'What's wrong?' asked Becky, about to roll her eyes.

'I've got no wardrobe. We've got no internal doors in this house. All my stuff is in boxes. My life is all over the place.'

'We'll get there – take a chill pill.'

'I just need to get my shit together, but I'm constantly chasing my tail. I'm way behind at work. And I'm way behind with the mountains. I'm panicking I might not make it.'

The past six days at work, including an all-weekend event, had left me feeling down. Everything was stacking up against me. The house move had thrown a massive spanner in the works at exactly the wrong time. My Fix the Fells job was hectic, with an ever-growing to-do list, and a series of freelance-writing deadlines was looming. A few evenings spent revising my peak-bagging schedule had started me doom-mongering too. It was touch-and-go whether I'd make it in six months. The task ahead was looking increasingly daunting. I knew that it didn't really matter if it took seven months, or six months and two weeks, but I was obsessing over it. I'd set out to do it in half a year and that's what I wanted to do.

'Don't beat yourself up about it. You'll figure it out – pull a few sickies or something. Or maybe just pretend you've climbed some of the peaks, no one would know,' suggested Becky from the sofa.

'Fair enough – that's Snowdonia "complete" then,' I said, laughing and pretending to tick off a swathe of Nuttalls in my notepad in one fell swoop. Becky's humour had reminded me not to take myself too seriously. It wasn't worth getting stressed over.

I set off the following morning for the Peak District in a more positive frame of mind. My camping gear was on the passenger seat of my VW Golf because, bizarrely, I had a single mattress crammed into the back. I'd borrowed it from Mum and Dad during the house move and needed to drop it back to Birmingham. The mattress wouldn't fit in lengthways so it was half folded, forming a shallow U-shape. It was as if I'd converted my car into the shittiest campervan of all time.

I had the next four days off work. My plan was to spend Thursday and Friday hiking in the Peak District, followed by a stop-over in Birmingham to drop off the mattress. On Saturday, I'd drive to Dartmoor to bag the two pesky Nuttalls located an inconvenient 800-mile round trip from my house and then, on Sunday, I'd cheer on Becky as she finished her 100km sponsored walk in the Cotswolds, before driving home. On Monday at 9am I'd be back at my desk. It was all go.

Torrential rain was pounding the windscreen as I drove through the town of Glossop towards the hike's starting point. The wipers, turned up to the fastest setting, glided frantically left and right in a futile attempt to cope with the downpour. I squinted my eyes, trying to make sure I wasn't about to run over a toddler or cat. This was not exactly the weather I'd hoped for.

I donned everything waterproof I had with me, grabbed my pre-packed backpack, and then bottled it. I couldn't face going outside. Instead I just sat there idly listening to my radio for 30 minutes, and then, during a brief respite, went for it. The lull didn't last for long. I was pummelled by wind and rain as I plodded past residential housing and a factory, emerging on to a track with high-sided walls. I entered open countryside and veered slightly left to the minor summit of Cock Hill, which reminded me of the time I completed the most phallic-themed walk of all time: walking from my home in Cockermouth to climb Great Cockup and Little Cockup in the Lake District.

After half a mile of featureless moors, I turned right on to the Pennine Way path and edged along the lip of Torside Clough, a high-sided ravine. The fellside was enveloped in a thick white-out, so I was denied any views to distract my mind from the creeping coldness of a damp body. I followed the stream east to a junction labelled John Track Well and then veered left along Wildboar Grain, before looping south over boot-swallowing boggy terrain to the flat 2,077ft summit of Bleaklow Head. It had been uninspiring, but at least that was one Nuttall down.

I stumbled briefly south-west, straining against the wind and driving rain, and dived for shelter at the Wain Stones. The two large boulders, located prominently on a smooth, weathered platform, resemble two heads puckering up, and thus are known as 'The Kiss'. I stood between the two sets of lips, as if I was eager to get involved in the action – but all I really wanted was a break from the weather. The boulders provided a little cover and I took the opportunity to chug on my water bottle and scoff a flapjack.

The marker posts of the Pennine Way guided me south to Hern Stones, where I veered off the national trail, aiming for my second Nuttall of the day, Higher Shelf Stones. I pressed on over a swampy maze of peat overhangs, muddy channels and wet gullies. As the mist swirled, my boots squelched through dark black peat and I felt like Frodo trekking through the Dead Marshes of *The Lord of the Rings*. I passed the tragic ruins of a Superfortress aeroplane that crashed on the mountain in 1948, killing the crew of 13, and eventually arrived at the 2,037ft trig point.

Rejoining the Pennine Way, I headed south above Crooked Clough to the Snake Pass road, crossed it, and climbed gently towards William Clough above Kinder Reservoir. I arrived at 7.30pm, needing to find somewhere to camp. Thankfully, the rain had subsided a little. I looked around for a suitable spot and genuinely contemplated setting up Dennis under the lip of a peat hag, but decided it was way too muddy. Eventually I settled on a space that wasn't particularly flat, but that was sheltered on three sides by rocky outcrops.

Like a Guinness World Records contestant trying to set a new best for the fastest erection of a Vango Banshee 200, I positioned the groundsheet, assembled and inserted the polls and pushed in the pegs in record time. I blew up my mat – the self-inflation mechanism had broken – and laid it out, with my sleeping bag on top and my rucksack to one side. I grabbed my cooking gear from my bag and set about boiling up some spaghetti, stirring it intermittently with my yellow spork. I bit off chunks of chorizo from the lengthy sausage and spat them into my pot, like some sort of caveman chef, and then added a powdered tomato soup as a sauce. It wasn't gourmet cooking but it was a hot and hearty meal – just what the doctor ordered.

I pulled off my hood, fed up with having my vision blinkered by a visor, and looked up at the skies. Drops of rain splashed on to my face. I shivered slightly. Dennis flapped in the wind. My sodden feet felt numb and my damp fingers ached. I took off my gloves and wrung them out, like a wet cloth. My drenched hair stuck to my forehead. Enough was enough. The Peak District had not been kind to me – and it didn't look like that was going to change any time soon. I slid into the haven of Dennis, battened down the hatches, and spent the evening watching Netflix on my iPhone. I felt bad for doing so, knowing I was breaking my self-imposed phone rules. But after a testing day in terrible weather, I was in desperate need of some morale-boosting entertainment.

✳ ✳ ✳

The Daily Adventure Journal of James

29/06/17: Maybe I should carry an emergency shelter with me. But not for emergencies – for eating lunch. I just couldn't find anywhere sheltered for lunch today, meaning I was chomping on horribly damp ham sandwiches while a gale-force wind and horizontal rain blew directly into my face. It was about as relaxing as dining inside one of those automatic car washes with gigantic rotating brushes.

30/06/17: Is it my navigational incompetence or does the British countryside consist of a confusing, crisscrossing, complicated maze of paths, trods, tracks and trails? One minute the path is clear underfoot, the next it has completely disappeared; one minute you think you know exactly where you are, the next you're presented with a crossroads of seven divergent trails, none of which is marked on the map; one minute you're convinced you're on an official track, the next you realise it's a sheep trod leading to precisely nowhere. It makes it so easy to lose your way. 'Not all who wander are lost.' Except for me. I'm lost as shit.

✳ ✳ ✳

The following morning I lay in my sleeping bag listening to the drumbeat of large raindrops on Dennis. The sound was strangely hypnotic and soothing. Conversely, the thought of going out in it was horrific and sinister. All my wet kit was – in the absence of anywhere to hang it up to dry – piled haphazardly in a sorry-looking pile in the corner of the tent. I boiled up breakfast in Dennis's tiny porch, which just about shielded me from the elements, and then crawled back inside to eat my double sachet of porridge and sip on my instant cappuccino. Feeling more awake, I squirmed and shuffled around on my back, like a fish out of water, trying to undress and put on dry clothes in a space that was too low to sit up in. I opened the door, took a deep breath – as if I were a footballer composing himself before a crucial penalty – and prepared to slip my feet into sodden boots. I always hated that moment. Really hated it. It was my daily bushtucker trial, something I desperately didn't want to do, but had to. So I reluctantly squeezed my feet into the damp, cold, foul interior of my Scarpas, with the words 'I'm a peak-bagger, get me out of here' racing around my mind, and prepared for the day ahead.

With Dennis hastily packed away, I marched south-east along the ridge towards Kinder Downfall. The best way to deal with the rain, wind and cold was simply to get moving as quickly as possible, so I strode out purposefully through the clag. From the waterfall I turned south, sticking to the high-sided gritstone edge, and arrived at the 2,077ft trig point of Kinder Low. But, alas, this was not the official Nuttall top. Instead, I had to head north-east over a pathless, peaty plateau aiming for the minor bump that marked the 2,087ft summit.

It was a desperate slog through a slippery, filthy, peat-splattered quagmire. If yesterday I was Frodo in the Dead Marshes, today I was the troll from *Labyrinth* in the Bog of Eternal Stench. Steep-sided slopes of exposed peat up to ten feet high, with lips of overhanging vegetation, formed mini valleys of mud. I tried to stick to the valley floors, splashing through a maze of wet gullies, but invariably they led to dead-ends or veered in the wrong direction. So I was forced to slip and slide up the crumbling hags, only to drop down the other side into a swampy hinterland, trapped again by the peaty prison. In the cloud and pounding rain, it was a desolate, unforgiving trudge, not helped by my inability to maintain a compass bearing. But, after repeated and frantic glances at the OS Maps app on my phone, I eventually found my way to the rather disappointing summit.

I stood atop Kinder Scout and felt happy that I could now walk out of the cursed Peak District.

It was a long loop back to Old Glossop. I returned to Kinder Low and turned south on the Pennine Way, before veering west down Oaken Clough and onwards to Kinder Reservoir. I continued generally north and north-west through the fields and foothills of the western edges of the Peak District National Park, passing a prominent sign that read 'Deep Bog Ahead'. That pretty much summed up the past two days. I tramped along a narrow trod with a stream flowing down it that covered my boots almost to the ankle. *Standard summer conditions in the English mountains*, I thought, and battled on, dreaming of sitting in my car with the heating on full blast.

Nearing the town, I passed through a field of sheep, crossed a stile and walked towards the brow of a misty hill. Suddenly, a herd of calves appeared out of the whiteness and charged towards me. I knew they were probably just being inquisitive, but I was bricking it nonetheless. And so, in a fitting end to my Peak District misadventure, I found myself sprinting hysterically for the safety of a fence ahead. With limbs flailing and fear etched on my face, I clumsily leapfrogged sideways over the wooden rail and landed face down in a muddy puddle. Apt. Very apt.

Four hours later, after dropping off the mattress, I knocked on the door of my friend Mo's flat.

'Mate, how's it going? Must be strange for you not to be on top of a mountain,' he said, smiling.

'All good, buddy. Now, are you ready to lose at darts or what?' I replied.

I've known Mo since Year 9 at school. He's one of my very best friends, a true mate I can depend on – and the only person I know with a weirder set of character traits and interests than me. I have a strange fusion of hobbies and passions: hiking, wild camping, mountains, obscure hip-hop, playing football, writing and West Bromwich Albion. Mo, on the other hand, takes it to a new level. He is a GP: highly qualified, intelligent and articulate. But he moonlights as a Saturday-night dance DJ in the shady corners of Oldham in Greater Manchester. He is from Iran, proud of his Persian routes, and a committed Muslim who prays five times a day. But he is also hip and western, with the latest skin-fade plus comb-over haircut; a wardrobe of garish River Island clothing; and a brand-new white Audi with blacked-out windows. He plays hockey, watches *Love Island*, holidays in Ibiza, and is obsessed with darts. It is a bizarre combination – and I love him for it.

I walked into the flat and was greeted with a hug and a big smile from Rachel, Mo's girlfriend, whom I hadn't seen for years. The three of us sat around the table, drank tea, chatted, laughed and reminisced about old times. I told them about my latest mountain antics and mishaps; they told me the story of their romantic recoupling, following a few years of separation. I was relishing the normality – an evening in, chilling out with good friends, with four walls protecting me from the lashing rain and gale-force winds. For dinner we popped out for a curry, basically a must-do when you're in Birmingham, and then, with Rachel watching Netflix on the sofa, Mo and I engaged in one of our long-standing traditions: a darts match. If I remember correctly, and if it's printed in a book it must be true, I won five sets to nil and Mo embarrassed himself with a pathetic display of tungsten incompetence. I definitely didn't lose. Honest.

At 7am on Saturday I left the flat, with Mo joking there was a 90 per cent chance I'd return to find my car windows smashed or the wing mirrors ripped off. Mercifully, I fell into the lucky ten per cent. My car was undamaged. I threw my stuff on to the back seat and sped off for Dartmoor, a unique national park in Devon in south-west England, covering an area the size of London and boasting over 160 distinctive granite tors. I'd never been before and I was excited about losing my Dartmoor virginity.

As I sped at 80mph down the fast lane of the M5, I sipped on a can of Red Bull and thought about what a ridiculous detour this was for just two Nuttalls. After what felt like an eternity, exacerbated by a couple of sat-nav issues, I parked up at Meldon Reservoir car park at 11am. I stretched my legs and set about packing my day-bag. It was a stunning day: the sky was a vivid blue, the air was tranquil, the sun shone brightly, and a heat haze shimmered in the distance. I plastered sun cream on to my face, neck and arms, filled my water bottles from a 5-litre container I had stashed in the boot and set off, the rainy Peak District a distant memory.

Wild ponies, granite tors, windswept moorland – I immediately warmed to the distinctive landscape of Dartmoor. It was a welcome change from the scenery I'd become accustomed to over the past 221 summits. The dazzling weather helped, naturally, and I realised that my impression of different peaks and national parks was massively influenced by the conditions on the day I happened to be there.

I crossed the reservoir dam and tramped up a track looping to the ridge of Longstone Hill, taking care to give a herd of cows a wide berth. At the head of a stream, I veered east over boggy ground and arrived at a red and white pole marking the start of the Okehampton military range, an area of land used by the army for live firing. I already knew, courtesy of the MOD website, that no drills were taking place today. But a metal sign next to the poles read rather alarmingly: 'Do not touch any military debris. It may explode and kill you.' Bloody hell. Was I about to step on an unexploded bomb? Did I need to scan the ground for shells, like a soldier in Afghanistan searching for IEDs? Then I thought about it logically. There were about 100 sheep that I could see within the so-called danger zone. None of them had three legs or major deformities – and they were nonchalantly wandering this way and that without a care in the world. I should be fine.

Treading gingerly nevertheless, I walked east over easy slopes of grass and heather and arrived safely at the slabbed platform of Yes Tor, which was adorned with a flagpole and trig point. I dropped down north briefly from the summit, seeking solitude, and sat on a boulder for lunch. I looked out over the expansive countryside. The idyllic rolling greenery of Dartmoor, scarred only by blemishes of grey rocky tors, dominated the foreground. In the distance flat plains continued for as far as the eye could see, making a jigsaw puzzle of interlocking, differently shaped fields of yellow, orange and green. To the right, the tiny white sticks of a wind-turbine farm caught my eye; to the left, a small village with a church spire stood out. But it was the sky that was most spellbinding. A hundred different shades of blue and white blended together, merging into a violet haze over the horizon. It was exquisite – and all the better for the hardship I'd endured in the Peak District. The highs are sweeter when you've experienced the lows.

The rest of the day didn't feel like mountain walking at all. It felt like a lazy Sunday stroll in some fantasy land where the sun always shone and the terrain was always gentle and forgiving. I dropped easily south to the 2,037ft top of High Willhays, my second and final Nuttall in Dartmoor, and the highest point in Britain south of the Brecon Beacons. The quickest way back to my car would've been to retrace my steps, but I wanted to prolong my Dartmoor experience. So I continued south, visiting Dinger Tor, a podium of granite with excellent views, and Lints Tor, a rocky spire that resembles a Jenga tower of stacked slabs. Next, I dropped down steeply to the West Okement River and turned right, following the water course north. The valley was deserted, quiet and charming, while the ancient stunted oak woodland of Black-a-Tor copse felt like a lost world, a glimpse of a forgotten era when Britain was covered in native trees. Thirty minutes later I emerged from the river valley to the reservoir. I turned right, crossed the dam again, and arrived back at my car. My dalliance with Dartmoor had come to an end.

I drove to Cheltenham that evening and stayed in a room I'd booked through Airbnb, hosted by an overly maternal but lovely pensioner who asked me about 17 times whether I wanted a rich tea biscuit to go with my brew. The following morning I supported Becky as she powered through the pain and blisters to complete her latest 100km sponsored hike. I actually walked with her across the finish line, which, amusingly, meant I was cheered on by the big crowds and congratulated by a series of strangers, despite having barely walked 100m let alone 100km. Half an hour later, I had a medal around my neck as I stood in the queue for the completers-only free buffet.

'How did you find it?' asked an exhausted-looking lady behind me.

'So tough,' I replied, rubbing my 'aching' legs. I'm a terrible person.

It was nice to catch up with Becky. We chatted, chilled out, cheered on the walkers crossing the finish line and ate a late lunch of massive burgers and chips, complemented with salad, chicken fajitas and all manner of tasty snacks and desserts. But, sadly, the good times couldn't last for ever and we parted ways at 4pm. Becky was travelling home by train. I was driving, with just 250 miles to go before I could relax on my sofa.

On the long drive home it suddenly dawned on me. I was exactly halfway through my list of Nuttalls – 223 mountains completed out of 446. That put a smile on my face. A pang of pride shot through my system and I could almost physically feel the determination to finish the job rising within me. At a service station, feeling curious, I turned on my laptop and loaded up my Nuttalls-log spreadsheet. I'd completed 44 days of walking and climbed 223 peaks. Dartmoor, the Peak District, the Cheviots, the Yorkshire Dales, the North Pennines (bar five summits) and the Black Mountains in Wales were all completed, and I'd climbed 131 of 171 Nuttalls in the Lake District. All I needed to do was climb another 223 mountains over the next 11 weeks and it'd be mission complete.

CHAPTER 14

CHASING ALIENS

Mountains 224–260

DATE	REGION	MOUNTAINS
Thursday 6 July	Berwyns	Moel Fferna 2,067ft (630m)
Friday 7 July	Berwyns	Pen Bwlch Llandrillo Top 2,037ft (621m) Cadair Bronwen 2,575ft (785m) Tomle 2,434ft (742m) Foel Wen 2,267ft (691m) Foel Wen South Top 2,254ft (687m) Mynydd Tarw 2,234ft (681m) Godor 2,228ft (679m) Godor North Top 2,215ft (675m) Moel yr Ewig 2,280ft (695m) Cadair Berwyn New Top 2,723ft (830m) Cadair Berwyn 2,713ft (827m) Moel Sych 2,713ft (827m) Post Gwyn 2,182ft (665m)
Saturday 8 July	Berwyns Arans	Foel Cwm Sian Llŵyd 2,126ft (648m) Y Groes Fagl 2,162ft (659m) Cyrniau Nod 2,188ft (667m) Cefn Gwyntog 2,018ft (615m) Stac Rhos 2,067ft (630m) Pen y Boncyn Trefeilw 2,119ft (646m) Foel Goch 2,011ft (613m) Trum y Gwragedd 2,008ft (612m)

DATE	REGION	MOUNTAINS
		Foel y Geifr 2,054ft (626m)
		Moel y Cerrig Duon 2,051ft (625m)
Sunday 9 July	Arans	Llechwedd Du 2,014ft (614m)
		Foel Rhudd 2,162ft (659m)
		Esgeiriau Gwynion 2,201ft (671m)
		Foel Hafod-fynydd 2,260ft (689m)
		Erw y Ddafad-ddu 2,861ft (872m)
		Aran Benllyn 2,904ft (885m)
		Aran Fawddwy 2,969ft (905m)
		Waun Camddwr 2,037ft (621m)
		Gwaun y Llwyni 2,247ft (685m)
		Gwaun Lydan 2,073ft (632m)
		Pen y Allt Uchaf 2,034ft (620m)
Monday 10 July	Arans	Glasgwm 2,559ft (780m)
		Pen y Bryn-fforchog 2,247ft (685m)

I didn't feel scared. Or did I? Doubts crept in as darkness descended over the remote mountainside. I was all alone, cocooned in my bivvy near the summit of Cadair Berwyn in North Wales. Strange night-time noises shattered the silence. The dark sky was eerily lit by a thin crescent moon. And my mind was filled with thoughts of other-worldly vessels and sinister beings.

In January 1974 loud bangs and bright lights were observed over this mountain. Was it a UFO crash, subsequently covered up by the government? Or an earthquake combined with a meteor shower, as per official statements? From my internet research prior to heading to the Berwyns I had learned of the so-called Roswelsh Incident, perhaps the most bizarre moment in the history of Britain's mountains – and it felt a little unnerving to be investigating it first-hand.

A flashing light appeared in the sky; it danced from left to right, fluctuating in intensity, and then seemed to hover for almost a minute. *Oh God, what the hell is that?* I panicked momentarily, as my mind careered into a black hole of catastrophising: *I'm about to be visited by an Alien Grey with an engorged head and black, almond-shaped eyes. Or beamed up into a spacecraft to be probed with all manner of paranormal instruments. Or abducted by a terrifying extraterrestrial reptilian.*

Then I snapped out of it and chuckled to myself. It wasn't a UFO. It was just a distant star, playing an optical illusion on a nervy wild camper. I consciously engaged the rational side of my brain and gave myself a pep talk. *C'mon James, pull yourself together, you don't even believe in aliens.* It worked. My worries dissipated and I slipped into the glorious state of relaxation that seems to come only with being in the mountains. A thousand stars twinkled in the black-blue night sky; a cold breeze ruffled my hair; and the very last of the sunlight painted the uneven horizon with an entrancing red hue. I wriggled around in my four-season sleeping bag, settling on a position that felt comfortable. I yawned, rested my head down, and felt privileged to be sleeping in the fells.

Rewind 48 hours and I had been sitting at my desk in Cockermouth, planning my next expedition. Surprisingly, after my hectic days off exploring the Peak District and Dartmoor, I'd got lots done back in the office from Monday to Wednesday, and now I had the next five days – Thursday to Monday – booked in for Nuttalls-bagging. I was meant to be plotting a route and getting organised, but I couldn't keep my eyes off internet articles about the Roswelsh Incident.

On the evening of 23 January 1974, so the story went, residents across North Wales reported loud noises and brilliant lights in the sky over Cadair Berwyn. Confusion reigned supreme. Had an aeroplane crashed into the mountain or a wartime German bomb exploded? Or was it something out of this world? An RAF search-and-rescue team was scrambled to the mountainside, but – according to official reports – they found nothing. Police descended on the area and investigations were launched. But, again, they came to nought. Instead, in the coming days and weeks, it was scientists who explained the phenomenon witnessed by hundreds of local people.

141

The bright lights had been a meteor descending through the atmosphere and burning up before it reached the ground; the loud noises had been caused by an earthquake that simultaneously struck in the Berwyn mountains with a magnitude of 3.5 on the Richter scale.

But not everyone was convinced by the official explanation and an alternative narrative, an extraterrestrial conspiracy theory, emerged. Newspaper articles included eyewitness accounts describing 'flying saucers emerging from the Irish Sea', a 'big glowing object sitting on the mountainside with a load of lights circling around underneath it', and even the military loading a crashed flying saucer on to a flatbed truck and taking it away. Official police logs included numerous 999 calls from villagers reporting an 'orange and red glow' and a 'large perfect circle' or similar on the mountainside. Key witness Pat Evans, a retired nurse, drove up to the mountain on the night, stating that she saw a 'huge ball glowing and pulsating' that 'had to be a UFO of some sort'. Self-proclaimed UFO investigators took it even further, claiming eyewitnesses saw 'alien beings emerging dazed from a crashed spaceship' and mysterious 'men in black' initiating a government cover-up in the rural area.

A total load of codswallop, I thought, but it was intriguing nonetheless. I had to stop procrastinating, however, and I refocused on route-planning. After an hour or so, an exciting master plan emerged. I was going to climb all 23 tops in the Berwyns and all 14 tops in the Arans in one big expedition, walking approximately 55 miles, ascending over 16,000ft, and sleeping wild in the hills for four nights. If I made it, I'd complete eight of the Nuttalls guidebook's day-walks in five days. The only potential spanner in the works? I'd designed a linear route, heading roughly south-west from Llangollen to Dolgellau, that linked all of the summits in a wiggly line on my map. But this meant I'd end up miles and miles from my car – I'd be relying on my thumb-wagging skills again.

My intention was to get going early on Thursday morning. But, as usual, everyday life got in the way. I waited in for a plumber to fix our leaking toilet, paid bills by online banking, sent long-overdue emails, renewed my car insurance last-minute, and obsessively packed the exact quantities of food I needed for the trip, laying out each meal individually in neat little piles on the kitchen counter. But, at 2pm, I eventually got out of the door and started driving towards the A66.

I slammed on the brakes and pulled over on a grass verge. It wasn't exactly a safe space to stop, but it'd only be for a minute. I'd spotted an old guy hitching on the roundabout. Perhaps this was karma? If I offered him a ride, it might bode well for my own hitchhiking endeavours in Wales. I looked in my side mirror as the man walked down the verge towards my car. He was about six feet tall, with a scraggly beard and wild hair. A gigantic army-surplus backpack, with a tent and sleeping mat wedged through the straps, was thrown over his shoulder. He was wearing dated, slightly scruffy clothing. But I wasn't worried. There was a calm, kind aura about the guy.

'Were you stopping for me?' he asked, almost apologetically.

'Sure, mate – hop in. Where you headed?'

'Keswick, if you don't mind?'

'No worries. I'm heading that way. What you been up to?'

'Shopping in Lidl.'

I was not expecting that answer. But I soon learned the story behind it. The hitcher, who I immediately warmed to, told me that he'd been living a wild, nomadic existence for the past 30 years. He had no home and instead lived in his tent, sleeping wild in the mountains. Currently, he was camped up in the remote, quiet hills between Thirlmere and Watendlath in the Lake District, but he split his time between Cumbria and Scotland. And every few weeks, he hiked out with his big backpack, hitched to the west coast, and stocked up with supplies from his favourite German discount supermarket.

We chatted – or, more accurately, I bombarded him with numerous questions – during the 20-minute journey. I was utterly intrigued. He told me of his backpacking travels in the '80s and '90s through South America and New Zealand. He explained that every few years, when he ran out of money, he worked intensively to boost his savings. He said that he didn't have a phone, or involvement with social media, or any real connection with the outside world. The only entertainment he needed was nature and the landscape. Many would have seen him as some sort of crank or vagrant detached from reality, but I found him inspiring. He was an old-school adventurer. He wasn't doing it for Instagram likes or for fame and fortune or for, ahem, a book deal. It was all just for the love of it.

Three hours later I parked up on a minor road in Cynwyd, a small village west of Llangollen. It was an ideal starting point for my journey on foot into the Berwyns, an often-ignored mountain range of high moorland to the east of Bala, lying just outside the boundaries of Snowdonia National Park. I made some last-minute changes to the contents of my backpack – why is it so bloody heavy? – and then set off east along the long tarmac road through Cynwyd Forest.

I veered off left and took a track through the dense trees. About half a mile later, I dropped my heavy backpack to the floor, stood still and listened to the sounds of the forest: the creak of a tall tree swaying in the wind; the rustle of leaves; the buzz of insects; the chorus of rhythmic, melodic birdsong – a symphony of tweeting, chirping and twittering. Dappled light danced on the ground, breaking through the canopy in beams and spots. I've always found forests enchanting places and this was no different. Compared with open hillsides, which can be bleak and barren, the forest was vibrant and breathing and full of life. I felt wired. My eyes darted left and right. I heard every sound. I noticed every movement. The forest gave me a tribal-like alertness, as if I was a Native American hunting prey, or watching out for bears, or tracking an enemy.

It was 7pm and I was feeling hungry. I stopped on the edge of the forest, sat on a mossy log and boiled up rice with sweet chilli sauce. The meal filled a hole, but it was spoilt slightly by a swarm of incessant midges that wouldn't leave me alone. Keen to escape the flying nuisances, I packed up quickly and crossed a fence at a stile on to open fellside. I took the North Berwyn Way east for a mile and a quarter to a path junction, and then turned left to climb along a fence over thick heather to the 2,067ft summit of Moel Fferna. One out of 37 Nuttalls ticked off.

Summer meant I had the luxury of long, light evenings and it enabled me to make up for my late start to the day by hiking until 9pm. I returned to the *bwlch*, the Welsh word for a mountain pass or col, and headed south along a narrow trod next to a fence. It was a beautiful evening, with the setting sun casting pink shades over the sky, and the Berwyns were empty and tranquil. I hadn't seen a soul. The peace was shattered, however, as a merlin – not the legendary Welsh wizard, but the UK's smallest bird of prey – circled high above me. Its shrill, chattering call sounded aggressive and angry. I figured I was accidentally hiking through its nesting ground, so I crept along carefully and finally walked far enough out of its territory to be deemed unthreatening. Night was rapidly arriving, so I bailed on my plan to bag a second Nuttall, and instead pitched Dennis in a sheltered spot in a hollow below a weathered excrescence of rock. I sipped on a hot chocolate and looked out over the looming darkness. My Berwyns adventure had started well.

The following morning, after a breakfast of porridge and an instant cappuccino, I texted Becky to let her know I was safe and sound, then decamped and climbed briefly back to the fence line. I glanced back at my camping spot, where a Dennis-shaped imprint was left in the squashed reeds and grass, and then tramped over rough moorland to the summit of Pen Bwlch Llandrillo Top. A disfigured sheep figurine, with half its face missing, was placed eerily on top of the cairn. In the lonely hills, it was an odd sight that freaked me out. So I pressed on hastily, eager to avoid an encounter with the sheep-toy mutilator.

I dropped south to the next col, where a memorial stone was located, and then climbed steadily up the rising ridge towards Cadair Bronwen. To my surprise, there was a hiker ahead of me – perhaps another peak-bagger or lover of lonely, wild places? I quickly caught up with the rambler and startled him with my presence. I don't think he'd seen me approaching.

'Morning, lovely day – where are you headed?' I asked, surprised by the person standing in front of me.

He was old, maybe in his late 70s, white, with a pale, gaunt, wrinkly face and a neat goatee. An army camouflage cap hid tufts of grey hair. He was wearing a collared walking shirt, green walking trousers, a camouflage-green gilet and an army-surplus-style jacket. Breathing heavily, he looked tired but, at the same time, happy and full of life.

'I'm climbing – or, should I say, trying to climb – Cadair Berwyn,' he replied.

'You'll get there, mate, just take it slow and steady. What brings you here?'

'I'm celebrating my 80th birthday today by climbing a Welsh mountain over 800 metres – but my fitness isn't what it used to be.'

'Wow, that's amazing. Happy birthday, my friend. That's really inspirational.'

'I hope I make it. I tried Tryfan last year but I made it only halfway up. Now I'm trying easier peaks. I had my heart repaired, you see, with a new valve. So I haven't got the speed or fitness of my youth any more. I walked for many years and climbed many of the Welsh mountains. I love them. And I wanted to summit a big one again for my birthday.'

I was about to butt in, but he continued his monologue. He seemed happy to have met someone to talk to – and I was more than willing to listen.

'I've also booked a helicopter flight over Snowdon and a hot-air balloon flight in Derbyshire to celebrate my big birthday. You only turn 80 once, after all.'

He was so inspiring – an octogenarian with a bucket list. He wasn't going out with a whimper, he was going out with a bang. I found myself hoping I'd be that effervescent when I was 80. We walked together for a while and chatted socially. I reassured him about the directions, which he seemed a little concerned about, and made sure he was OK physically. His breathing had returned to normal and he seemed strong enough for the climb ahead. I was confident he wasn't about to have a heart attack. So I bade him farewell and shouted, 'Good luck' as he climbed gradually south-west aiming ultimately for Cadair Berwyn.

I was completely out of water. I hadn't filled up since I'd left my car, so I veered north over pathless slopes looking for a stream marked on my map. It had dried up, so my thirst would have to go unquenched. I retraced my steps, stopping briefly for a snack of dried apricots, and then ascended gentle terrain to the 2,575ft summit of Cadair Bronwen and onward to the *bwlch* before Cadair Berwyn. This was where my route-planning was far from logical. I was going to do a high-level horseshoe in reverse, starting at the top, descending a ridge into the valley, and then ascending the second ridge back to the top. But never mind. So be it.

Walking the ridge east was productive and I ticked off four Nuttalls – Tomle, Foel Wen, Foel Wen South Top and Mynydd Tarw – in just 50 minutes. At the last one, I stopped for what felt like a well-deserved lunch of tortilla wraps smothered in Nutella, followed by banana chips, juicy raisins and a large slab of milk chocolate. As I ate, my eyes were drawn to the striking ridgeline of Cadair Berwyn. It was the best mountain scenery of the range, without doubt. Feeling full and lethargic, I dropped steeply south-east through fields and arrived at a farmyard, where I was greeted by a hellish cacophony of barking dogs who sounded as if they wanted nothing more than to rip a trespassing English hiker to shreds. I was immediately petrified, but thankfully the canines were locked in wooden kennels. I eyeballed one dog. It looked possessed by a demon, pacing around maniacally, standing on its hind legs, baring its teeth, and barking ferociously. I got out of there quickly.

I took a footpath south-west and filled my water bottles in the Afon Lwrch, before climbing through a series of sheep fields up the eastern slopes of Godor. I plonked my left boot atop the small cairn of the 2,228ft summit and then pressed on over tussocky grass to the insignificant bump of Godor North Top and the grassy knoll of Moel yr Ewig, located high above the waters of Llyn Lluncaws. The terrain steepened as I climbed over slightly rockier ground and up a gully to finally regain the main ridge I'd left hours earlier. Sadly, I couldn't fully enjoy the 'lovely airy walk' along the ridge, as described in the guidebook, because cloud had descended. But it still felt good to ditch my bag under a rock and tramp over easy, flat ground on an out-and-back to the twin tops of Cadair Berwyn.

Remembering the Roswelsh Incident, I headed off-piste and started exploring the mountainside. I wasn't entirely sure what I was looking for. Maybe a previously undiscovered spaceship crash site? Or a strange glowing rock from a distant planet? Or perhaps a trail of alien sludge to follow that might just lead to a fleeting glimpse of an other-worldly being? But I didn't find anything – and I got bored very quickly. After all, this was real life, not *Stranger Things*. So I decided to press on.

I headed south briefly to the 2,713ft top of Moel Sych, before completing a long loop of the high ground circling Afon Disgynfa to arrive at the summit of Post Gwyn, my 13th and final Nuttall of the day. I was exhausted. It was a nice evening, so I decided to bivvy. I laid out my bag on the flattest, softest, bounciest grass I could find and busily prepared for a night under the stars, trying not to think extraterrestrial thoughts.

At 6am I opened my eyes, bleary and half-asleep. I wasn't using a pillow, so my face was almost perfectly horizontal to the ground. This was life from the bivvy perspective: an up-close-and-personal interaction with the mountain. All I could see were tufts of grass, like towers of green and yellow spiky blades. I raised my head slightly to reveal the gentle grassy slopes of Post Gwyn and a horizon coming to life with the onset of daylight. The mountainside was wonderfully still and quiet. All I could hear was the rush of a cold wind. I was all alone, undisturbed by my fellow man and unperturbed by the hassles of everyday life. It felt joyous to be waking up in the wild, as if I was tapping into a deep desire to be connected to the landscape.

As my brain caught up with my body, it slowly dawned on me where I was. I thought about the night before in the Berwyns. Had I seen anything extraterrestrial? Had I heard anything paranormal? The answer, definitively, was no. I felt a little disappointed. My alien investigation had been a damp squib. I had nothing interesting to report; no revelations or discoveries; no conclusions to draw in the ongoing mystery of the Roswelsh Incident. Had an alien spaceship really crashed on Cadair Berwyn in 1974, or had it simply been a meteor shower and earthquake? I was none the wiser.

My porridge bubbled on my camping stove as I sat in a small wind shelter behind my bivvy. I stirred my 3-in-1 Nescafé – a pre-mixed sachet of powdered coffee, milk and sugar – and dropped two sweeteners into my mug, turning it into a 5-in-1. It was a gorgeous morning: blue skies, bright sunshine, a light wind, and fluffy white clouds casting shadows over a landscape of green hills rolling away to the horizon. I felt relaxed, happy and energetic. Little did I know I'd be a broken man by the end of the day.

I descended steeply south-west along a stream, taking the opportunity to replenish my water supplies, and emerged over pathless slopes on to a long farmyard drive. A solitary wheelie bin stood at the end of the drive and, glancing around to check that a moody Welsh farmer wasn't watching me, I ditched my plastic bag of rubbish. It always felt great to reduce the weight of my bag, even if only minimally.

Unable to hitch a ride, I hiked along the Milltir Gerrig Pass road for a mile and a half and then turned left on to a 4x4 track that offered pleasant views down the U-shaped valley of Cwm

Rhiweirth. The morning had started easily enough, but that was all about to change. I struggled north-west over rough, thick heather to the 2,126ft top of Foel Cwm Sian Llŵyd. My Nuttalls guidebook described it, rather savagely, as 'a very boring mountain indeed' where 'only the dedicated peak-bagger will be tempted to explore further'. John and Anne weren't wrong – and this was only the start of my energy-sapping, soul-destroying battle with the Berwyns' heather.

The rest of my day was a war of attrition with the western Berwyns above Penllyn Forest, a group of eight Nuttalls covered in deep, thick, almost impenetrable heather. There were few paths and even fewer redeeming features. The highest point was only 2,188ft, the mileage was modest, and the ascents were puny, but somehow the rough tramping over dense heather was utterly exhausting. It was the toughest hiking of my challenge to date.

I headed south from Foel Cwm Sian Llŵyd, aiming for the next Nuttall, Y Groes Fagl. Progress was painfully slow. It was like wading through treacle. The heather was thigh-deep and all-encompassing. Sometimes it would hold my weight and I could walk momentarily along the soft, bouncy tops. Then I'd step on an unsteady clump that would collapse and I'd sink down into a purple-flowered entrapment. Consequently, every step involved lifting my legs higher than normal, as if I was vaulting over thousands of heathery hurdles. I continually jarred my ankles on uneven ground and scratched my legs on prickly branches. All I needed was a little trod through the impassable vegetation, an avenue through the maze, but there was none. It felt like an eternity of hard graft over Cyrniau Nod, Cefn Gwyntog and Stac Rhos before I finally collapsed at the 2,119ft summit of Pen y Boncyn Trefeilw. I was spent.

As I shovelled peanut-butter crackers, dates, cranberries, steak crisps, jelly babies and two Twix bars into my face, the sun warmed my skin and I looked out over the so-called Boring Berwyns. The remoteness and solitude were palpable – but the walking was just too arduous. If only I'd chosen the Marilyns list of mountains I wouldn't be faffing around with these cursed summits. It had been a real battle – and I definitely felt as if I'd ended up on the losing side.

Mercifully, a bulldozed forestry track gave me easier passage west to the Hirnant Pass, a narrow road linking Lake Vyrnwy with Bala. I followed the road north for about half an hour, feeling ecstatic to have firm tarmac underfoot, and then veered west up a steep grassy rake next to a forest. My lungs heaved and my calves burned as I gained the brow of the hillside and decided to stop for a hot chocolate and biscuits. It was gentler walking over the heathery ridge, with a heaven-sent trod guiding the way, and I easily ticked off a trio of Nuttalls – Foel Goch, Trum y Gwragedd and Foel y Geifr. I slumped against the last one's OS trig point and clenched my fist in victory. I'd completed the 23 tops of the Berwyn mountains.

But I still had the minor issue of climbing the Arans, a range of 14 Nuttalls stretching principally in a long, high-level ridge from Llanuwchllyn to Dinas Mawddwy. I started with another painful slog over heather-clad, pathless slopes – a no man's land of boggy, featureless high ground that linked the Berwyns to the start of the Arans. I headed south-west to the bump of Cefn Coch, which was too low for Nuttall status, and then veered south, aiming for Moel y Cerrig Duon, the easternmost top of the Arans.

Then I hit a wall. Not literally. I just felt drained and light-headed and totally devoid of energy. So I stopped, took a break and boiled up some dinner. That gave me the boost I needed and I continued along a stream to a *bwlch*, where I spotted a fox. It looked straight at me intensely, as if it was weighing up its next move or carefully considering the threat I posed. I held its gaze. But dusk was falling and I was keen to find a place to camp. I didn't have time for a staring contest. So I stepped forward, breaking the stalemate, and the fox bolted, its tail bobbing up and down above the sea of heather into the distance. I pressed on to the 2,051ft summit, my first Nuttall ticked off in the Arans, and then lazily set up camp. I was so tired

I could barely enjoy the sunset, with the serrated horizon of distant peaks turning a fiery orange, as if lit up by volcanic eruptions of glowing magma.

I woke late, having slept like a log. The previous day's exertions had knocked me out cold. I had a leisurely breakfast before lazily packing Dennis away, and then assessed the damage caused by my war with the Berwyns. Both my kit and my body were falling apart. The waist-harness buckle had broken on my backpack, meaning it frequently came loose, jolting the weight of the load on to my unsuspecting shoulders; I'd ripped my tent bag and the tent outer sheet while straddling myself over a barbed-wire fence; and my inflatable sleeping mat had developed a puncture, effectively rendering it useless. My toes were developing blisters; the soles of my feet ached horribly; my back was sore; and I felt very lethargic. But I knew I needed to persevere. I hauled my rucksack on to my back, nodded to the ground – as if to thank it for a good night's sleep – and headed south-west for the road at Bwlch y Groes and the start of Snowdonia National Park.

It was a hike of two halves, to borrow a football cliché. The morning was spent ticking off four Nuttalls – Llechwedd Du, Foel Rhudd, Esgeiriau Gwynion and Foel Hafod-fynydd – in the eastern Arans. It was a tad dull. The weather was overcast, a mix of sunny intervals with light showers, and my views were shrouded at times by low cloud. The windswept moorland was pleasant enough but far from spectacular, and I found myself contemplating the less glamorous sights you see while out peak-bagging. It's not all sweeping ridges, spiky mountains, epic skylines and stunning sunsets. In fact, I suddenly realised, I spent a lot of time looking at the most mundane of stuff: rows of rotten fence posts, tossed-away banana skins, discarded rolls of fencing wire, dead sheep, Coke cans lining a mountain road, shrivelled tea bags in a wind shelter, animal bones, blown-away sweet wrappers, sheep droppings, the deflated shell of a 'Happy 60th Birthday' balloon. It sounds utterly bizarre, but on monotonous mountainsides those were the things that sometimes caught my eye and captured my attention.

Everything changed in the afternoon, however. As I dropped down the western slopes of Foel Hafod-fynydd towards the tarn of Creiglyn Dyfi, the clouds dispersed, the sun appeared and the Aran ridge was revealed in all its glory. No more rounded grassy lumps to trudge over for me. This was real mountain territory once again – shattered crags, rivers of scree, sheer gullies and a knobbly, rocky ridgeline with expansive views.

I took the steep grassy sweep to the right of the tarn that breached the long eastern line of precipitous cliffs and provided safe passage to the ridge. After three days of seeing only one other hiker, I was annoyed at the presence of two large groups of ramblers, as if they'd gatecrashed my party, spoiling my solitary enjoyment of the fells. Perhaps I was turning into some sort of hermit, scared by the sight of other humans? Or maybe, after all the pain and toil of the heather-smothered Berwyns, I simply felt I deserved a special, personal moment on the sunny Aran ridge.

It didn't disappoint at all. The broad grassy ridge, studded with rocky outcrops and scattered boulders, was my favourite section of walking, outside of the Lake District, so far. I topped out of the grassy entry point almost exactly at the summit of Erw y Ddafad-ddu, the first Nuttall, and ditched my bag next to the cairn. I turned right and completed an out-and-back to Aran Benllyn, feeling invigorated by the scenery, as if I was back where I belonged – in the uncompromising, soul-stirring, exciting mountains. Next I continued south, sticking to the edge of the cliffs and peeping down rocky chutes to the lake below, and finally arrived at Aran Fawddwy.

At 2,969ft, it is the UK's highest mountain south of Snowdon and falls an agonising 31ft short of the magical 3,000ft mark. I stood alone, next to the OS trig point, and gazed out over the surrounding peaks. It was a magnificent viewing platform. To the north were Snowdonia and the Arenigs, to the south were the Pumlumon mountains of central Wales and to the west were Cadair Idris and the Rhinogs. It was a scene of grandeur and beauty, but also, for me, trepidation. I still needed to climb so many of these peaks. It was a daunting visual representation of how far I still had to go.

Trying not to dwell on that never-ending panorama of not-yet-bagged Nuttalls, I followed a fence line south-west, aiming for the summit of Waun Camddwr. It was baking hot and I could feel my neck burning as I dropped off the ridge and emerged on to a boggy plateau. I threw my backpack to the ground, downed a litre of water, and searched for my sun cream. Damn it. The bottle was virtually empty. No matter how hard I shook it, nothing came out – I needed to cut it in half and scrape the dregs out with my fingers. But I didn't have a Swiss Army knife. Double damn it. So, in some sort of unhinged attempt to avoid skin cancer, I found myself repeatedly stabbing an Ambre Solaire bottle with a piece of slate, raising the dagger of rock high into the air and repeatedly driving it downwards like a frenzied killer. It was surprisingly difficult to pierce the plastic container. But I managed it finally and victoriously smothered the cool white cream on to my neck, face, arms and legs.

Adequately shielded from harmful UV rays, I plodded along planks of wood – conveniently placed at the boggiest parts of the bog – and reached the somewhat disappointing top of Waun Camddwr. I retraced my steps briefly north-east and then turned right, following a fence over easy terrain to the next Nuttall of Gwaun y Llwyni. That was the boring leg to two minor tops done and dusted.

I was back on a ridge. To my left was flat grassy ground; to my right, crags and fields of scree dropped precipitously to the Afon yr Hengym valley. I walked safely along the edge, captivated by the myriad little streams flowing down the steep slopes, scarring the mountainside with a network of watery veins, and reached the memorial cairn at Drws Bach.

It was an evening to die for. I grabbed my DSLR from the bottom of my bag and got trigger-happy, snapping over 100 photos.

And then I put the camera away and simply sat still, savouring the moment. Two birds with scythe-like wings and forked tails – possibly swifts or swallows – flew acrobatically above me, ducking, diving, twisting and turning with immense grace and fluidity, the air whooshing with their every move. The sun was still warm on my skin. A light, cooling breeze blew. I ran my hands over the dry, dusty ground and looked north back to the Aran ridge. Grassy slopes glowed a mix of green and gold in the bright sunshine; Creiglyn Dyfi tarn twinkled like a giant coin of silver; and the fissured crags, naked rock and vertical chutes of the eastern cliffs cast a sinuous, creeping shadow beyond their scree base. There was no one else around. I was having that special, intimate moment with the Aran ridge I'd craved.

✳ ✳ ✳

The Daily Adventure Journal of James
09/07/17: How do you know you've spent too long alone in the mountains? I'm pretty sure I found out today. It's when you look at a herd of sheep and find yourself contemplating which ewe is the prettiest.

10/07/17: Sometimes, when I'm perched on a rocky outcrop or strolling along a sun-drenched ridge, I find myself thinking I must look like a real adventurer now, an intrepid hero, an absolute hiking legend. But, more often than that, I find myself thinking I'm a disgrace. Such as when I'm in a public car park, stripped down to my boxers, washing myself with wet wipes, looking like a pale, skinny, dishevelled Gollum-like creature, while passing parents give me disapproving stares and shield their children's eyes from the harrowing sight.

✳ ✳ ✳

From paradise to hell in the blink of an eye – that's how it felt the following morning as I woke up to terrible weather. I'd spent the evening, as dusk gilded the fells in a beguiling light, descending east to the 2,073ft summit of Gwaun Lydan before traversing south-west to set up camp atop my final Nuttall, the 2,034ft Pen y Allt Uchaf. But I'd witnessed dark clouds rolling over late at night, and by morning the fells of yesterday were no more. Heavy rain fell, hill fog cloaked every view, the wind raged – and, to make matters worse, I was out of chocolate and sweets for the day. I'd overeaten during my struggles in the Berwyns. I decided I'd have to walk my way back to civilisation as quickly as possible.

I hit the deck three times as I descended wet, slippery grassy slopes west into the quiet valley of Cwm Cywarch. I had only two more Nuttalls to complete – Glasgwm and Pen y Bryn-fforchog in the southern Arans – but it still felt like a long way to go, especially as I also had the obstacle of hitchhiking 25 miles back to my car to negotiate.

Sticking to a public footpath, I picked my way north up the valley and through a farmyard towards the start of the Glasgwm climb. Feeling fatigued and brain-dead, I was mentally on another planet until a barking farm dog jolted me back into the land of the living. It was an angry, agitated hooligan of a Welsh hound. With a flurry of growls, it ran around a fence, confronted me and started jumping up. It wanted me out of there – quickly. I was bricking it. And so, with a flurry of cowardly yelps, in a blur of panic I sprinted for safety beyond a gate, leaving my manly pride firmly in the farmyard.

I spent the next 15 minutes dreaming up ridiculous, outlandish outcomes if other adventurers I admired had encountered that hound. In my fantastical stories, Charlie Walker befriended the canine and rode it like a horse to the summit; Ben Saunders got it to pull his backpack like a sleigh; Sean Conway challenged it to a race to the top – and won; Anna McNuff gave it a big hug, defusing the stand-off with her infectious, flamboyant positivity; and Alastair Humphreys handed it a bivvy bag and went off for a microadventure with his new best friend.

The vast cliffs of Craig Cywarch – a sprawling mass of overhanging bluffs, perpendicular chutes, heathery platforms and near-vertical sheets of bare rock – looked Jurassic, as if the sight of a pterodactyl taking to the skies from the lumpy crags wouldn't have been a surprise. But I couldn't fully enjoy its remote, rugged splendour. I was feeling completely drained of energy as I slowly ascended past a series of waterfalls and emerged at the col. I checked my phone and loaded up the trio of Facebook, Twitter and Instagram in turn, desperate for a momentary distraction from this grey, rain-battered mountainside. Utterly drenched and freezing cold, I wanted only to tick off these final two tops and go home to bed.

I crossed a stile and climbed steeply south-west along a fence to reach a small lake and, finally, the rocky knoll of Glasgwm's summit. I had one more Nuttall left. I wolfed down some damp peanut-butter crackers and the unappetising remains of my bag of trail mix, and then forced myself to plod onwards for Pen y Bryn-fforchog. My sodden boots squelched through muddy swamps, large drips of rainwater trickled down my face, my wet body shivered, and my lungs felt heavy and laboured, as if they were about to stop working. The rain persisted and the clag was down, making navigation difficult. But using fence lines as a handrail, I slowly veered west and south around the edges of a forest and reached my final 2,247ft top. It was a glorious relief. I'd made it – all 37 mountains in the Berwyns and Arans climbed in five days.

An hour and a half later, after a slow descent over pathless fellside and agricultural fields to Rhydymain, I was standing on the A494 trying to hitch a ride. It was a long and slightly complicated route back to my car parked in Cynwyd. Still soaked and cold, I was worried. How long was this going to take? How many lifts would I need?

As it turned out, I made it back to my Golf in a trio of rides. First, a man in his 40s, with a docile Staffordshire Bull Terrier in the back, picked me up in an old banger of a white-panel van. He lived in Central Wales but his girlfriend was from Liverpool. They were meeting up halfway for a romantic rendezvous in Bala. He dropped me in the town, enabling me to raid the local Spar for sugary snacks, and then I headed to the northern tip of the lake, aiming to hitch further north-east on the B roads. A forestry worker in a pick-up truck pulled over for me and asked where I was heading.

'Cwee-nid,' I said, more than a little unsure of my Welsh pronunciation.

'Where?' he replied in a thick Welsh accent, looking confused.

'Cwhy-nwhyd?' I tried.

'Eh? There's nowhere called that around here.'

'Hang on. Let me show you on my phone.'

'Oh, Cun-wid – why didn't you say?'

I jumped into the truck, which was strewn with an alarming array of discarded Costa coffee cups, Red Bull cans and empty fag packets, and chatted away with my new friend, laughing about my terrible Welsh pronunciation. I asked him questions about his job; he asked questions about my hiking challenge. It was a fun journey, with rock music blasting out of the stereo, but sadly he couldn't take me the whole way. So, feeling newly educated on the Welsh language, as well as strangely high from the caffeine-and-tobacco-infused atmosphere of the truck, I jumped out at a crossroads and bade the forester farewell.

Three minutes later, a builders' merchant lorry, loaded up with pallets of bricks and bags of gravel next to its hydraulic arm, pulled over at the side of the rural road. Had it responded to my thumb-wagging? I opened the passenger door, used the steps to haul myself up to the high cabin, and leaned in.

'Hi mate, I'm trying to get back to my car in, erm, Cun-wid – any chance of a lift?'

'Good luck finding your car in Cun-wid – it'll have been nicked by now,' said the driver, smiling cheekily.

I laughed awkwardly, not entirely sure whether he was joking, and paused, somewhat tongue-tied.

'Hop in, mate, I'm doing deliveries that way anyway, no problem.'

My car was still there. And it wasn't propped up on bricks, or missing a wing mirror, or any of the other scenarios my driver had joked about. I changed clothes, downed water, shovelled a Snickers into my mouth, and sat in the driver's seat with the heating on full blast. I smiled. I'd made it back. Thirty-seven Nuttalls in five days – my best peak-bagging stats to date. It was a huge step towards my ultimate goal – and it felt like I was back on target to make it within six months.

CHAPTER 15

SLEEPING IN A SWAMP

Mountains 261–283

DATE	REGION	MOUNTAINS
Tuesday 18 July	Brecon Beacons	Cefn yr Ystrad 2,024ft (617m) Allt Lwyd 2,146ft (654m)
Wednesday 19 July	Brecon Beacons	Waun Rydd 2,523ft (769m) Bwlch y Ddwyallt 2,474ft (754m) Fan y Big 2,359ft (719m) Cribyn 2,608ft (795m) Pen y Fan 2,907ft (886m) Corn Du 2,864ft (873m) Craig Gwaun Taf 2,711ft (826m) Y Gyrn 2,031ft (619m) Fan Fawr 2,408ft (734m) Craig Cerrig-gleisiad 2,064ft (629m) Fan Frynych 2,064ft (629m) Fan Llia 2,073ft (632m)
Thursday 20 July	Brecon Beacons	Fan Nedd 2,175ft (663m) Fan Fraith 2,192ft (668m) Fan Gyhirych 2,379ft (725m) Fan Hir 2,497ft (761m) Fan Brycheiniog 2,631ft (802m) Picws Du 2,457ft (749m) Waun Lefrith 2,221ft (677m) Garreg Las 2,083ft (635m) Garreg Lwyd 2,021ft (616m)

I returned in a zombie-like state to the Fix the Fells office for three days from Tuesday to Thursday, struggling through each shift as if it was a lifetime of admin and emails. Friday was spent in front of my laptop in Cockermouth's Starbucks, frantically working on the 100-page toolkit I'd been commissioned to write for the Berlin-based NGO; and on Saturday morning I finished off a magazine feature about my bushwalking adventures in Tasmania for *Outdoor Enthusiast* magazine.

By Saturday evening, in true could-my-life-get-any-more-hectic? style, I was 300 miles away in a cottage on the Pembrokeshire coast with Mum, Dad, my Becky, Tom, his wife Becky, Adam, his girlfriend Cath (who needs to change her name to Becky before being allowed into the family), and Tom's children, Daniel and Samuel. It was the Forrest clan's annual summer holiday, organised without fail by my dad, and I was joining in the fun for Sunday and Monday. I was sad not to be able to stay for the whole week – but this was just another in a long line of sacrifices I was making in the name of peak-bagging.

It was a fun two days of family time in a mini holiday complex: feeding the goats and donkeys, ambling down country paths, watching dolphins from the secluded cove of Mwnt beach, going out for coffee, competing for bragging rights in intense table tennis, cricket and penalty shoot-out contests with Dad, Adam and Tom, and pretending to be Jaws while swimming with the kids in the indoor pool. Every evening there was a big get-together over dinner, with someone different cooking each night. Thankfully, my carefully crafted reputation as a terrible chef paid dividends and I was politely spared the cooking duties, which meant that I could gorge myself on Mum's chilli con carne and Cath's sausage roll without having to return the favour. The perfect crime.

But the good food, bantering conversation and family-time normality of the Pembrokeshire break couldn't last. I had a date with the mountains of South and Central Wales. I'd used my annual leave to give myself the next seven days, Tuesday to Monday, off work and

I was hoping to bag as many Nuttalls as possible. The Brecon Beacons were the first mountains on my radar. My plan, according to the route I'd created on OS Maps, was to walk a wavering line westwards from, very roughly, Aber village to the A4069, ticking off all of the range's 23 Nuttalls. I estimated it would take three to four days to hike the 45 miles required and then hitchhike back to my car.

Bidding farewell to everyone, I drove east towards Merthyr Tydfil feeling a little melancholy. It was always sad saying goodbye to loved ones and I felt selfish for prioritising mountains over them. But, equally, I knew this was something I wanted to do – no, needed to do – and that helped reduce my sense of guilt.

As I tootled along, I thought about an incident the previous day. Mum, Dad, Becky and I had been walking along the Wales Coast Path towards the dramatic headland above Mwnt beach. I led everyone through a field, following a handful of other tourists, thinking it was the correct path. Out of nowhere a Land Rover appeared, beeping its horn repeatedly, and an irate farmer jumped out, shouting, 'Oi oi oi, what are you doing? What is wrong with you people?' Clearly we'd taken a wrong turn. It was an honest mistake and the signage was far from clear. But, regardless, we were angrily turfed out of the field with a barrage of expletive-laden abuse, as if we'd just trampled over the graves of the farmer's relatives. Maybe we had? Do farmers bury their loved ones on their own land? Anyway, there was a certain irony that I'd hiked 260 mountains without offending a single landowner, only to be fiercely berated on a gentle afternoon seaside stroll.

I parked up at Pontsticill Reservoir, a few miles north of Merthyr Tydfil, and prepared myself for the off. The Brecon Beacons are a range of rounded, grassy hills, broken in places by steep escarpment edges that stretch for over 20 miles on an east–west axis across South Wales. The Brecon Beacons National Park includes the summits of the Black Mountains to the east, but I'd already ticked them off in April. So my focus was on the 23 Nuttalls in the national park's central Fforest Fawr region and the confusingly named Black Mountain region to the west. The first summit on my hit list was Cefn yr Ystrad, a solitary top infuriatingly located out on a limb to the south of the main line of mountains, thus adding an extra six miles to my route.

Weighed down by a backpack full of food, I set off at 2pm and climbed an easy path to the two gigantic, ancient cairns of the 2,024ft top. I surveyed the mountains of the Brecon Beacons, which spread out into the distance to the north-west. I associated the range with hardcore SAS expeditions and remembered tragic headlines of three men who died from heat illness on a training exercise here in 2013. But the rolling green tops looked distinctly unthreatening from this angle.

I descended north to the quarries of Cwar yr Ystrad and Cwar yr Hendre. They seemed bleak and eerie, almost post-apocalyptic. Derelict buildings, collapsed piles of concrete, and the deeply scarred landscape had a *Mad Max* vibe. I picked up a path continuing north to Talybont Reservoir and, on a whim, decided to veer around the southern tip of the water rather than take a much longer anti-clockwise loop north. This 'short cut', however, meant I'd have to climb the pathless southern slopes of Allt Lwyd, my next Nuttall – and I soon regretted that decision. I found myself wading through waist-high ferns, scratching my exposed legs with a hundred tiny paper cuts on stems and twigs. Shorts were a bad choice. And it almost certainly took longer than if I'd just stuck to the main path. I should have known better. My mountain 'short cuts' invariably ended up in some sort of calamity or delay or life-threatening scenario. But I made it through the jungle of bracken, emerged on to open fellside and plodded onward to the 2,146ft summit.

I continued north-west on an enjoyable, narrowing ridge and arrived at the start of a flatter summit plateau. From the nose of the ridge, I turned right and walked along the edge to an impressive, dome-shaped cairn at Carn Pica, before veering left and finding a place to camp. I set up Dennis, boiled up two sachets of instant noodles – which had cost 20p each but tasted like they should've cost

2p each – and settled down for the night. My Brecon Beacons expedition had got off to a steady start.

❋   ❋   ❋

The Daily Adventure Journal of James

19/07/17: You've had a 'proper' day in the mountains only if you've completed this checklist of must-do activities: fallen on your arse; straddled a barbed wire fence (with your 'crown jewels' coming dangerously close to being shredded by the spiky metal spurs); fled like a coward from an overly friendly cow; been fooled by a false summit; seriously questioned your life choices while being battered by repulsive weather; eaten your body weight in flapjacks; skimmed a stone in a tarn or lake; taken off layers and put said layers back on at least 13 times; and wandered over seven separate cairns to make sure you've visited the 'true' summit of a top. I ticked them all off today. Go me.

20/07/17: I always take only my integrated cooking-pot when I go wild camping. I never carry a separate pan, simply to save weight. But I'm beginning to think I should. Mainly because, with only one pot, my morning porridge tends to have a vile aftertaste of yesterday evening's dinner; or my tea has blobs of porridge floating in it. Trust me, there's a reason why Quaker Oats don't sell chicken jalfrezi-flavoured porridge pots.

❋   ❋   ❋

I woke to detestable weather: torrential rain, gusting winds and a ubiquitous clag. Urgh. I reluctantly decamped and, fully waterproofed up, headed out into the heavy rain weighed down by a heavy backpack and a heavy heart. I was feeling low. Why the hell had I exchanged the warmth – both literal and emotional – of a family holiday in favour of being brutally battered by the weather in the

Brecon Beacons? Was I enjoying this? How nice would it be to be sipping on a coffee right now with my brothers, or strolling along a sunny beach with Mum and Dad?

The whole day was a laborious, dull trudge. I climbed briefly north-west to tick off Waun Rydd and then descended west to the 2,474ft top of Bwlch y Ddwyallt. I stuck to the high-sided edge leading to the summit of Fan y Big, the only mountain with a name implying it could accommodate the girth and length of Lord Hereford's Knob. Located just 20 miles apart, the two dirtily named fells were a duo in my mind, ideally made for each other, perfect bedfellows. Or maybe that was just me passing time with strange thoughts.

I pressed on to Cribyn, cursing my luck that I couldn't see the scenery, some of the best in the region, and then slogged onwards for Pen y Fan. At 2,907ft, it is the highest point of the Brecon Beacons, but I didn't like it. Despite the bad weather, the summit was swarming with groups of loud, annoying, over-excited school kids – and I was just totally fed up with being cold and drenched. My waterproof jacket was leaking and I wasn't sure why. Was the driving rain getting through the large hood, which was designed to accommodate a helmet? Or had the lining failed? Or was it something else? Either way, my underlayers were getting damp, making it impossible to get warm, while the constant precipitation made stopping for a morale-boosting snack or hot drink a futile exercise. The mountains were doing my head in. I wanted to scream.

Deciding that the only option was to smash out as many miles as possible, I nipped easily to the summit of Corn Du and then swung left on a detour to bag Craig Gwaun Taf, one of those mountains with an ever-changing status. John and Anne originally thought it qualified as a Nuttall when they visited it in 1986. But with the onset of new metric maps, Ordnance Survey's official data saw it fall short of the criteria and it was excluded from the Nuttalls' books, only for a re-survey in November 2016 to promote it finally into the elite. I found myself wishing it hadn't been, as I tramped through horrible conditions on an out-and-back to the top, before making a semicircular loop north-west, west and then south-west to Y Gyrn. Next, I dropped down out of the hills to the A470 at the Storey Arms and dived under a bus shelter, my saviour from the harsh Welsh weather.

I wasn't the only one who'd been dealt an unforgiving hammering by the Brecon Beacons. Two Americans from New Jersey were sitting in the bus shelter, a glazed look of post-traumatic shock written across their faces. They looked like they'd just been through a heavy-duty cycle in a giant washing machine. Another set of unsuspecting, ill-prepared tourists chewed up and spat out by the inhospitable British mountains, I thought. The man's glasses were steamed up and covered in small droplets of rain; his black hair was plastered flat against his forehead; and his beige chinos were so damp they'd clearly darkened by several shades. His oriental wife was meek and quiet, as if the mountains had delivered such a harsh lesson she'd lost the ability to speak, make eye contact or think straight.

We chatted for a while. They'd planned to climb Pen y Fan but had got only halfway before beating a hasty retreat with their tails between their legs. I joked that they'd had the 'true' Brecon Beacons experience and managed to inject some light-hearted positivity into the conversation. We shared a tasty Welsh cake and some dried fruit – and they both seemed to perk up. Perhaps a little too much, as the man dropped a packet of cheese slices on to the floor.

'Oh crap,' he said, looking frustrated.

'Unlucky,' I offered, unhelpfully.

'I don't want to waste them,' he added, picking up the muddy cheese slices. 'Do you think sheep would eat cheese?'

And so, with the bizarre sight of a clueless American tourist throwing orange squares of cheddar over a fence at a clearly baffled Welsh sheep, I left the bus shelter and climbed the north-east ridge between steep crags to the 2,408ft summit of Fan Fawr. I turned right and tramped through the continuing rain to Craig Cerrig-gleisiad and Fan Frynych before picking up the Beacons Way path to Fan Llia.

Enough was enough. It had been a long, boring day. No views. No excitement. Just rain and wind and then more rain. But I'd completed 12 Nuttalls – a good haul – and it was now time for some shelter. I set up Dennis on a flat patch of grass next to Afon Llia and settled down for a quiet night reading a Jack Reacher novel and watching episodes of *Narcos* with the Netflix app on my iPhone.

I physically retched the following morning at the disgusting sight in front of me. A massive black slug had somehow got itself stuck in the narrow slit in the lid of my all-in-one integrated camping stove and pot. The slit, like the opening at the top of a travel mug, was there to enable you to chug on hot drinks or drain pasta or rice. I used it for both purposes. But now a trail of slug mucus was smothered liberally across the red lid and the offending gastropod was firmly entrapped in the narrow slit. How the hell had it managed that? The slit was at least ten times smaller than the girth of the slimy beast, so it must have shape-shifted to squeeze through. And now the parts of its body above and below the slit had engorged into a bulbous, gooey, gloopy mass of grossness. My morning coffee, I feared, was going to be akin to a mucus-smothered snogging session with a slug.

Leaving the lid to one side and hoping the slug would somehow free itself, I boiled up golden syrup porridge with water from the stream. It didn't go down too well. I couldn't get the nauseous slug thoughts out of my mind. It was a nicer day, so I laid out my damp waterproofs and tent sheets on a stone wall, hoping they would dry out in the morning sun, and slowly prepared for the day ahead. I was taking things at a leisurely pace in a bid to give my gastropod nemesis more time for a much-needed act of escapology. But it didn't work. The slug was in the same position as an hour previously. Damn it. I tried to nudge it through with my thumb but that just felt as if I was going to squash its body. I sprinkled water on to it, hoping that would lubricate its escape, but it didn't work. Other adventurers negotiate crocodile-infested rivers, scorpion-strewn deserts and forests full of bears, and here I was being outwitted by a slug. Half convinced

167

I should guillotine its body with a sharp rock and be done with it, I finally opted to put the lid and slug in my plastic bag of rubbish and let it escape slowly through the day.

I passed Maen Llia, a huge Bronze Age standing stone, and climbed west over grassy slopes, aiming for Fan Nedd, my next Nuttall. I was now in Fforest Fawr territory, the moor-like, rounded hills of the central Brecon Beacons – a remote, quiet area that is far less frequented than the peaks further east. But, as I neared the 2,175ft top, that tranquillity was shattered by the roar of a red and white HM Coastguard rescue helicopter. It landed just 50ft away from me, so close that I could feel the powerful downdraft of the rotor blades. I watched as the pilot and crew skilfully completed what I presumed were training exercises.

On a wide track dissecting Fan Fraith and Fan Gyhirych, my next two Nuttalls, I saw a group of young army recruits. Covered in camouflage paint and carrying rifles, they were hiking silently in single file with steely looks on their faces. I wondered if I had that same determined, single-minded aura or not, as I descended west through quiet forest and stopped for lunch among the dense trees. Feeling re-energised by the plethora of tasty snacks I'd just consumed, I descended an overgrown public footpath – a veritable jungle of brambles that had probably not been walked on for decades – and arrived at the hamlet of Glyntawe on the A4067.

My morning had been productive. I was making good progress west and I had only six more Nuttalls left to complete the Brecon Beacons. The sun was shining and I felt happy and excited about the walk ahead of me. I took the opportunity to check my rubbish bag. Result. Houdini the slug had, finally, squirmed its way through the impossibly small gap, thus enabling me both to reclaim ownership of my lid and to release the slimy creature safely into the overgrowth of the road's grassy verge. Everything was working out all right. Maybe this Brecon Beacons trip wasn't going to be a total wash-out after all. I boiled up some water and, feeling relaxed and content, sipped on a sugary hot chocolate. Little did I know that I was in for a hellish, morale-crushing night.

Known collectively as the Carmarthen Fan, the next five Nuttalls – Fan Hir, Fan Brycheiniog, Picws Du, Waun Lefrith and Garreg Las – were the most enjoyable section of Brecon Beacons walking for me. I hiked along the striking escarpment edge, basking in the sunshine and praising the gods for the blue skies that had arrived. I sat on the lip of the Bannau Sir Gaer cliffs, dangling my legs and gazing down as the wind made beautiful swirling, rippling patterns on the surface of Llyn y Fan Fach. It almost looked like the mythical Lady of the Lake – a local Welsh legend not to be confused with the King Arthur tale – was about to appear from below the surface. But, sadly, she didn't – and the only thing that emerged were menacing dark clouds blowing in over the mountains.

By the time I'd veered south on the Beacons Way, heading for Garreg Las, the weather had turned awful, bringing the same old hated trio of heavy rain, strong winds and pervasive cloud. It was exactly what I didn't want. But, rather than get annoyed, I let the frustration fuel my fire and I marched onward, determined to tick off my final two Nuttalls. I reached the large cairns of Garreg Las's 2,083ft summit and then left the usual Carmarthen Fan route, instead aiming west for the outlying top of Garreg Lwyd. There were only three miles between the two summits but it seemed to take for ever. With my head down and my arms folded under the straps of my backpack – a crouched, defensive posture I used to try and minimise my exposure to the elements – I staggered through the storm and stumbled, somewhat disorientated, to the summit, my 23rd and final Nuttall in the brutal Brecon Beacons. I was exhausted, freezing, drenched and dejected – and totally ready for dinner and bed. But the ground was strewn with rocks everywhere I looked. So I descended briefly north-west and, in an act of minor desperation, settled on a patch of black, hard, peaty mud that was relatively flat and rock-free. I pitched Dennis and dived inside, using the porch to quickly boil up a tin of

Heinz ravioli for dinner. With my hunger satisfied, I crawled inside my sleeping bag feeling slightly apprehensive. Dennis was swaying and flapping wildly in the wind, while diagonal rain slammed into the tent as if it was trying to pierce the fabric. It was going to be a rough night.

At 4am a rough night became a disastrous night. Dennis, after hours of relentless pressure, finally buckled. The central pole snapped, collapsing the tent into a flimsy, spineless mess, and waking me instantly from a fitful sleep. But that was just the start of it. What had started out as a relatively firm dirt platform for Dennis had transformed into a soft, squelchy, disgusting quagmire. Basically, I was lying face down in a peaty swamp. Dank, muddy water was seeping up through the groundsheet, soaking everything in its black, foul-smelling wake.

I opened the zip of the misshapen tent and created a slither of an exit point. I crawled through it on all fours, my hands sinking into the cold, thick mud, and tried to shimmy my feet into my sodden boots, located in what used to be Dennis's porch. Half in the tent, half out of it, I was doing a strange downward-dog yoga pose, with my nose inches from the peaty, puddle-strewn bog. The wind howled and the rain lashed down remorselessly. Cold water trickled down my neck. Dark mud splattered over my clothes and skin. And I thought to myself, *What the fuck am I doing with my life?*

CHAPTER 16

LIAM'S MANGOES

Mountains 284–294

DATE	REGION	MOUNTAINS
Friday 21 July	Central Wales	Pen y Garn 2,001ft (610m)
Saturday 22 July	Central Wales	Gorllwyn 2,011ft (613m) Drygarn Fawr 2,103ft (641m)
Sunday 23 July	Central Wales	Y Garn 2,244ft (684m) Pumlumon Fawr 2,467ft (752m) Pumlumon Fach 2,178ft (664m) Pen Pumlumon Llygad-bychan 2,385ft (727m) Pen Pumlumon Arwystli 2,431ft (741m)
Monday 24 July	Central Wales	Bache Hill 2,001ft (610m) Black Mixen 2,133ft (650m) Great Rhos 2,165ft (660m)

Six hours later, I was tucking into a breakfast wrap and a large latte in McDonald's, wearing several layers of dry clothes, feeling toasty and cosy, and giggling at a TV show on my laptop. The location was a characterless retail park in Merthyr Tydfil, that much-maligned South Wales town. The skies were black and stormy and my fellow customers seemed to be drunks, tramps or screaming toddlers. But it still felt like paradise compared with the godforsaken top of Garreg Lwyd.

I'd made it to Merthyr by means of a long and painful combination of road walking and hitchhiking. At 4.05am I'd decamped as quickly as I could, entering a survival-like mode of urgency that involved abandoning any hope of keeping either myself or my stuff dry and mud-free. Then, with my backpack crammed full, weighed down by 10kg of equipment and an extra 10kg of mud and rainwater, I hiked north-west for 15 minutes through torrential rain to the A4069. Haunted by the sight of several perfect wild-camping spots with good shelter on the descent to the road, I turned left and plodded south, aiming for the small town of Brynamman. It was sod's law that several cars passed me heading north for Llangadog, but not a single one did so in my direction. So I pounded the tarmac for three miles. My mind was troubled. Why the hell had I camped in such an exposed spot? What on earth was I thinking, setting up on that peaty mud platform? Why hadn't I hiked out of the fells and camped in the shelter of one of the shake holes or disused pits next to the road?

In a trance-like state of fatigue and post-traumatic stress, I made it into the town and turned left to pick up the A4068. I found a lay-by and started wagging my thumb. Drenched from head to toe, I can't have looked like an attractive prospect as a passenger. But, thankfully, a rather rotund, silver-goateed army adventure instructor picked me up in his 4x4. We chatted about his job, the army and the Brecon Beacons. He moaned about bureaucracy, funding cuts, and the switch from in-house adventure instructors to freelancers, but sounded excited about the weekend ahead. The SAS guys from Hereford would be in the Brecon Beacons in force, he said, undertaking a training and selection exercise. If only I'd got the fortitude of an SAS recruit, I thought, I wouldn't be feeling quite so beat.

My new friend dropped me off at a road junction before turning north for his work at Sennybridge. I hiked along a grassy verge, passing the time by analysing whether there were more disposable Costa cups or Coke cans discarded on the roadside. Each time an HGV whizzed past, a wall of air hit me, followed swiftly by a spray of muddy puddle water from its tyres. I didn't care – I couldn't get any wetter. I arrived at the road I needed, found a lay-by and put out my thumb, looking downtrodden and desperate. My pathetic appearance seemed to work. A builder stopped in his large white Transit van. He was tall and well-built, maybe in his late 20s, with a mop of messy but cool hair, dark stubble and a mischievous, friendly look to his face.

'Thanks for stopping,' I said, sliding open the side door to stash my sodden backpack.

'I saw you before, mate, and drove past. But I felt guilty so I turned around. I just couldn't leave you standing there in this storm. You looked like you'd been destroyed by the weather.'

'Thank you so much for the lift – are you heading towards Merthyr Tydfil?'

'Sure, no worries.'

I jumped in the passenger seat, adding, 'Did I shut that side door properly?'

'Should be fine, mate.'

Two minutes later, the side door suddenly swung open as we were doing 60mph on the A465. Oh God – this was my fault. Surely a cement mixer or ladder was about to fall into the busy road, causing a fatal multi-car pile-up. My new friend, however, was on the ball. He slammed on the brakes and the sudden change in speed jolted the sliding door forward, slamming it shut. Without missing a beat, he said, 'Job done,' like a Hollywood superhero delivering the perfectly timed one-liner, and sped back up to 60mph with a slightly narcissistic smirk on his face. If I was ten per cent as cool as this guy I'd be happy, I thought.

'What are you up to today?' I asked, rubbing my hands together and warming them in front of the heating vents.

'As little as possible – my boss is away and I've got the Friday feeling,' he joked. 'I'll drop you into Merthyr, that way I can delay starting work a little longer.'

'Absolute legend,' I replied, developing an instant man-crush on my driver.

From a large roundabout to the west of the town, I had just over three miles left to travel north-east back to my car at Pontsticill Reservoir. I walked half the way down a minor road before getting one final lift. I hadn't even put my thumb out when a massive coach pulled over next to me and the automatic door slowly opened.

'You shouldn't be walking in weather like this,' said the Scouser driver. 'It's diabolical. Get in – I'll give you a lift.'

He dropped me off in the village, before heading off to pick up a group of school children from an adventure centre. I walked the final quarter of a mile back to my car which, fittingly, was now surrounded by a gigantic puddle of water. My Brecon Beacons expedition was over. Thank God. And good riddance – I'm never, ever, ever returning.

Back in McDonald's, I read my Nuttalls guidebook, downloaded maps to my phone and scribbled together a hotchpotch plan in a notepad. With the 23 Nuttalls in the Brecon Beacons already in the bag, I set my sights on Central Wales. I had four days left to play with and only 11 Nuttalls to climb – three in New Radnor, two south-west of Rhayader, one close to Devil's Bridge, and finally the five Pumlumon fells to the east of Nant-y-moch Reservoir. All of these peaks fell within the Cambrian Mountains range, a homogeneous area of uplands in Mid Wales, except for the three Nuttalls in the isolated Radnor Forest, to the north of New Radnor.

As much as I passionately wanted to have a day off walking, I decided I'd spend the day climbing Pen y Garn, a solitary 2,001ft summit to the east of Devil's Bridge, leaving three simple day-walks for Saturday, Sunday and Monday. Plan sorted. All I needed to do was resupply and find somewhere to sleep. There was absolutely no way

I was prepared to head out wild camping again. After five minutes on Google, I had the address of a nearby supermarket scribbled in my pad and a bed booked at the Mid Wales Bunkhouse.

I parked up by a huge stone arch, which commemorates the Golden Jubilee of George III, and reluctantly forced myself out of my car. It felt akin to being horrifically hungover but still having to get up for work and face the world. There followed a dull trudge along a long forestry track before a brief slog over pathless, thickly vegetated slopes to the summit, which offered views to an eerie farm of wind turbines, as if tall, white, spinning robots were invading the countryside. I retraced my steps to the forestry road, turned left and plodded back to the car. It was only a short amble, but I felt utterly exhausted. So I switched on my phone, loaded up a Spotify playlist and blasted out some motivational tunes through my headphones. Once more I felt guilty for using my mobile in the mountains and breaking my own rules. But as the challenge became more physical and more defined by terrible weather, the more I found myself searching for some way to break the monotony. Inevitably, I turned to my phone and, on that afternoon in particular, I just don't think I'd have made it up Pen y Garn without the music.

By early evening I was chilling at the Mid Wales Bunkhouse, a quirky independent hostel located between Rhayader and Llanidloes. I had a major drying operation under way – clothing draped over radiators, sleeping bag hanging from a top bunk, tent sheets spread out on the floor, more clothing hung over a drying line outside, and my boots filled with scrunched-up balls of newspaper. Irrecoverably damaged items – my soiled book and a paper map – were in the bin, while my newly cleaned camping accessories were drip-drying on the kitchen dish-drainer. This post-expedition admin was taking ages. But I felt good. The bunkhouse was warm and cosy and I had a curry in the microwave for dinner.

At 10pm, just as I was about to settle down for the night, there was a knock on the window from a dishevelled-looking cyclist. 'How do you get into this place?' he asked. 'I can't find the entrance.' I chuckled and explained how to find the front door.

The man who emerged looked like the cycling version of me after my Garreg Lwyd incident: freezing, drenched and forlorn. A glazed look in his eyes told of hardship endured. Rainwater shed from his clothing on to the hallway floor, like a mini waterfall. He was wearing a cycling helmet, yellow high-vis jacket and shorts. He was in his 30s, with light brown, wavy hair and a scraggly beard. He looked utterly exhausted.

'C'mon in, pal. Get yourself warm and dry. Do you want a brew?' I asked.

'That'd be perfect,' he replied, running his hands through his wet hair, the rainwater slicking it back like Brylcreem.

He certainly didn't look like a cyclist. He wasn't kitted out in all the lycra and accessories money can buy. Instead, he had more of a hipster-on-a-spontaneous-adventure vibe, or maybe it was bohemian-on-a-journey-of-self-discovery. I was particularly taken aback by his footwear. No clip-in cycling shoes for this guy. Instead, he was wearing a pair of brilliantly polished black leather shoes. He looked like a kid on his first day of school.

'Nice shoes,' I said. 'I've heard all the professional cyclists wear them.'

'Haha, you don't see Bradley Wiggins in these, do you? I was so desperate for dry feet this morning, I bought these from a charity shop. They were the only ones in my size.'

'Did it work?'

'Nope. Pretty pointless strategy – my feet are still absolutely soaked.'

'I can totally relate to that. I'm James, by the way, good to meet you,' I said, reaching out to shake my fellow adventurer's hand.

'You too – I'm Liam.'

We spent the evening sharing tales of our adventures. Liam, a former teacher who now resided in the Catalonian countryside, near

Barcelona, running his own bread-baking workshops, was cycling from John O'Groats to Land's End. He'd had two spare weeks in Britain and decided, somewhat on a whim, to go on a big adventure. It was a makeshift, do-it-yourself expedition. He freely admitted to learning on the go and making it up along the way. I admired his adventurous spirit, despite his lack of skill and experience. It reminded me of my own approach. He just did it with a cooler beard and fuelled by more mangoes, judging by the way he was feasting on the luscious fruit.

'Mangoes? Not the classic expedition food,' I suggested.

'I've cycled with these bloody heavy mangoes in my panniers for about 400 miles, since Oban in Scotland, waiting for them to ripen,' replied Liam, taking the mick out of himself. 'Basically I'm the absolute epitome of a middle-class adventurer.'

'Oh my God, that's hilarious. But why?'

'I just really fancied mangoes. I'm such a hipster.'

'I get it, pal. On adventures, sometimes you really need a treat, no matter how illogical. Every adventure needs a mango morale-boost.'

✸   ✸   ✸

The Daily Adventure Journal of James
22/07/17: Today I found myself constantly ogling the beautiful cottages and grand country houses in the villages and hamlets I walked through. I must stop. It always leads to excruciating pangs of house envy. Alternatively I need to (a) retrain as a corporate banker in London so I can afford to buy one, or (b) get hitched to a doddery old grandma who owns one such cottage, in a blatant case of inheritance gold-digging.

✸   ✸   ✸

The next three days were a blur of mindless hiking. I felt like a professional footballer whose childhood love for the game had morphed into a serious job, requiring hard work and sacrifice – a profession with elements of stress and drudgery, like any other. I was a professional hiker now. This wasn't about cheerful sun-drenched Sunday afternoon strolls in the fells. Climbing Nuttalls was my nine-to-five, a task to get done, a job I had to work at diligently even when I didn't feel like it.

On Saturday I climbed Gorllwyn and Drygarn Fawr in the Elan Valley, battling over desolate, pathless moorland. The fells were remote and tranquil, which I enjoyed, but the landscape was somewhat featureless – and certainly far less entertaining than the scenes of drunken debauchery I encountered on my journey back to the bunkhouse. Rhayader, which had been empty and quiet just the day before, was swarming with hordes of revellers in the streets, swilling pints, chanting and bantering around in fancy-dress costumes. For a second I thought it was just a normal Saturday night in rural Central Wales, before discovering it was the town's annual carnival. I contemplated hanging around for a while. But after seeing a blue Smurf snogging the face off Dorothy from *The Wizard of Oz*, while Mario threw up in the corner and Luigi pretended to hump the Tin Man doggy style, I decided a shy and sober peak-bagger probably wouldn't fit in.

On Sunday I ticked off the Pumlumon fells, the highest points of Central Wales, visiting the source of the River Severn in the process. It was a slow plod. I enjoyed my lunch perched on a rock overlooking Llyn Llygad Rheidol, but in general I found myself underwhelmed by Central Wales. The Cambrian Mountains, which fill the gap between their more famous neighbours of Snowdonia and the Brecon Beacons, used to be known as the 'Green Desert of Wales'. It certainly felt arid and boring to me.

By Monday at 2pm I was nearing my 34th and final Nuttall of the past seven days – another gigantic step towards the finish line, keeping me roughly on track for my six-month target. I'd spent the morning climbing to the 2,001ft top of Bache Hill and onward to the ugly building and transmitter mast of Black Mixen, before tramping along the edge of a forest and veering left over boggy heather. Finally, I could see the trig point of Great Rhos, maybe 100ft ahead. I took about 40 steps and arrived, placing my hand on the concrete plinth with a smile on my face. I suddenly felt really emotional. I was welling up, but in a good way. A dizzying sense of euphoria and pride and inspiration descended on me. Despite all of the hardship and epic fails of this latest expedition, the mountains could still lift my heart and make my soul sing.

CHAPTER 17

DODGING BOMBS

Mountains 295–305

DATE	REGION	MOUNTAINS
Saturday 5 August	North Pennines Western Fells	Tinside Rigg 2,047ft (624m) Long Fell 2,046ft (624m) Little Fell 2,454ft (748m) Mickle Fell 2,585ft (788m) Murton Fell 2,215ft (675m)
Tuesday 8 August	Lake District Far Eastern Fells	Selside Pike 2,149ft (655m) Branstree North East Top 2,208ft (673m) Branstree 2,339ft (713m) Tarn Crag 2,178ft (664m) Grey Crag 2,093ft (638m) Harrop Pike 2,090ft (637m)

I crashed back down to reality the very next day. Still feeling jaded from my calamitous misadventures in Wales, I returned to Fix the Fells duties for five days from Tuesday to Saturday. On Sunday I relaxed and pottered about, before spending Monday and Tuesday the following week on freelance-writing jobs and Wednesday to Friday back with my Fix the Fells hat on. I was playing catch-up for the time off I'd had while I'd been in Wales, working the equivalent of full-time for those two weeks.

Physically I was fulfilling my work duties, mentally I was away in the fells. On those all-too-frequent moments in the office when my mind wandered away from the immediate task at hand, I reflected on my Nuttalls challenge. I thought about what was going well, what was going badly, how I needed to change and improve, and, more than anything, contemplated whether I was being true to my original vision.

I felt as if I had lost my way somewhere along the line. On occasion, I listened to music while walking, checked Instagram from beautiful mountainsides and watched Netflix lying in my tent at night. I'd wanted to disconnect from social media and reconnect with the great outdoors, but now the irresistible lure of my phone was hooking me back in. I knew I was reaching for that little black rectangle of entertainment far too often when out in the fells – and I was breaking my self-imposed rules for phone use in the mountains. Although I wasn't using it for hours on end, I'd definitely become liberal with the original 30-minute limit.

Why was this happening? I concluded it was because I wasn't rejoicing in the mountains as much as I had earlier in the challenge. More and more of the climbs were becoming a chore, a joyless drag that I endured rather than enjoyed. Of course, there were still amazing highs – like that euphoric moment on Great Rhos in Central Wales – but they were becoming few and far between. And the monotony and terrible weather were pushing me back into the comforting arms of my iPhone's entertainment. It was a mindset and attitude change that worried me.

One evening after work I went for a long stroll at dusk through Cockermouth. It was the downtime I needed to get my troubled thoughts straight. As I ambled through the Memorial Gardens on the banks of the River Derwent, it all became clear. I was putting myself under too much pressure. I was climbing 446 mountains in six months on my days off from work – a relentless schedule by anyone's standards. It was inevitable that not every climb would be hiking bliss. That was where the physical and mental challenge kicked in – and if a Spotify playlist or some Netflix entertainment helped me get through it, then so be it. I didn't have to be a hillwalking hermit, totally detached from the outside world.

Nevertheless, I made some new promises to myself. I would keep my internet phone use to the original limit of 30 minutes per evening, but give myself some leeway, listening to music and watching Netflix shows when I was really struggling. I thought that was a fair compromise. As for the impending creep of mountain apathy, I pledged simply to stop obsessing about it. Instead I would stay positive, take the rough with the smooth, relish the highs without dwelling on the lows, and, ultimately, focus on the physical pleasure of the exercise when the rain, wind and cloud denied me the spiritual pleasure of the mountains. I felt happier after that, as if I had refocused on my original goals.

I was reflecting on three other issues too: how my body was coping, how effectively I was integrating a big adventure with my everyday life, and whether I was on target to hit my six-month deadline. Physically, I felt I was holding up remarkably well. I was fit, strong and injury-free. I could walk for hours on end without too much trouble and, without wanting to belittle the physical challenge, I wasn't climbing the Himalayas. Yes, I felt exhausted at times, but ultimately the mileage and ascents were within my physical capabilities. My knees were the only slight cause for concern – they creaked and ached when I was descending. However, my new pair of graphite walking poles seemed to take the strain off and nipped the problem in the bud. They also made me look like a bona fide hiking geek. All I needed was a sit mat, an over-the-neck map holder, a compass dangling from my backpack strap, an unfashionable beard and a high degree of social awkwardness and I'd really fit the geeky-rambler stereotype.

Concerning my strange double life of adventure and normality, I was just about managing. There was no downplaying it – my existence was hectic and stressful. I was constantly chasing my tail and, at times, it felt completely overwhelming. But I was getting by. I hadn't been sacked, my house hadn't fallen down, I hadn't been arrested for failing to insure my car. I was behind on things, certainly, and I would have to catch up on a lot of personal admin and household chores after the challenge. My efficient approach and ruthless prioritising, however, meant I'd figured out a way to fit it all in. Just.

Finally, as far as my target of finishing in six months was concerned, I felt as if I was approximately on schedule. The situation was ever-changing. At times it seemed as if everything was under control and I was cruising towards the finish line. At other times – when work or home commitments increased significantly – I found myself seriously concerned about falling behind. But I knew the deadline was never seriously in doubt. My anxieties and fears were probably more emotional than actual and my master plan of 82 days dedicated to hiking, as established at the beginning, was a solid strategy. As long as I stuck to that I was confident I'd make it.

After a fortnight of self-reflection, I'd come to terms with my worries and felt happier about everything as Saturday arrived, my next day booked for Nuttalls-bagging. My plan was to tick off the five Nuttalls I had left to climb in the North Pennines: Tinside Rigg, Long Fell, Little Fell, Mickle Fell and Murton Fell. Located mostly within the MOD's Warcop Artillery Range to the east of Appleby-in-Westmorland, this walk was going to be far from straightforward.

Public access to the 9,700-hectare site, used almost every day by the army for live-firing, was limited to Sunday afternoons and 12 designated weekends a year. I already knew that the Saturday fell on one such access weekend – but even so, walking was permitted only on public footpaths. And, alas, the rights of way didn't visit any of the summits. Access to Little Fell was available only on an annual guided walk; Mickle Fell could be climbed only with a special permit; and Tinside Rigg and Long Fell, though a bridleway passed close by, still lay hundreds of feet off the right of way. The latter two, both elevated to Nuttall status in 2016 after new surveys, were actually classified as 'optional summits' by John and Anne because of the access difficulties. Murton Fell, conversely, could legally be climbed under the Countryside and Rights of Way Act because it fell narrowly outside the military range's boundary. The whole thing was a confusing mess, an administrative nightmare I couldn't get my head around. Who knew climbing a mountain could be so complicated?

Needless to say, I hadn't been organised enough to apply for a permit or find out when the annual guided walk took place. My hectic double life wasn't conducive to such structured pre-planning. So I was just going to go for it and see what happened. I didn't intend to fall short of my 446-mountain challenge on a bureaucratic technicality and, hopefully, I wouldn't step on an unexploded bomb or get shot by an army sniper for trespassing.

I was feeling slightly nervous as I drove towards Hilton, a village three miles east of Appleby-in-Westmorland. The sight of a discarded tank on the side of the road and a multitude of red MOD danger signs hardly allayed my fears. Perhaps I was being paranoid, but I felt there was a deserted, eerie, clinical atmosphere to the countryside, as I tramped warily north-east on a track alongside Scordale Beck. I looked left and right, ahead and behind, half expecting to see a camouflaged commando rise out of the vegetation wielding a machine gun. I placed every step carefully, concerned I might be about to tread on an undischarged shell.

But soon the perilous aura of Warcop dissipated, replaced by the atmosphere of a quiet, unassuming, tranquil day of walking over remote moorland. I turned right after a mile and a half and headed south-east on the bridleway over Swindale Edge and onward to a col close to the tops of Tinside Rigg and Long Fell. This was where I needed to leave the safety of the right of way. I tentatively veered south-west off the bridleway, taking three carefully placed steps, and paused, half expecting something to happen. Was a SWAT team about to abseil out of a helicopter, surround me with their automatic rifles, and throw me in jail for trespassing on military property? Was a red laser dot from a distant sniper about to appear on my forehead, causing me to soil my Montane trousers? No, was the answer. It was a total anticlimax. Nothing happened. So I plodded on easily and ticked off the two minor tops. Parts of the hillside were strewn with shells, some lodged diagonally in the ground, others buried under the thick grass. But they were relatively easy to avoid and, while it was a little unnerving, thankfully nothing exploded. I felt as if I was a total badass, breaking the rules and laughing in the face of danger. I hadn't felt this rebellious since the time I took a 5p plastic bag from a Tesco self-service machine without paying for it.

Back at the bridleway, I retraced my steps north-west and turned right to follow Siss Gill towards Little Fell. I passed a hiker taking the same route in the opposite direction. I assumed he wasn't someone official, or the only person on the annual guided walk. It was apparent I wasn't alone in bending the rules to explore these fells.

The rest of the day passed without incident. I ticked off Little Fell easily and then stuck to the high ground, taking the curved ridge to the 2,585ft top of Mickle Fell. To my right was a scarred plateau, a pockmarked boggy hellhole that looked like a half-exploded battlefield. According to locals, Warcop had been used to train troops for the Falklands. Staring at that scene, I could certainly believe the mountainside had seen some intense training operations. From Mickle Fell I tramped over pathless moorland and progress-slowing heather, aiming for Murton Fell. I followed a series of streams,

Fisher Sike, Swarth Beck and Master Sike, that offered slightly easier passage to the 2,215ft summit, and then I picked up the main path along Scordale Beck back to my car in Hilton. That was the Warcop Artillery Range fells completed and, simultaneously, all 36 Nuttalls in the North Pennines ticked off. I was relieved. I'd been worrying that Warcop was going to be a spanner in the works, a potential stumbling block for my challenge. But I'd negotiated it safely – and I'd done it without losing a single limb. Result.

✳   ✳   ✳

The Daily Adventure Journal of James
05/08/17: For every hour of walking I complete, I think I spend at least 15 minutes taking off and putting on layers. This is how it went today: I'm too hot, take off down jacket; I'm even hotter, take off micro-fleece; *God, it's windy on this ridge*, put micro-fleece back on; take a break at the summit, put down jacket back on; it starts raining, put on waterproof; sun comes out, strip off yet again; and so on and so forth. More costume changes than a Lady Gaga concert.

✳   ✳   ✳

With one stumbling block out of the way, I felt motivated to tick off another – Pillar Rock, the imposing craggy tower that juts out of Pillar's north face and is separated from the bulk of the mountain by a vertical chasm. Located in the Lake District's western fells, it is the only Nuttall that requires technical climbing skills and ropes. My friend Richard Fox, the lead ranger for the Fix the Fells programme, originally offered to join me on a climb after work on the Monday, but a back injury meant a last-minute withdrawal. And so, against my better judgement, I found myself travelling to Ennerdale to scope out the scramble alone.

To save time, I cycled rather than walked the four miles along forestry tracks from the Bowness Knott car park towards the start of the climb. Like all self-respecting adventurers, I did it on a high-quality bicycle – an old-school, violet-coloured, elegantly shaped woman's bike I'd bought for £15 from Facebook the day before. To really complete the look, I should've installed a wicker basket on the front (perhaps containing a French baguette and a bouquet of flowers) and worn a flowing dress complemented with a silk floral scarf. Instead I was wearing grey hiking trousers and a blue and red down jacket. A poor effort.

I ditched the rusting, half-broken bike on the side of a track and began climbing diagonally through forest. An hour or so later I reached Pillar Rock, feeling anxious. I had no ropes. My technical climbing skills were nil. And, despite a forecast predicting a 95 per cent chance of clear skies, it was raining heavily. The rocks under my feet were grimy and slippy. The route ahead – classified as a Grade 3 scramble or moderate rock climb – looked daunting. Competent scramblers could do it without ropes. But could I?

I breathed out deeply, composed myself and descended into a gully safely. I skirted across steep but stable ground and reached the start of the climb. I hauled myself halfway up a rocky wall and peered over a ledge at the route ahead, known as the Slab and Notch. I suddenly felt utterly exposed and vulnerable. My legs turned to jelly. My boots struggled to grip the greasy rock. My forearms shook as I clung on to the crag. I had a vision of falling – helplessly, hopelessly, fatally – to a painful end in the abyss below. Had I become so obsessed with the Nuttalls that I was willing to risk my life for the mission?

I didn't want to die – not now anyway. I had a delicious pizza in the fridge for dinner. I just couldn't risk not tasting that sweet combination of barbecue sauce, spicy chicken and red onions ever again. So I bailed on the Pillar Rock attempt. As annoying as it was, I knew I was way out of my depth. Grade 1 scrambles – maybe Grade 2 at a push – were within my limits, but this felt too close to catastrophic for my liking. So I beat a hasty retreat into Ennerdale, retrieved my purple bike and cycled back to my car. On the final stretch, along a gravel road on the shores of the lake, I momentarily sped past an embarrassed woman squatting in the woods. We caught each other's eyes for an awkward split second. Thirty seconds later I whizzed past her two sons, who were both in hysterics in the knowledge that I'd just rumbled their mum's forest wee. My Pillar Rock climb had been a complete failure this time around, but I knew I'd be back soon – I didn't give up that easily. And, despite my disappointment, I pedalled back to my car smiling at the thought of two little boys engaging in a spot of maternal Schadenfreude.

The following day, after a shift in the office in Threlkeld, I decided on an impromptu post-work hike to take advantage of the long evenings and to boost my Nuttalls total. It was a functional, efficient walk – rather than free and joyful – in Lakeland's far eastern fells. From the shores of Haweswater, I climbed in trainers, shorts and T-shirt with a small backpack over boggy, muddy ground to the tops of Selside Pike, Branstree North East Top, Branstree, Tarn Crag, Grey Crag and Harrop Pike. The weather was overcast and the scenery appeared dull. But it didn't matter. The exercise filled my body with happiness-inducing endorphins and I absolutely relished the sense of achievement of taking on another mini physical challenge and succeeding. What's more, I knew I'd passed the big 300 mark. It felt epic.

Back in my car, I greedily forked a chicken pasta meal from Morrisons into my mouth and opened the Nuttalls spreadsheet on my laptop. I excitedly reviewed how far I'd come and how far I had left to go. I'd ticked off 305 Nuttalls, leaving 141 still to climb with just over a month left. England would be complete in just five walks' time. I felt close to my target of 256 English mountains. Wales, however, was a different matter. I had 28 walks and 107 mountains still to tick off. They were split by John and Anne into several distinct groupings: 23 Nuttalls in the Carneddau, 12 in the Glyders, 12 around Snowdon, 11 in Moel Hebog, 15 in the Moelwyns, 13 in the Arenigs, 9 in the Rhinogs and 12 around Cadair Idris. But I wasn't concerned about the slightly daunting stats. I had two weeks of annual leave booked for a mad blitz of Welsh peak-bagging. I was confident it was going to be an epic mountain odyssey to spectacular Snowdonia.

CHAPTER 18

BOY RACERS AND MIDDLE-FINGER SALUTES

Mountains 306–363

DATE	REGION	MOUNTAINS
Friday 11 August	Carneddau	Tal y Fan 2,001ft (610m) Carnedd y Ddelw 2,257ft (688m) Drum 2,526ft (770m) Pen y Castell 2,044ft (623m)
Saturday 12 August	Carneddau	Craig Eigiau 2,411ft (735m) Pen Llithrig-y-wrach 2,621ft (799m) Craiglwyn 2,044ft (623m) Creigiau Gleision 2,224ft (678m) Creigiau Gleision North Top 2,080ft (634m)
Sunday 13 August	Moel Hebog	Moel Hebog 2,569ft (783m) Moel yr Ogof 2,149ft (655m) Moel Lefn 2,093ft (638m) Mynydd Mawr 2,290ft (698m)
Monday 14 August	Snowdon	Crib Goch 3,028ft (923m) Crib y Ddysgl 3,494ft (1065m) Snowdon 3,560ft (1085m) Yr Aran 2,451ft (747m) Y Lliwedd 2,946ft (898m) Y Lliwedd East Peak 2,930ft (893m) Lliwedd Bach 2,684ft (818m) Gallt y Wenallt 2,031ft (619m)

DATE	REGION	MOUNTAINS
Tuesday 15 August	Glyders	Tryfan 3,010ft (918m) Y Foel Goch 2,641ft (805m) Gallt yr Ogof 2,503ft (763m) Glyder Fach 3,261ft (994m) Castell y Gwynt 3,189ft (972m) Glyder Fawr 3,283ft (1,000m) Y Garn 3,107ft (947m) Foel-goch 2,726ft (831m) Mynydd Perfedd 2,664ft (812m)
Wednesday 16 August	Glyders Carneddau	Elidir Fawr 3,031ft (924m) Carnedd y Filiast 2,694ft (821m) Carnedd y Filiast North Top 2,365ft (721m) Pen yr Ole Wen 3,209ft (978m) Carnedd Dafydd 3,425ft (1044m) Foel Meirch 2,625ft (800m) Yr Elen 3,156ft (962m) Carnedd Llewelyn 3,491ft (1064m) Foel Grach 3,202ft (976m)
Thursday 17 August	Carneddau	Garnedd Uchaf 3,038ft (926m) Foel-fras 3,091ft (942m) Llwytmor 2,785ft (849m) Bera Bach 2,648ft (807m) Bera Mawr 2,605ft (794m) Drosgl 2,487ft (758m) Gyrn Wigau 2,110ft (643m) Pen yr Helgi Du 2,733ft (833m)
Friday 18 August	Snowdon	Moel Eilio 2,382ft (726m) Foel Gron 2,064ft (629m) Moel Cynghorion 2,211ft (674m) Llechog 2,356ft (718m)
Saturday 19 August	Moel Hebog	Y Garn 2,077ft (633m) Mynydd Drws-y-coed 2,280ft (695m) Trum y Ddysgl 2,326ft (709m) Mynydd Tal-y-mignedd 2,142ft (653m) Craig Cwm Silyn 2,408ft (734m) Garnedd-goch 2,297ft (700m) Mynydd Graig Goch 2,000ft (610m)

'You look exactly like Will Young,' said the 70-year-old female hiker, as I passed her on the path.

'Is that a good or bad thing?' I replied, chuckling.

'Definitely good, but you're much more handsome – and you've got lovely blue eyes,' she added, leaning on her walking poles.

I wasn't expecting to pull in the remote tops of the northern Carneddau, but it was happening. Grandmas always seemed to have a soft spot for a Will Young doppelgänger. And, ever since his *Pop Idol* win in 2002, people were constantly telling me I was the perfect double for the 'Evergreen' singer.

'Just don't ask me to start singing "Light My Fire" or "Leave Right Now" – I've got a terrible voice.'

'Oh, go on, please.'

'OK, but only if you join in. We can harmonise.'

Sadly, that playful encounter was the highlight of my first three days in Snowdonia. My hikes on the Friday, Saturday and Sunday were drab and lacklustre. The tops were in cloud, denying me any morale-lifting views, and the constant rain slowly gnawed away at my positivity. I felt low-spirited, unable to escape the thought that I was a prisoner to the challenge, forced against my will to climb mountains in abhorrent weather. Work stresses were nagging at the back of my mind too, which didn't help. I even spent two mornings working on my laptop at Betws-y-Coed YHA, trying to shift some of the unfinished Fix the Fells and freelance-writing tasks that were troubling me.

It was an unlikely source that helped me to stay upbeat in those early days in Snowdonia – Twitter. One evening I tweeted a picture of me looking drenched and downhearted on Creigiau Gleision, with the caption 'Is this fun? Am I enjoying this?' My Twitter friends reminded me that it was 'Type II Fun' – miserable while it's happening but fun in retrospect. They were right. Despite being thrashed by the merciless weather while hiking an 11½-mile loop of the quiet eastern Carneddau, I still felt pangs of pride and happiness on completing the walk.

Though none of the mountains stuck in my mind on those three damp, dull walks, one incident certainly did. On the Sunday, looking like a drowned rat, I returned from a blustery, rain-battered climb of Moel Hebog, Moel yr Ogof, Moel Lefn and Mynydd Mawr to Snowdon Bryn Gwynant Hostel, my home for the night. I was desperate for a hot shower and some dry clothes. I tried the front door but it was locked. Damn it. Where was the piece of paper with the door code? Shit. I'd left it in the dorm room. Just what I needed. I rang the bell. No answer. I banged on the door, knocked on windows and shouted – but to no avail. The whole place was empty.

I wandered round to the right of the building and walked down a dark alleyway filled with a messy jumble of discarded junk and outdoors equipment. I noticed the kitchen window was slightly ajar. Leaning over a pile of mouldy old kayaks, I wedged my arm through the gap and managed to contort my hand into a position to flick open the lock – one of those thin metal bars with multiple holes. I was in. Feeling like a burglar, I took a big stride forward and managed to place one muddy trainer in the kitchen sink. My other leg was balanced on a teetering pile of canoes and, erm, 'Little James' was positioned perilously over the concrete windowsill. *How the hell do I get myself into these predicaments?* I thought. I was one slip away from doing the splits in a testicle-crushing gymnastics move. But, thank God, I made it inside before anyone turned up. Which was lucky because I imagine there is nothing quite like the sight of a sweaty peak-bagger doing crotch lunges through a window in a pair of running leggings to put you off your dinner.

After three days of rain, my Snowdonia adventure took a turn for the better on Monday. It was a glorious sunny day and there was no doubt in my mind which walk I wanted to do – the classic Snowdon Horseshoe. John and Anne praised it as 'without doubt the finest ridge walk in Wales', and it included an exhilarating scramble along Crib Goch's knife edge up to Snowdon before looping home via the sheer cliffs of Y Lliwedd. As a schoolboy I'd climbed the highest mountain in Wales, but I hadn't repeated the feat for many years. And I'd never done Crib Goch, an iconic Grade 1 scramble that topped many Snowdonia bucket lists, nor ticked off the entire Snowdon Horseshoe. But now I had a chance to do them all in near-perfect conditions. I'd hit the jackpot.

From the Pen-y-Pass car park, which was buzzing with the jovial camaraderie and exuberant banter of numerous hiking groups, I headed west on the Pyg Track. The path was busy, filled with a snaking line of walkers ahead, all chatting away and looking forward to a day of adventurous, outdoorsy fun. But I didn't mind the crowds. There was a supportive, almost mischievous atmosphere in the air: strangers sharing jokes, friends helping each other out, bags of Fruit Pastilles being handed around. It felt more like the start of a carnivalesque running event than a quiet day in the hills to me.

At a signpost I turned off to my right and climbed to the start of the Crib Goch scramble, bumping into a man I'd seen in the northern Carneddau.

'Can't believe my eyes,' he said, his face red with frustration and anger. 'There's so many people here. It's like Piccadilly Circus.'

I nodded and laughed. He was right. The mountain was heaving with walkers. But it was a beautifully clear day, in August, in the middle of the school holidays, on a mountain visited by almost half a million people a year. It was to be expected. And I wasn't going to let the crowds ruin my experience. This wasn't time for silence and solitude; this was time for eye-watering panoramas and adrenalin-inducing adventure.

Crib Goch was everything I hoped it would be and more. It was like Striding Edge on steroids: a saw-toothed arête with knee-wobbling levels of exposure and an intoxicating sense of adventure. I first scrambled over bulky slabs, picking the line I thought was easiest up the buttress, and clumsily hauled myself on to the crest of the ridge using my hands, arms, knees and feet. The precariousness hit me in the face. This was serious stuff – near-vertical cliffs to my right, lethal drops to my left, and in the middle a sharp pointed edge to cautiously creep along. Edge was the right word. I felt on the edge of my comfort zone, on the edge of Snowdonia, on the edge of euphoria, on the edge of death.

I teetered carefully along the serrated extremity of the ridge, using my hands for stability and shuffling on my bum whenever it seemed sensible to do so. At times I felt very vulnerable, one trip away from a painful demise; at others I felt completely safe, with a firm footing and excellent handholds. But, more than anything, I had an unrelenting feeling of excitement and adrenalin flowing through my veins, as if I was drunk on the adventure. I was loving every minute it.

I made it to the middle of the scramble, a 3,028ft spot height that qualifies as a Nuttall, and then tiptoed cautiously onward to the rocky turrets and craggy towers of the Pinnacles. The crowds queued up on occasion, when scramblers froze in fear for a second or took their time on a tricky manoeuvre, but I wasn't bothered. I used the breaks to gaze dewy-eyed at the rugged beauty of Snowdonia: the sweeping ridgeline of Garnedd Ugain ahead; the stepped corrie below, holding the shimmering tarns of Glaslyn and Llyn Llydaw; and the domineering and majestic summit of Snowdon to the left.

From the col at Bwlch Coch I looked back at Crib Goch, mesmerised by its imposing outline. To me it was the jagged, scaly, impenetrable backbone of a dozing dragon, the stuff of Welsh legend. It was the red beast from the Wales flag, solidified in mountain form. But I couldn't sit and stare for ever. I had seven more Nuttalls to bag. The exposure relented somewhat as I scrambled steeply to the next peak – Crib y Ddysgl – before veering south-west and south over Bwlch Glas aiming for the roof of Wales, the 3,560ft top of Snowdon. I'd be lying if I said I cared much for the summit, with its hordes of train-hopping, café-visiting tourists, but I did warm to the friendly atmosphere. There was a palpable sense of communal achievement in the air, as if we'd all experienced something special together.

I descended momentarily south on the main horseshoe circuit but ignored the usual path to the left for Bwlch Ciliau, instead taking the descent to Bwlch Main. This was where my peak-bagging exploits were forcing me to take an illogical route. To save a day of walking, I wanted to bag the lonely top of Yr Aran, an isolated but shapely peak lying nearly two miles to the south of Snowdon. I edged along the cliffs of Clogwyn Du down to a small tarn and then climbed steeply to the 2,451ft summit, feeling as if the detour had drained me of energy. So I scoffed a syrupy flapjack and a handful of sugared mango slices, before going cross country over pathless slopes to pick up the Watkin Path beyond Afon Cwm Llan and climb steadily to rejoin the horseshoe route at Bwlch Ciliau.

The rest of the walk, edging along the sheer north face of Y Lliwedd high above the dancing surface of Llyn Llydaw, was breathtaking. I hiked happily east over a trio of Nuttalls tops – Y Lliwedd, Y Lliwedd East Peak and Lliwedd Bach – feasting on the expansive views. This quieter section of the horseshoe was an extraordinary viewing platform. Snowdonia's pure majesty and grandeur were laid out in front of my eyes, invigorating and uplifting. Across the expanse, Crib Goch rose like a fin from the opposite ridge; minuscule hikers, mere dots in the distance, crept along the arête, silhouetted against an azure sky; sunlight brightened crags, cliffs, scree and grass with a dreamy hue; and the mighty Snowdon, the undisputed lord of the range, soared proudly over it all.

Two hours later, after a detour off the classic horseshoe route to bag the 2,031ft top of Gallt y Wenallt, I was back at the YHA making vegetable curry in the kitchen and chatting to Bethany, a petite 20-something with short blonde hair with pink streaks, a lip piercing, brown eyes and a pretty smile.

'How was your day?' I asked, frying up onions and peppers in a pan and stirring my bubbling pot of rice.

'Amazing in this weather – I've been practising nav skills for my upcoming Mountain Leader assessment,' replied Beth.

That took me by surprise. She was wearing baggy, patterned harem trousers and a multi-coloured woolly top. Her style had a hippy-bohemian twist. For a split second I found myself thinking she'd got lost on the way to a vegan yoga festival and accidentally ended up in Snowdonia. She didn't look like a mountain person. Then I stopped that train of thought in its tracks. It was completely sexist of me and I was annoyed at myself for even thinking it. Adventure was no longer the preserve of privileged white men with beards. The old stereotypes no longer applied. The world of adventure should be open to everyone: people from different backgrounds, genders, ethnicities, sexualities and appearances. That was something I supported wholeheartedly and, while male-centric bias might still apply to a certain extent, I wanted to be part of the movement towards equality rather than harbouring outdated prejudices. After all, so many of my adventure inspirations were female: Anna McNuff, Sarah Outen, Lizzie Carr, Sophie Radcliffe and many more. I quickly added Beth to that list.

We chatted over dinner and she told me about her life. She lived in the Eden valley in Cumbria and worked as an outdoor instructor at the Robinwood centre in Alston, teaching archery, climbing, kayaking and all manner of outdoor activities to groups of schoolchildren. When she wasn't at work, she hiked up mountains, climbed rock faces and explored Britain on mini adventures. Her love for the outdoors was infectious. And she looked stylish with it, too. In comparison, donned in plain black hiking trousers and a black micro-fleece, I was the epitome of a bland, tasteless, unstylish hiking geek. I needed to up my game.

✳   ✳   ✳

The Daily Adventure Journal of James

15/08/17: When I'm out wild camping, every now and then I need to send a text to a family member. But, thanks to sod's law, this invariably coincides with me losing all reception. And so, like today, I tend to find myself leaving Dennis and wandering aimlessly and barefoot around the rainy mountainside, climbing on to boulders and up dangerous crags while holding my phone to the skies in the hope of one bar kicking in. 'How did James die?' my teary mum asks the mountain rescue team-leader. 'He fell off a cliff trying to send a text to his brother Tom.' 'What did the text say?' 'You're a knob.'

16/08/17: After so much time walking in the mountains of Britain, I've come to recognise a series of hiker stereotypes. A few of my favourites are: the first-timer, who usually wears jeans, Converse trainers and an expression that says, 'What the hell am I doing here?'; the warring couple – one loves hiking, the other hates it, the latter is being dragged along by the former, and they both look like they want to push their partner off a cliff; the geeky rambler who has a waterproof map-case around his neck, a compass in his hand and a style that screams 40-year-old virgin; and the 'rad' adventurer, who generally wears bright orange trousers, an electric-blue down jacket and a backwards Pata-Gucci (Patagonia) cap while using the word 'bro' at least 17 times per sentence.

❋   ❋   ❋

Twelve hours later and I was lost on the north face of Tryfan, struggling to find safe passage to the ridge. The initial climb from the busy A5 on the shores of Llyn Ogwen was disorientating. I took the footpath to the left of Milestone Buttress, clambered through a boulder field and, accidentally, found myself scrambling dangerously up a steep, wet, awkward gully. There were criss-crossing trods here, there and everywhere. I'd obviously picked the wrong one. Weighed down by a backpack full of camping gear and supplies, I was far from agile, but I just about made it out of the slippery flume without incurring any significant injuries and emerged on to the north ridge proper.

It was another day of near-perfect conditions in Snowdonia. I was planning to climb all 12 Nuttalls in the Glyders over the next two days, with a wild camp in the middle. It promised to be another glorious outing – my chance to complete more classic Snowdonia peaks in bright sunshine. Second in popularity only to Snowdon, the Glyders are an enticing group of mountains wedged between the Llanberis and Nant Ffrancon passes. Named after the twin peaks of Glyder Fach and Glyder Fawr, the range includes six peaks over 3,000ft, the dramatic Tryfan – Britain's favourite mountain according to readers of *Trail* magazine – and the much-photographed, impossibly balanced slab known as the Cantilever Stone. It is a world of rock and not much else: giant fields of jumbled boulders, rivers of scree, fissured cliffs and crags, and innumerable wonky turrets, spiky towers and fine summits.

The Grade 1 scramble up Tryfan's fortified north ridge felt like a heroic entry on to the range; a hands-on, adventurous climb over pillars of rock and tangled webs of stacked boulders. It was much less exposed than Crib Goch, but the absence of a knife edge to guide me actually created difficulties of its own. With views up obscured, I could never quite tell where the rocky chute I was climbing led to, or if I was about to become stranded on a slabbed wall that suddenly increased in difficulty.

But I slowly scrambled on, crested the North Tower and topped out on Tryfan's summit, where two columns of rock – known as Adam and Eve – adorn the highest point. As legend has it, if you jump from one to the other you are granted the Freedom of Tryfan. But it is a nerve-jangling test of your mettle. The gap between the twin monoliths is too wide for a step. Instead it requires a terrifying, am-I-about-to-die? leap with both feet off the ground. And there is a precipitous drop beyond the second column, meaning a poorly placed landing could be catastrophic. I watched a dad make the jump easily, sparking applause and whoops from his family and friends, and I contemplated going for it. But I'd stood on the first pillar years before, only to chicken out and climb back down. I didn't fancy another embarrassing withdrawal in front of a bigger crowd, so I wimped out again, in the knowledge that I'd probably just been out-adventured by a 47-year-old accountant and dad-of-two from somewhere like Slough.

I dropped south to Bwlch Tryfan and, rather than continuing straight ahead on the main drag to Glyder Fach, I veered left and traversed east towards the small tarn of Llyn Caseg-fraith. From this angle, Tryfan was an imposing triangle: a pyramidal fin of grey rock, an adventure playground of crags and cliffs. It was so captivating I couldn't keep my eyes off it. Tryfan is a revered mountain: admired, respected, and held in the highest esteem. Everest legends George Mallory and Sir Edmund Hillary even used it as a training ground. And, like them, I could feel myself being lured in by the mountain's magnetic attraction.

I ditched my bag next to a boulder and completed a slow out-and-back to bag the Nuttalls of Y Foel Goch and Gallt yr Ogof. After 15 minutes of wandering around like a headless chicken looking for my bag, which I couldn't locate, I eventually found it and headed west, aiming for the main Glyders ridge. I hopped from boulder to boulder towards the first of a trio of 3,000ft tops – Glyder Fach – where an anxious woman was struggling to haul herself on to the highest point of the summit's bizarre pile of jutting boulders. Half laughing, half crying, the woman finally crested the summit, straddling her legs around its base, bear-hugging it with her arms, and slowly edging forward in a manoeuvre that reminded me of a dog scratching its arse on the floor. I was joined by three middle-aged guys from Bewdley, in Worcestershire, and we all laughed and joked.

'That was the least graceful arrival at a summit,' I teased. 'Ever.'

'Still counts,' added one of the Worcestershire contingent.

'See you then, good luck getting down,' joked another.

'Please don't leave me here,' added the lady in a jokey way but with a serious undertone.

Needless to say, we didn't leave her stranded. Walking as a fivesome, we continued west to the spiky, fang-like pinnacles of Castell y Gwynt, which we awkwardly scrambled up, and then pressed onwards to the day's final 3,000-footer, Glyder Fawr. It was ridge walking at its finest, with phenomenal views, but our time together was brief. Insisting on leaving me with a bottle of beer for my wild camp, the three guys from Bewdley and the woman veered north-east back to the A5 and reality, while I stayed high and continued north-west on the increasingly quiet ridge. I easily bagged the tops of Y Garn, Foel-goch and Mynydd Perfedd, before setting up camp on a grassy slope under the shadow of Elidir Fawr. I tucked into a Wayfayrer chilli con carne as the sun set over the Menai Strait, adding pinks, oranges and reds to a landscape of greens and browns. It was tranquil and beautiful. I had the whole of Snowdonia to myself – exactly how I wanted my epic day in the Glyders to end.

The following morning was overcast and cloudy and the walking was functional. It felt as if all the excitement had happened yesterday and today I was left with the chore of getting myself back to the A5. I climbed Elidir Fawr first, cooked breakfast in a wind shelter, headed north for the twin Nuttalls of Carnedd y Filiast and Carnedd y Filiast North Top, and then made a meal of my descent to the road over steep, boggy, slippery ground. I hitched back to my car, getting a lift off a lovely couple who seemed astonished that I was sleeping wild in the hills, and dived into the refuge of my Golf as rain showers arrived. I ate cheese salad wraps for lunch and checked the forecast on my iPhone. It did not look at all promising. In fact, it was looking slightly dangerous, but I didn't have the luxury of any leeway in my schedule. An afternoon off was not feasible. So I replenished my food supplies, hoisted my backpack over my shoulder, and headed back out into the drizzly conditions, determined to bag the 14 Nuttalls of the central and western Carneddau over the next two days.

Three hours later I was seriously ruing my decision. Gale-force winds were throwing me all over the place, knocking me to the ground and playing havoc with my balance. Diagonal rain was lashing into my face and thick cloud had left me woefully disorientated. The best I could do was stumble, like an unsteady drunk, taking one ungainly step at a time. I leaned into the wind, as if bracing for a rugby tackle from an ugly brute of a forward, and crept along the edge of precipitous cliffs from Yr Elen towards Carnedd Llewelyn. The wind would relent momentarily, only to suddenly gust over the cliffs with formidable power. I threw myself to the ground, lying horizontally with my face in the grit and my hands clasping at rocks in a bid to prevent myself being blown down a crevasse. Why the hell hadn't I just stayed in the valley? This wasn't a joke any more, this was getting serious. In such apocalyptic weather, the mountains seemed utterly inhospitable. They felt hostile, harsh and unwelcoming – not a safe place for humans to be.

These were the worst conditions I'd ever walked in. I had an empty feeling in my stomach, as if something really bad was just around the corner. But, rather than being overwhelmed by fear, an adrenalin-charged survival instinct seemed to kick in. I was alert and focused, wired by an inherent sense that I was in trouble and just needed to get through it, no matter what it took.

Lying down, shivering and soaked to my core, I grabbed my iPhone out of my jacket pocket. I wiped droplets off the waterproof case and, in an almost hysterical flurry of finger-tapping, desperately tried to open the OS Maps app. Was I going in the right direction? Where was the nearest escape point? What was the fastest way out of the mountains?

Finally the map tiles loaded and I just about got my bearings. Then my battery died. I looked to the heavens in exasperation. I wanted to scream out expletives at the top of my voice. Why was this happening to me? I was boiling with anger and frustration. But I had my trusty powerpack with me. Taking rudimentary shelter next to a boulder-covered slope, I hooked it up to the phone, and waited for the device to spark back into life.

I studied the maps carefully. I'd already ticked off Pen yr Ole Wen from the western edge of Llyn Ogwen, a calf-burning climb on to the broad high ridge, before continuing north to bag Carnedd Dafydd and Foel Meirch and then slowly staggering east above the cliffs of Ysgolion Duon, aiming for Yr Elen. I pinpointed my exact location. I was en route back from the 3,156ft top of Yr Elen heading towards Carnedd Llewelyn, Wales' third-highest mountain at 3,491ft. I took a bearing, making a mental note to give the cliffs to my left a wide berth, and decided I'd climb to the summit before making a plan of action. There was no way I was going to wild camp in these conditions. That would be foolhardy. I needed to get out of the mountains and get out quick. It then leaped off the map and caught my eye: a small black square next to the word 'Shelter' just to the north of Foel Grach. Perhaps that could be my saviour from this abominable weather.

As I neared Carnedd Llewelyn a trio of sodden figures emerged out of the mist and shouted towards me, waving for attention. I headed over to see what the problem was. They were three young Dutch backpackers, perhaps in their early 20s, carrying huge backpacks, wearing jeans, and looking shaken and scared.

'Can you help us?' said a blond guy, the leader of the pack.

'We tried to get back down to the road but we couldn't find the path,' said another, trying to stop his teeth chattering and his body from shivering. 'It just became steep cliffs and too dangerous, so we came back up to the ridge, and now we're totally lost.'

I reassured them that everything would be all right, hiding the fact that I was panicking a little myself, and promised to get them on to the right track. We walked together briefly, hiking in single file without talking, each individual engrossed in a personal battle against the wind and rain. Then we ducked into a wind shelter and I laid out my map to show them the path heading south-east for the A5 via Pen yr Helgi Du. I added that they should take great care along the narrow ridge above Ffynnon Llugwy Reservoir, then I popped out of the shelter briefly with the blond guy to identify the start of the path. They seemed happy with the plan and, perking up, began joking about their navigational cock-up as well as fantasising about a hot shower back at their campsite near the base of Tryfan. I wished them luck, praying I wasn't going to see their faces on the news the following day in a mountain-disaster story, and prepared to head north for Foel Grach.

'Just before you go,' called a Dutch accent, 'take this – it's a Netherlands delicacy.' He handed me a coin-shaped liquorice sweet.

'Seems like a fair exchange for saving your lives,' I joked, and turned away into the driving rain, hoping to God the shelter I was aiming for had a roof.

Twenty-five minutes later, having visited the 3,202ft summit of Foel Grach, I zig-zagged over boulders and between outcrops towards that little black square marked on the map. After a few nervy minutes of confusion, I breathed a sigh of relief as I stumbled across the refuge. It was part of the mountain. Built into the slope and made of mossy, lichen-covered grey rock, the shelter blended beautifully into the mountainside. I unbolted the brown door and opened it tentatively. The interior was cavernous, dark and dingy, with a damp smell. The only sound was the repetitive plop of a drip from somewhere within. The only furniture was a wooden bench. The walls were grimy and mouldy and the floor was splattered with the muddy footprints of recent day visitors. It was far from luxurious and, classified as an emergency shelter rather than an overnight bothy, technically I wasn't supposed to stay the night. But I was putting my situation in the emergency category. And, despite being just a basic, empty, characterless shell, the shelter still felt like a life-saving haven from the brutality of the mountains.

I woke in a daze, temporarily unsure where I was. It had been a cold night, lying on the hard rock slabs of the refuge's floor. But, cocooned as I was in my sleeping bag, which I'd laid out on top of my tent sheets and sleeping mat, it hadn't been too bad. I was safe and dry and felt reasonably well rested. I stirred and stretched, as my eyes grew accustomed to the darkness, and sat up. A sliver of light pierced through the gap at the bottom of the door, shining a thin, bright line of hope across the dark, wet floor. I walked barefoot to the door and opened it. I couldn't believe my eyes – here were perfect blue skies, bright sunshine and not a hint of wind. It was a different world, a total transformation. I'd made it through the storm and come out on the other side.

The rest of the day was a breeze: a relaxing, drama-free, precipitation-free tramp over grassy slopes to bag seven Nuttalls in the tranquil central Carneddau – Garnedd Uchaf, Foel-fras, Llwytmor, Bera Bach, Bera Mawr, Drosgl and Gyrn Wigau – before climbing Carnedd Llewelyn again and descending out of the range via my final top of Pen yr Helgi Du. At the A5 a grandmother responded to my hitchhiking pleas and gave me a lift west, adding wonderfully, 'I never leave anyone in need on the roadside.' Then, back at my car, in a gust of wind I lost my grip on a plastic bag. It flew through the air only for another hiking grandma to catch it one-handed, in a Jedi-like show of nonchalant reflexes, and return it to me with the damning put-down, 'Here, have your filthy bag back.' Aside from those two brief and entertaining encounters, the day had been unremarkable – and that's exactly what I'd wanted. I was hoping the rest of my Snowdonia adventure would be similarly incident-free.

And it was. On Friday I climbed the four Nuttalls – Moel Eilio, Foel Gron, Moel Cynghorion and Llechog – to the west of Snowdon, watching on as the dinky mountain train chugged and puffed its way up the steep slopes. I had a massive portion of burger and chips at Pete's Eats café in Llanberis and then spent dusk walking up to Llyn Dwythwch to wild camp in a sheep pen. On Saturday, I headed for the Nantlle Ridge, a long, airy ridge heading south-west from Rhyd-Ddu. The weather was cloudy but pleasant, and I hiked over the undulating ground with a smile on my face, happy in the knowledge that this walk would see me hit my target of 58 Nuttalls bagged and four ranges – the Carneddau, the Glyders, Snowdon and Moel Hebog – completed in my first week in Snowdonia. I ticked off Y Garn first, scrambled up the soaring crest of Mynydd Drws-y-coed next, and then pressed on over the glorious ridge ever south-west to tick off Trum y Ddysgl, Mynydd Tal-y-mignedd, Craig Cwm Silyn, Garnedd-goch and Mynydd Graig Goch. But, with the last summit in the bag, I made one final error. There was no easy way to loop back to Rhyd-Ddu from the end of the ridge and, feeling fatigued from nine intense days of peak-bagging, I decided to go for the lazy option. I descended west over pathless slopes to the main road and started wagging my thumb, intent on hitching north on the A487 and east on the B4418 back to my car.

It didn't go well. As I stood on the wide grassy verge waiting for a ride, a pimped-out Ford Fiesta signalled and slowed down. *That was easy*, I thought, reaching for my backpack. The driver, a teenager with gel-spiked hair and a marijuana-leaf T-shirt, leaned out of the window and gestured as if to say, 'Jump in, pal.' Loud hip-hop blasted out of the sub-woofers and clouds of vaping smoke billowed from the orange and black car. Who was this wannabe gangster? The Welsh version of Snoop Dogg – Snoop Dafydd maybe? I was a little apprehensive but I went for it regardless. I should've listened to my instinct. Just as the car slowed to a stop, the boy racer flipped me the middle finger, burst out laughing and sped off with a roar from his engine. Dickhead.

Sadly, he didn't immediately spin out of control, crash down the roadside embankment, and land head-first in a field of cow shit, as I hoped. *Perhaps it was a one-off*, I thought, and continued to wave my hitchhiker's thumb in hope. I shouldn't have bothered. Every boy racer in North Wales, it would appear, was cruising up and down the A487 on that Saturday evening. And the sight of a hitchhiking rambler was simply too good an opportunity for drive-by bullying for them to ignore. Two further pimp-my-ride drivers greeted me with the middle-finger salute, while one incredibly polite boy racer opted to merely flick me the 'V' and another, clearly a banter-merchant, shouted 'bus wanker' in an inspired *Inbetweeners* gag.

And so, after all the highs and lows, the adventure and solitude, the beauty and euphoria, the wild camping and nature, the rousing summits and airy ridges, my 58-peak Snowdonia adventure ended with me plodding along a noisy, ugly A-road being sworn at by Snoop Dafydd and his boy-racer friends. Not exactly the way I'd hoped to celebrate. But I wasn't bothered. I'd taken a huge stride towards the Nuttalls peak-bagging record – and it made me feel on top of the world. No amount of obscene gestures could spoil that.

CHAPTER 19

MAPLESS AND CLUELESS

Mountains 364–391

DATE	REGION	MOUNTAINS
Wednesday 23 August	Moelwyns	Allt-fawr 2,290ft (698m) Moel Druman 2,218ft (676m) Ysgafell Wen 2,205ft (672m) Ysgafell Wen North Top 2,195ft (669m) Ysgafell Wen Far North Top 2,133ft (650m) Cnicht 2,260ft (689m) Cnicht North Top 2,251ft (686m) Moel-yr-hydd 2,126ft (648m)
Thursday 24 August	Moelwyns	Moelwyn Mawr 2,526ft (770m) Craigysgafn 2,260ft (689m) Moelwyn Bach 2,329ft (710m) Moel Penamnen 2,034ft (620m) Manod Mawr North Top 2,159ft (658m)
Friday 25 August	Moelwyns Arenigs	Manod Mawr 2,169ft (661m) Moel Siabod 2,861ft (872m) Foel Goch 2,005ft (611m)
Saturday 26 August	Arenigs	Arenig Fawr 2,802ft (854m) Arenig Fawr South Top 2,743ft (836m) Arenig Fawr South Ridge Top 2,336ft (712m) Moel Llyfnant 2,464ft (751m) Foel Boeth 2,021ft (616m) Gallt y Daren 2,031ft (619m)

DATE	REGION	MOUNTAINS
Sunday 27 August	Arenigs	Carnedd y Filiast 2,195ft (669m) Waun Garnedd-y-filiast 2,133ft (650m) Carnedd Llechwedd-llyfn 2,110ft (643m) Arenig Fach 2,260ft (689m) Dduallt 2,172ft (662m) Rhobell Fawr 2,408ft (734m)

After a night of sleeping in a forest, I drove to Lytham St Anne's, near Blackpool, on Sunday and spent three joyous days relaxing with Becky. We ambled along the sandy beach, played the penny-drops, read the papers in Costa Coffee, and went out for pizza every night. It was just what I needed to recover from the exertions and calamities of Snowdonia. But, sadly, the break couldn't last for ever. I didn't want to leave. I didn't want to climb any more mountains. I didn't want to be tired, cold, wet and alone again. But I had another battle to fight with the mountains of Snowdonia and so, on Tuesday night, I reluctantly packed up my bags and set off for the CellB Hostel in the town of Blaenau Ffestiniog.

I shared a dorm with a friendly German biker who was touring Britain on a massive BMW. Unfortunately, his snore was about as loud as his motorbike, and I had a terrible night's sleep. In fact, it was so bad that at one point I left the dorm with my duvet and tried to sleep in the kitchen. But I was too worried an unsuspecting guest would walk in to grab a glass of water, trip over my body and head-butt the kitchen worktops. So I switched to the large bathroom, lying on the tiles wrapped up in my duvet. But that was even worse. The lights were on a motion sensor and whenever I shuffled or wriggled, even in the slightest, the room would be suddenly bathed in a blinding glow. Lying perfectly still, as if in a straitjacket and bed restraints, was not particularly conducive for dropping off, while the intermittent dazzling spotlight was like a form of torture. I had no choice but to return to the roaring, revving sounds of the

German's 1600cc, six-cylinder snore. There was some serious torque on that thing. I barely slept a wink.

Feeling drained and light-headed, I sat on my bed at 8am slurping gloopy porridge into my mouth and flicking through my guidebook. I had the next five days in Snowdonia and I wanted to complete two mountain ranges: the Moelwyns, a group of 15 Nuttalls extending north-east from Porthmadog to the isolated and highest top of Moel Siabod south of Capel Curig; and the Arenigs, a group of 13 Nuttalls to the north and west of Bala. I decided, somewhat randomly, that I'd start with the Moelwyns, and a two-day loop of the tops to the west and east of Blaenau Ffestiniog seemed like as good an idea as any. I laboriously packed up my rucksack for the mini expedition, drove to the Crimea Pass and set off.

The next 24 hours were instantly forgettable. Nothing happened. I walked, it rained, I ticked off one Nuttall, then two, then three, the wind blew, my boots squelched, I plodded on north, then west, then east, then south, I ate lunch, I hiked up, I hiked down, I hiked on the flat, my Nuttalls tally grew to four, then five, then six, I scoffed snacks, I made tea, I rested, I plodded on, I rested again, I marched on, I set up camp, I boiled up dinner, I slept, I woke up, I walked some more, and then some more, and then some more. That was it. Even Cnicht, the so-called Welsh Matterhorn, didn't break the monotony.

Only one incident broke my rhythm and progress. With the 11 Nuttalls to the west of Blaenau in the bag, I tramped along the town's main road heading east, aiming for the quarried landscape containing three Nuttalls: Moel Penamnen, Manod Mawr North Top and Manod Mawr. The weather was gross, clouds obscured all views, my body was weak and sleep-deprived, and I was suffering from a case of post-seaside blues. And then things got worse. As I struggled over steep, rough ground covered in thick bracken, I reached for my iPhone to check the OS Maps app. The screen was blank. *That's odd,* I thought, *I'm sure I had 80 per cent battery.* I attached a powerpack to charge it up. Nothing. I tried another powerpack. Still nothing.

My phone was well and truly crocked. And, in a textbook schoolboy error, I hadn't printed out hard copies of the map. In addition, I'd just walked off the very edge of the OL17 Snowdon map in my bag. I was now without a map, in disorientating low cloud, attempting to explore the confusing labyrinth of scoured, gouged, blasted mining land to the east of Bala. Surely this was a recipe for disaster. I was up the creek without a paddle. Or, more accurately, up the mountain without a map. Mapless and clueless – that summed me up as an adventurer, I thought.

I sat for about ten minutes, dripping wet in the drizzly rain. I frantically stuck the charger cable in and out of my phone, time and time again, but with no luck. I then used every last ounce of willpower I possessed to stop myself from smashing my phone on the nearest boulder and screaming profanities at the top of my voice. After calming down, I thought about a plan of action. Option one was to carry on regardless and risk getting horrendously lost; option two was to retrace my steps into the town and buy a map. In fact, I ended up with option three, which was to walk down into the town, wander around for ages, waste loads of time, not find a single shop that sold maps, and then head back into the hills to risk it anyway.

However, I'd grabbed my Nuttalls guidebook from the car, and that included a rudimentary map and basic walk description. I hoped it would suffice, as I climbed a tarmac road into Maen Offeren Quarry. The right of way ahead, which was wildly overgrown with rhododendrons and thick vegetation, passed to the left of the derelict manager's house, before emerging into a world of ruined buildings, old mining machinery, and discarded drums, cables and rails. It was an eerie place to be as dusk was descending over the misty mountainside. I half expected to see the ghosts of long-dead miners appear and bring the disused workings back into twilight operation.

I followed a ruined wall and marched over pathless moorland to bag the 2,034ft top of Moel Penamnen, before dropping east to the edge of a forest at Foel-fras. I stopped to hurriedly prepare a dinner of Heinz beef ravioli in tomato sauce, only for my gas canister to run out. *I'm a total idiot*, I thought, before deciding to make light of my latest bout of incompetence. 'Dinner is served, sir, an exquisite selection of unheated ravioli parcels, filled with succulent cold beef and complemented with a rich, creamy, tepid tomato sauce, and served on an indulgent bed of slightly stale, mould-flecked bread rolls. It arrives with the warmest compliments of the chef. And, as always, we hope you enjoy the ambience of this rain-battered hillside in the middle of nowhere.'

I plodded on, swinging south and aiming for the 2,159ft summit of Manod Mawr North Top. It was easy to locate, thanks to a fence that led to the top. The next summit, Manod Mawr, proved far trickier. I tried to keep my bearings as I skirted around Graig-ddu Quarry, but I quickly became disorientated in a confusing landscape of bulldozed roads, deep excavations and steep-sided scars. I was utterly lost and surrounded by quarry cliffs all around me. Cloud prevented me from seeing the way out and, right on cue, heavy rain started to fall. So I decided to bail and instead set up camp in Dennis on the flattest, least stony patch of ground I could find, hoping the morning would be kinder.

❋   ❋   ❋

The Daily Adventure Journal of James
24/08/17: How do you judge the credentials of a long-distance hiker? I think I now know. It's not speed, or kit, or navigation skills, or anything like that. It's how confidently, upon re-entering civilisation, they can walk into a pub, use the toilet and steal a toilet roll without buying a drink. It's something I am now proficient at. It's probably my main adventure skill, to be honest.

26/08/17: When I'm lying in my tent after dark and I hear a rustling sound outside, the way I react has changed over the course of this challenge. At the beginning I would've been totally freaked out – 'It's a demonic badger about to rip me to shreds! I don't want to die! Please, God, help me!' Now, after so many nights in the wild, I think very differently. I either ignore it and go straight back to sleep, or think, *Please, God, let it be a demonic badger about to rip me to shreds. I want to die, because then I won't have to go peak-bagging tomorrow.*

✷   ✷   ✷

Strong winds slammed into Dennis and rain pattered on his outer sheet as I roused myself early the following morning. Out of sheer stubbornness, I plugged the charger cable into my phone and, to my immense surprise, it worked. I whooped with joy. And so, half an hour later, I was tramping along a winding quarry road, clutching my iPhone in front of me and watching the glorious little red arrow guide me in exactly the right direction through the confusing landscape. A tipper lorry was coming in the opposite direction.

'You're not supposed to be here,' said an angry-looking man, leaning out of the cab window of his gigantic truck.

He was the spitting image of Ross Kemp and I was a little scared. It flustered me. For a second I thought about embarking on a rambling explanation about lost maps, broken phones and a peak-bagging record, but I feared it might go over his (bald) head. Another part of me wanted to reply, 'Did you used to be in *EastEnders*?' but I worried that could lead to violence. Yet another part of me was desperate to climb into the cab and gently rub his immaculately polished, shiny head, but obviously I wasn't going to do that. So, instead, I settled for a rather abrupt and boring option.

'Sorry, pal,' I said apologetically, 'I'm just heading to the public footpath. Is that OK?'

He nodded reluctantly and waved me on. I continued down the track and picked up a right of way south-west of Llyn Pysgod and then climbed south to belatedly bag the summit of Manod Mawr.

After all the worry and uncertainty of the previous day, it felt great to have finally made it. I descended gently north-west in a good mood, and followed a disused incline through derelict mine workings back to Blaenau Ffestiniog. I sat in my car, eating cereal and sipping on a cup of sugary tea. It was only 9.30am and I already felt as if I'd been through a lot in the day. Somehow I needed to pluck up the motivation for a split day of peak-bagging, with one walk in the morning and another in the afternoon.

My morning's task was Moel Siabod, an isolated mountain close to Capel Curig that is both the northernmost and the highest peak of the Moelwyns. I really enjoyed it. After two days of unexceptional walking, including several long slogs over pathless terrain, it felt great to be back in proper mountain territory: the well-worn paths were clear and firm underfoot, the hill fog and rain had lifted, and the scenery was rocky and stirring. With a spring in my step, I walked to the right of a pretty lake, its shores alive with the mauve flowers of blooming heather, and climbed past a deep quarry pool and old slate workings to Llyn y Foel. Ahead, an amphitheatre of crags and cliffs enclosed the lake, with the rough eastern ridge of Daear Ddu rising prominently towards the summit. This was to be my route to the top and it looked enticing. I crossed a boggy section to the base of the scramble and began ascending the narrow arête, shimmying up faces of rock, weaving in and out of jumbled boulders, and edging along grassy ledges. I was smiling again, finally. This was a fun day out in the mountains, rather than a box-ticking, peak-bagging duty I couldn't get out of.

I stopped on a small bedrock platform, gazing down a precipitous gully towards the lake, and ate a lunch of chicken salad wraps, raisins, banana chips, marshmallows and a Boost chocolate bar. Casting my eyes intently across the landscape, as I tended to do out in the wild, I spotted a tourist struggling up an incredibly steep scree gully to the north. It looked a foolish and dangerous approach. He kept stopping and looking back quizzically, as if asking himself, 'Is this really the path?' I studied the scene further and his mistake looked an easy one to make. A clear trod looped to the north of Llyn y Foel, before petering out just below the gully. I imagine he'd taken that trod, presuming it was a genuine route, and then persevered into the gully to find himself in a spot of bother. Nevertheless, he made it out safely, but it was a stark reminder of how easy it is to make mistakes in the mountains of Britain – and that, sometimes, the best approach is to recognise your error and head back down, rather than stubbornly continuing.

I made it to the 2,861ft summit, retraced my steps down Daear Ddu – a ridge so good I had to do it twice – and soon collapsed back into my VW Golf in Capel Curig. That was the Moelwyns ticked off, but my day wasn't over. I still had an afternoon's hiking to complete and my first Nuttall in the Arenigs, Foel Goch, to climb. I always found these split days difficult. The stop-start approach was physically exhausting, more so than doing one long walk for some reason, while mentally it was almost impossible to remotivate myself for the second shift of peak-bagging. Several handfuls of crumbly flapjack, which I had stashed in my car still in the oven baking tray, helped massively, however. And after a slow plod through boggy, swampy, reed-covered ground, I gained the 2,005ft summit of Foel Goch, a solitary top north-east of Bala, and could finally rest for the day.

There was, however, one obstacle left to negotiate – the walk to the Co-op food store in Blaenau Ffestiniog, where I was staying the night in the CellB Hostel again. It was the school holidays and, evidently, the forecourt of the supermarket was *the* place to hang around if you were a bicycle-riding, Adidas-tracksuit-wearing, phone-music-blaring teenager from the town. Trying to pick up a pint of milk was like running the gauntlet of a hundred under-age yobs: a desperate dash for the automatic doors before anyone says, 'What you looking at?', or gobs in your face, or accuses you of being a paedo. At least, that was what I was envisaging as I neared the entrance with my eyes down.

215

But nothing happened and I picked up a microwaveable dinner of beef stew with dumpling. Not feeling very sociable, I ate alone in my dorm room and then went to bed early, ecstatic that there wasn't a German biker in sight.

At 10 the following morning, I sat in my car downing a cookie-dough-flavoured milkshake as a pre-hike reward and read about the Arenigs in my guidebook. I had 12 summits left to bag, spread across three suggested day-walks. My plan was to complete them in two days. I decided to spend Saturday walking an 11½-mile route to tick off the six Nuttalls around Arenig Fawr, followed by a split Sunday, walking the Arenig Fach fells in the morning and the isolated tops of Dduallt and Rhobell Fawr in the afternoon. The night between I would wild camp, perhaps near Carnedd y Filiast. It felt like a good plan. I loaded up the Met Office app and checked the forecast. Sunny intervals for both days. Get in. Perhaps my Snowdonia adventure would end on a high?

I walked west and south through fields of sheep, before turning steeply uphill alongside a fence. Without difficulty, I gained the snout of the ridge and continued over gentler terrain, veering right to arrive at the trig point and large wind shelter of Arenig Fawr's 2,802ft summit. I dropped south to cash in my three-for-the-price-of-one offer, bagging Arenig Fawr South Top and Arenig Fawr South Ridge Top, and then stopped for a brief break. A thick band of white cloud filled the sky, with small patches of blue sky breaking through intermittently. I looked south to a lumpy and bumpy landscape, dotted with a series of small tarns, while distant peaks and rolling countryside spread out to the horizon. It wasn't spectacular scenery but I was just happy to have views and to be dry. I chugged on my water and tucked into a Tupperware box of wild blackberries I'd picked from brambles near to where I'd parked. They were juicy and tasty, but I was completely put off when I noticed a small army of squirming grubs on their surfaces. Perhaps I should have accepted the extra protein but, like a true wimp, they made me feel squeamish.

Daydreaming about getting home, sitting on my sofa with a tub of Ben & Jerry's ice cream and watching trashy TV, I dropped west to a boggy col and climbed up to the rocky knoll of Moel Llyfnant, a good platform from which to gaze back at the grand, dominating mountain of Arenig Fawr. I descended to the edge of a forest, giving a herd of cows a wide berth, and then climbed, yet again, to bag the final two summits of the day. The repeated ascents, descents and re-ascents that came with peak-bagging were exhausting and mentally draining, but I made it to the tops of Foel Boeth and Gallt y Daren to finish off my day's summits.

Back at my car, I drove east briefly on the A4212, parked in a lay-by next to the northern shores of Llyn Celyn, and set about packing my backpack for a night of wild camping. Some of my kit – Dennis, my sleeping mat and my Vango sleeping bag – were still damp, so I laid them over the car doors and bonnet to dry in the bright sunshine. The rest of my kit was scattered around the car in haphazard fashion: piles of food laid out on the concrete, multi-coloured dry bags hung over the wing mirrors, two pairs of boots resting on the car roof, and myriad smelly socks, gas canisters, bottles of water and all manner of other camping accessories strewn across the pavement. It was a comical scene of organised chaos that I felt perfectly summed up the state of my life.

Finally my stuff was sorted, my bag was packed and the roadside chaos was no more. I plodded east along the grassy verge of the busy road, passing time with my new hobby – looking for discarded McDonald's coffee cups so I could steal the free-coffee loyalty stickers. I found three, as well as a small, cuddly toy monkey with a big smile and sticky-out ears. I contemplated adopting him as my new wild-camping companion for the night. He could be someone to chat to, confide in and share the good and bad times with, as Tom Hanks does with Wilson in *Cast Away*. But I decided I was too old, too mature and too boring for that.

I turned off the grassy verge to switchback through a dense forest on to the open mountainside. I climbed on a stony track over slopes of thick heather, aiming for Carnedd y Filiast, and just as dusk was descending I found a nice spot to set up Dennis. It was a tantalising wild camp. There was almost a stunning cloud inversion, but it didn't quite materialise; then there was almost a glorious sunset, but the clouds rolled over to block the view. It felt like a so-near-yet-so-far situation. I wasn't too bothered, though. I had pasta with chorizo and spicy tomato sauce on the boil, it wasn't raining nor was it cold, and I'd made it to the final leg. There was only one more day to go to complete my challenging two-week, 86-mountain trip to Snowdonia.

I woke up, ate porridge, drank coffee, decamped and then nipped east to bag the tops of Carnedd y Filiast and Waun Garnedd-y-filiast, before retracing my steps west over a boggy plateau to summit Carnedd Llechwedd-llyfn. I felt like the only man in Snowdonia as I tramped south-west along a fence over lonely back-country land. A solitary fox – its red fur and white tail bobbing up and down as it ran away – was the only creature I shared the mountains with. I arrived at the base of the Arenig Fach climb, chomped on a chunk of cucumber, downed a litre of water, and prepared myself for what looked like a brutal ascent over Berwynsesque thick heather and steep, pathless slopes. By the time I emerged at the 2,260ft summit I was dripping in sweat, my calves were burning, my lungs were heaving and I felt utterly exhausted.

Back at my car an hour or so later, I had a decision to make: option one was to drive to Bala, chill out, watch Arsenal versus Liverpool in a pub and finish the Arenigs the following day; option two was to go hell for leather and tick off my final two summits in the Arenigs that evening. Somewhat reluctantly, I went for option two, eager to stay ahead of the game. But it was a glorious sunny evening and, donning trainers and running gear, I made swift work of the 9-mile route. From the remote Cwm yr Allt-lwyd, I jogged east and then north to summit Dduallt, before descending over pathless heathery slopes and cutting through a thick forest to finally climb along a wall to gain the 2,408ft summit of Rhobell Fawr.

Briefly placing my hand on the trig pillar, I turned away and collapsed on to a patch of soft grass for a much-needed rest. I lay down, using my backpack as a makeshift headrest, and listened as my heavy breathing slowed. I looked up at the sky, marbled blue and white, the two colours fusing in a swirling, streaky pattern. It was one of those skies that put a smile on my face. I angled my head slightly. In the foreground a grassy knoll, dotted with rock outcrops and edged by a winding dry-stone wall, was bathed in a golden glow, while majestic massifs rose in the distance, standing dramatically against the horizon and displaying their spiky summits, pitted shoulders and extensive ridgelines as if for my pleasure alone. It was a grand scene – and I sensed that euphoric end-of-expedition feeling descend on me once again, like a dizzying wave of pride and joy. I'd done it: 86 Snowdonia mountains ticked off in one epic adventure. And now I had only 55 Nuttalls left to complete my mission.

CHAPTER 20

A HANDSOME CRAG

Mountains 392–416

DATE	REGION	MOUNTAINS
Friday 1 September	Lake District Far Eastern Fells	Place Fell 2,155ft (657m) Rest Dodd 2,283ft (696m) Rampsgill Head 2,598ft (792m) Kidsty Pike 2,559ft (780m) High Raise 2,631ft (802m) Wether Hill 2,198ft (670m) Loadpot Hill 2,201ft (671m)
Saturday 2 September	Lake District Far Eastern Fells	Yoke 2,316ft (706m) Ill Bell 2,483ft (757m) Froswick 2,362ft (720m) High Street 2,717ft (828m) Rough Crag 2,060ft (628m) Harter Fell 2,552ft (778m) Kentmere Pike 2,395ft (730m)
Monday 4 September	Lake District Western Fells	Pillar Rock 2,560ft (780m)

DATE	REGION	MOUNTAINS
Friday 8 September	Lake District Southern Fells	Wetherlam 2,503ft (763m) Black Sails 2,444ft (745m) Swirl How 2,631ft (802m) Great Carrs 2,575ft (785m) Grey Friar 2,526ft (770m) Brim Fell 2,612ft (796m) The Old Man of Coniston 2,634ft (803m) Dow Crag 2,552ft (778m) Walna Scar 2,037ft (621m) White Maiden 2,001ft (610m)

I clung to the greasy rock for dear life. My legs turned to jelly and I breathed frantically, trying to compose myself. Torrential rain was pounding down and a biting wind was swirling. I was a walker out of his comfort zone, teetering on the edge of Pillar Rock. My climbing technique was non-existent and my mindset was nervy. Where on earth was the next handhold? This was exposed and gnarly. One slip would be fatal, except for the fact that I was connected to the crag by all manner of climbing gadgets and gizmos. But I was strangely exhilarated too. It felt gloriously adventurous to be taking on this iconic Lakeland climb, especially after botching my previous attempt a month earlier.

Pillar Rock is a striking, imposing tower of rock; a seemingly impenetrable column that juts out of the mountain's north face like a dark, craggy cathedral. It rises some 500ft from the hillside and is separated from the mass of Pillar by a vertical chasm. Hence Pillar Rock is classified as a separate top, a mountain in its own right, and as such is the only Nuttall in England or Wales requiring rope work and climbing skills. First ascended in 1826 by Ennerdale shepherd John Atkinson, it is the birthplace of rock climbing in the Lake District and remains an inspiration to many mountaineers, as well as a target for Nuttalls enthusiasts. But many peak-baggers miss out Pillar Rock, because they either can't be bothered to hire a guide or don't fancy the exposure of the climb, and thus fall tantalisingly one short of completing all of the Nuttalls. There was no way that was going to happen to me. I'd bailed on my solo Pillar Rock attempt in August – but now I was back with someone who actually knew what they were doing. Nothing was going to stop me summiting this time around.

Rewind to 9am when I met Aled, my instructor from AB Mountains, on the green in Wasdale. 'Are you ready for a big mountain day?' he asked me, seeming both excited and anxious, while glancing at the moody clouds above. My life was in this man's hands so I sized him up: silver glint in his hair, red Arc'teryx jacket, mountaineering boots, and a Batmanesque utility belt of nuts, cams, slings, carabineers and quickdraws – he looked the part. I quizzed him on his credentials and learned that he'd cut his teeth as a climber in his native North Wales in the 1980s, bunking off school to explore some of Britain's best cliffs and crags, before gaining over 20 years' experience as a professional in the outdoor industry. My mind was at ease as we set off into the clag and drizzle.

We hiked along Mosedale before veering right on to the Black Sail Pass. It was cold and wet with minimal visibility, not exactly the clear, bone-dry conditions I'd been praying for. At the col we turned left, skirting past Looking Stead, and reached the beginning of the High Level Route. This was where the action started. We traversed on an undulating path, which was rough but not technically difficult, to Robinson's Cairn, a memorial to the respected fellwalker and climber John Wilson Robinson, the man who discovered this thrilling route.

Aled and I chatted away, trying to ignore the rain and the roaring wind. He asked about my challenge and I told him about my two recent hikes in the Lakes: a loop of seven Nuttalls from the delightful Martindale on Friday, followed by the classic Kentmere horseshoe ridge walk on Saturday.

'How were they?' asked Aled. 'Did anything interesting happen?'

'Really good, thanks, decent weather, fun days in the fells, but nothing out of the ordinary – I've climbed so many mountains now it's beginning to feel like my nine-to-five routine.'

'When on earth do you have time for work?'

'Put it this way: I got back from a long Snowdonia expedition on Sunday night last week, worked for four days in a row from Monday to Thursday, went peak-bagging on Friday and Saturday, worked again on Sunday, and now I'm here with you. Totally hectic, mate.'

We stopped chatting when we reached our next challenge, the Shamrock Traverse, a tilted rake featuring a heart-in-mouth shuffle across a slab of wet rock with precipitous drops on one side. We negotiated it safely and, finally, glimpsed Pillar Rock through the hill fog. Alfred Wainwright called it 'the most handsome crag in Lakeland'. I found it more fear-inducing.

To the untrained eye, it looked impassable. The buttress of Pisgah, which adjoins the main bulk of the mountain, would provide easy access to our destination, but for the plunging rift of Jordan Gap. This vertical cleft creates a distinct separation between Pillar and High Man, the highest point of Pillar Rock, leaving the summit tantalisingly out of reach for hikers. To the right, picking a route through a labyrinth of gullies, ledges, steps and outcrops seemed equally unlikely. But that is where we were headed – and, thank God, Aled knew the way.

We scrambled down scree to below Jordan Gap, in conditions that could accurately be described as biblical, and wolfed down a sandwich, donned harnesses and helmets, and ditched our bags. Let the real climbing commence. We were taking on the Slab and Notch route, the easiest climb to the summit of Pillar Rock. It is classed as either a Grade 3 scramble or a moderate rock climb. Either way, roping up was essential. The consequences of a fall would be catastrophic.

Aled headed up first, demonstrating his 'trad climbing' prowess by nimbly ascending a rocky wall while simultaneously looping slings over spiky outcrops and shimmying nuts into boulder crevices. In the absence of bolts on the natural rockface, these contraptions were our lifeline and I was grateful for their confidence-giving qualities. I progressed upwards slowly and deliberately. With Aled supporting me, I easily made it past the point at which I'd bailed on the idea of a solo climb back in August. That felt good. I was getting closer. My fingers dug into the cold, bare rock, and my boots searched for a secure footing on the slippery surface. The wind buffeted my jacket and raindrops rolled down my face, as I tightly hugged an outcrop. There was no doubting it, this was truly getting up close and personal with the mountain.

We reached the slab, a sloping face of smooth rock that, in this weather, was more than tricky to negotiate. It almost felt as if the mountain was willing me to slip and glide down the oily slide into the void below, never to be seen again. Or maybe it was just me being morbid. We crossed without incident, safely roped to the rock at all times, and continued ever upward. A few steps and another slab later, we climbed a vertical wall to reach the notch. The crux of the climb was over and I let out a loud sigh of relief.

The rest was a blur. We ascended further vertical cracks, skirted ledges and climbed rocky steps and staircases, drenched from head to toe in the unrelenting rain. Every now and then I froze on the rock, unable to find the next grip, but Aled's calm encouragement always helped me find a way forward. There were no views whatsoever, not even a glimpse down to the forested slopes of wild Ennerdale, but perhaps this was a blessing in disguise. Vertiginous vistas would have only added to my overwhelming sense of exposure. We rounded a corner, climbed a section with good holds, and emerged into a gully above the Great Chimney. It was nearly over – all that was left was a simple scramble to the summit.

I placed my foot atop the small cairn and raised my arms high in ecstasy. I knew a scary abseil to Jordan Gap still lay ahead, but this was my moment of triumph. I'd conquered Pillar Rock, albeit on my second attempt. John Atkinson climbed it in 1826. I climbed it in 2017. My success paled into insignificance compared with his pioneering ascent but there was one thing we must have shared – the magnificent, life-affirming sense of achievement felt by making it to the summit of Lakeland's most handsome crag.

Still reliving my first foray into the world of climbing, I returned to the Fix the Fells office from Tuesday to Thursday. On Friday I headed to Coniston, completing a 13½-mile walk and bagging ten Nuttalls, including the Old Man of Coniston. The tops were continuously shrouded in cloud and I was drenched by a series of torrential downpours, but I got it done. I felt happy to be ten summits closer to the finish line.

✳   ✳   ✳

The Daily Adventure Journal of James
02/09/17: Lots of hikers are total gear geeks. They like to talk at great length about the difference between 550 and 900 down fill density or debate the merits of a Gore-Tex 28,000mm/24 hours waterproof rating. They are the sort of people, I imagine, who for a special treat spend their weekends waxing their walking boots or polishing their tent poles (and I'm not being euphemistic). I, on the other hand, have been wandering around 446 mountains in a pair of waterproof trousers with 23 holes in them, a leaky pair of women's Scarpa boots, and a metal-framed backpack from 1997. All the idea, no gear.

✳   ✳   ✳

Back in the safety of my cosy home in Cockermouth, I spent Saturday morning on adventure admin: updating my journal, drying out kit, washing clothing, ticking off summits on my log, and organising myself for a final week of peak-bagging. A plan of action was in place.

To hit my target of finishing the Nuttalls in exactly six months, I needed to stand atop number 446 on Saturday, 16 September. That left me with six days free for peak-bagging and I had 30 Nuttalls left to climb: nine in the Rhinogs, 12 in the Cadair Idris range and nine in the Lake District.

Luckily, my bosses had agreed to let me have the whole of the next week off, in lieu of the double shifts I'd be working later in the month at the Ambleside Festival of the Fells. So my schedule was simple. I'd head to North Wales from Monday to Friday to bag my final 21 Welsh peaks, before returning for one last peak-bagging walk in my home territory of the Lake District. I'd deliberately saved the Scafell group for last, meaning that Scafell Pike – England's highest and, perhaps, most iconic peak – would be my 446th summit. I felt that would be a fitting way to end.

C H A P T E R   2 1

THE FINAL SUMMIT

Mountains 417–446

DATE	REGION	MOUNTAINS
Monday 11 September	Rhinogs	Y Garn 2,064ft (629m) Moel Ysgyfarnogod 2,044ft (623m) Foel Penolau 2,014ft (614m)
Tuesday 12 September	Rhinogs	Rhinog Fawr 2,362ft (720m) Rhinog Fach 2,336ft (712m) Y Llethr 2,480ft (756m) Crib-y-rhiw 2,198ft (670m) Diffwys 2,461ft (750m) Diffwys West Top 2,106ft (642m)
Wednesday 13 September	Cadair Idris	Tarrenhendre 2,080ft (634m) Tarren y Gesail 2,188ft (667m)
Thursday 14 September	Cadair Idris	Maesglase 2,218ft (676m) Cribin Fawr 2,162ft (659m) Waun-oer 2,198ft (670m)
Friday 15 September	Cadair Idris	Gau Graig 2,241ft (683m) Mynydd Moel 2,831ft (863m) Cadair Idris 2,930ft (893m) Craig Cwm Amarch 2,595ft (791m) Cyfrwy 2,661ft (811m) Tyrrau Mawr 2,169ft (661m) Craig-y-llyn 2,041ft (622m)

DATE	REGION	MOUNTAINS
Saturday 16 September	Lake District Southern Fells	Lingmell 2,625ft (800m) Middleboot Knotts 2,306ft (703m) Round How 2,431ft (741m) Great End 2,986ft (910m) Ill Crag 3,068ft (935m) Broad Crag 3,064ft (934m) Sca Fell 3,163ft (964m) Symonds Knott 3,146ft (959m) Scafell Pike 3,209ft (978m)

'What have you been up to recently, James?' asked my cousin Kerry.

I was leaning on the bar, sipping an ice-cold Tiger beer, dressed in leather shoes, smart black trousers and a grey chequered shirt with a skinny tie. My hair was neatly styled and I'd had a shower just one hour earlier. It was a strange sensation for me to be socialising. The occasion was my dad's 60th birthday party at The Blue Piano restaurant in central Birmingham. I felt like a fish out of water. A part of me thought I'd spent so much time alone in the mountains that I'd forgotten how to function in normal society.

'Not much really, just climbing 400 mountains,' I said.

'I don't know how you do it,' she replied. 'It's amazing.'

'I love being out in the great outdoors and climbing mountains – it's just awesome,' I answered, as my brothers wandered over.

'Is James boring you with his hiking tales?' piped up Tom.

'Can you remember what it's like to be in a place with electricity?' added Adam.

'Where are you staying tonight, James? In your tent on the grass verge outside?' continued Tom.

Back in the city, news of my mountain exploits was garnering two very different responses: either respect, admiration and awe, as if I was an inspirational adventurer truly making the most of life; or ridicule and mockery, as if I was an oddball rambler perfectly placed to be the butt of a joke. I didn't mind, though. It was good banter and

I relished the chance to have a laugh with my friends and family, let my hair down, and be normal for once. It was great.

Feeling slightly ropey the following morning, I headed to a coffee shop and spent the morning tying up a few loose ends: sending emails, finishing off a writing job, creating routes and downloading maps. I had a late lunch with my parents, packed my bags and set off in the early evening to Dolgellau, where I'd booked a bed in a bunkhouse for two nights. My plan was to get an early start the following day to begin bagging the Rhinogs, a range of nine boulder-strewn, heather-clad Nuttalls to the east of Harlech, centred on the gripping duo of Rhinog Fawr and Rhinog Fach.

By 9am I was tramping up from Ganllwyd in heavy rain, passing the raging 65ft-high Rhaiadr Du waterfall and aiming for the 2,064ft summit of Y Garn, an isolated top on the eastern edge of the Rhinogs range. After making an idiotic navigational error and walking the wrong way off the summit, I completed the five-mile route by walking about seven miles. But it didn't really matter and by lunchtime I was parked up at the end of a minor road to the north of Harlech, ready for the second leg of my split day of peak-bagging. I walked down an old mining track into the northern Rhinogs, as wild goats roamed across the open fellside to the left and right. I passed between the twin lakes of Llyn Eiddew-bach and Llyn Eiddew-mawr and emerged into a rocky world. I gained the ridge, picked my way to the summit of Moel Ysgyfarnogod, and continued onward to the striking top of Foel Penolau, which is surrounded by near-vertical cliffs but accessible by scrambling up a gully.

Back at the car, I answered a call from my adventure buddy Joe, who was hoping to join me in the Cadair Idris range, while I idly took off my muddy boots and sorted out my backpack. Somewhere during that process I managed to lose my car key. I couldn't find it anywhere. I emptied the entire contents of the car, crawled on my hands and knees to look under the bodywork, and searched the surrounding boggy undergrowth like a police investigator combing a field for evidence, my levels of frustration and exasperation rising with every passing minute. Clearly the mountains were scrambling my brain and I was struggling to cope with the most basic of everyday tasks. Half an hour later I was still keyless. It was utterly infuriating. I wanted to break stuff. Violently. Especially myself for being so calamitous.

I'd almost given up hope but, before calling a locksmith, I decided to try one last thing. I climbed on to the back seats and arched myself over into the boot, adopting the same downward-dog yoga pose I'd used to escape from my collapsed tent in the Brecon Beacons. I slid my fingers into the gap where the boot door met the car frame. I edged them left. Nothing. I edged them right. Still nothing. I tried even further right, just in case. Jackpot – there it was. My key was wedged into the smallest of gaps, as if it was deliberately hiding from me in a cruel bid to test my patience. I managed to grip it between my index and middle fingers and joyously extracted it from its secret chamber.

I felt unbelievably happy. And relieved. And blessed. Now I could actually make it home. I wasn't going to be entrapped by the rugged Rhinogs. I was no longer destined to be dinner for the circling posse of famished feral goats. I laughed to myself. Maybe I was going to climb 446 mountains in a grand peak-bagging adventure, but my greatest moment of euphoria would prove to be *not* losing my car key.

✳ ✳ ✳

The Daily Adventure Journal of James
11/09/17: While browsing rural service stations I hereby formally give myself permission to glance at the top shelf of naughty magazines without feeling guilty. After filling up with petrol in Dolgellau today, I found my wandering eyes doing such a thing, only to be greeted with erotic images of a different kind – copies of *Tractor* magazine.

✳ ✳ ✳

I slept well in the bunkhouse, which I luckily had all to myself, meaning there were no snorers to disturb my much-needed rest. And I was grateful for that. I needed to be on top of my game for the day's challenging hike. I was heading into the Rhinogs again. I'd completed three Nuttalls yesterday, but today I was targeting the stars of the range: Rhinog Fawr and Rhinog Fach, as well as four other tops. I checked my guidebook. It would be an 11-mile walk with 4,400ft of ascent, over 'some of the roughest and toughest walking to be found anywhere in Wales', including miles and miles of 'deep heather and ankle-twisting rocks', according to John and Anne. It sounded simultaneously exciting and exhausting.

The drive to Cwm Nantcol, at the end of a minor road south-east of Harlech, seemed to take for ever. First, I had to cross the wooden toll bridge at Penmaenpool, which I was not expecting at all. With Radio 1 blasting out, I initially sped past the payment booth, like a boy racer trying to avoid the hefty 40p charge. I realised the error of my ways, reversed, apologised, and spent an awkward few minutes searching for money in my car. In the meantime, the elderly attendant was having a conversation with Radio 1 DJ Nick Grimshaw, mistaking an on-air phone call from my radio for a real-life hands-free call I was missing. We laughed about the misunderstanding and then laughed again as I handed over 40p in 5ps and coppers.

The next delay came on the roads nearer to my destination, which were gated, presumably to stop livestock escaping. This made the stop-start journey jerkier than a bus ride down Broad Street in Birmingham's city centre. There were six metal gates in total. For each one I had to drive up, get out, open the gate, secure it so it didn't slam into my Golf in the strong wind, hop back in the car, drive through, jump out again, close the gate, dive back on to the driver's seat, drive on – all six times over. But at least free entertainment was provided. A farmer had pinned laminated signs to the gates, stating: 'This is not the way to the waterfalls. Dispose of your sat nav in the nearest bin.'

I parked in a farmyard and headed north past an old building, through fields and over a ladder stile. The weather was far from brilliant. The sky was grey, the air had a cold chill, and the sun was nowhere to be seen. But I was happy. It wasn't raining and the cloud line was high, so I had excellent visibility across the range. Below a sheepfold, I picked up a cairned path and climbed the south-western shoulder of Rhinog Fawr, avoiding the impenetrable ground on all sides. Excited about what the rest of the day might entail, I arrived at the 2,362ft summit and stopped for a drinks break and a snack. The view south to Rhinog Fach held my attention. It wasn't beautiful or postcard-perfect, like many of the places I'd walked. It was rough around the edges. But it felt wilder, more remote and more arduous than anywhere I'd been before. The sense of isolation, exploration and adventure was palpable – and I loved it.

Helicopter crashes were on my mind, as I descended east briefly on a clear path. I remembered reading in the news about a tragedy earlier in the year, when a millionaire businessman crashed his Airbus helicopter into Rhinog Fawr, killing himself and his four passengers. It was a morbid thought and I promised myself that I would return safely to my loved ones after this final week of solo peak-bagging. As I tried to locate a safe way to descend south over a steep, tangled, rocky maze, it was easy to see why the reclamation of the bodies and the helicopter wreckage had been such a challenge for the rescue crews. This was genuinely rough and remote country, an unkempt lumpy, bumpy wilderness that felt a very long way from civilisation. Using my hands at all times, I scrambled over gigantic boulders, exposed faces of rock and sliding rivers of scree, before picking up a gully that guided me neatly down into Bwlch Drws-Ardudwy.

Plonking myself down on a mossy mound, I used my backpack as a backrest and tucked into my lunch: ham salad wraps, trail mix, dried cranberries, banana chips and two Snickers. I hadn't seen a soul all day, not even at the farmyard where I'd parked, and the *bwlch* felt very remote. It would've been wonderfully tranquil too, if it hadn't been for the harsh, repetitive bleat of a feral goat. Was it in pain? Or angry? Or having fantastic sex? Or was that just the noise wild goats made? I had no idea.

Ahead, the rough ground of Rhinog Fach looked like a chaotic landscape of crags, scree, heather and bracken, rising over 1,000ft from the col. Thankfully, a decent path, relatively clear underfoot, guided me safely over the steep rocky terrain to the 2,336ft summit. I felt low on energy, exhausted by the tough walking over rough ground, but I felt happy too. I'd ticked off the two jewels of the Rhinogs, Fawr and Fach. It had been my favourite section of walking for ages and I felt like an explorer pioneering a new route through an isolated, harsh, forgotten land. It was so good I'd completely forgotten that I was peak-bagging.

But, sadly, the reality of Nuttalls box-ticking came back to slap me in the face. I still had four summits to tick off. I couldn't bail here, with my memories of the rugged Rhinogs undiluted. Instead, I needed to head south, where the rough character of the range relents into the softer, grassier, smoother tops of Y Llethr, Crib-y-rhiw, Diffwys and Diffwys West Top. I feared it was going to be boring. The initial steep descent towards Y Llethr, however, was enjoyable, with plunging views down rock slabs to the tarn of Llyn Hywel, followed by excellent panoramas back to the twin peaks of Fawr and Fach. But the rest of the walk was, as expected, a featureless, grassy trudge. To compound matters, a stormy downpour utterly drenched me just as I was nearing my car, as if the mountains were reminding me that they were in charge and I should always respect them. After a challenging adventure in the wild Rhinogs, it felt like an apt ending to the day.

Following a lazy morning sending emails and sipping on a vanilla latte in Starbucks off the A470 near Dolgellau, I arrived at the village of Abergynolwyn at midday. The Rhinogs were complete and now I had my sights set on the Cadair Idris range, a group of 12 Nuttalls in the southernmost section of Snowdonia National Park between

Dolgellau and Machynlleth. I wanted to tick off two today, the deserted and unfrequented Tarren hills, leaving the remaining eight Nuttalls for an overnight adventure with Joe.

I was no longer feeling the time pressure. I knew I'd make my self-imposed six-month target as long as I stuck to the master schedule I'd planned. And today was an easy day, with only two Nuttalls on my to-do list. From the village car park, I climbed up the steep minor road towards Nant Gwernol station, part of the Talyllyn heritage railway, a remnant of the area's slate-mining history. I had a moment of déjà vu as I passed a raised platform of land in attractive woodland. I suddenly remembered that I had bivvied at that spot a few years previously during one of my weekend trips from Birmingham. The memories flooded back. I recalled exactly where I'd slept, what I'd eaten, what I'd done and how it'd felt. It was strange to think back to that earlier version of myself, an adventurer in training, honing his skills and developing a deep love for wild places. Little had I known back then that this is what it would lead to – a crazed 446-mountain peak-bagging mission. What would 2014 James have thought of 2017 James? I liked to think he would have been super proud.

I climbed steadily through forest on a wide track with sharp switchbacks left and right, before scrambling steeply over a shaley slope and up a gully through the cliffs on to the ridge above the forest. The sky was blue and the sun was shining as I tramped easily along a fence to the summit of Tarrenhendre. One Nuttall down, one to go. Enjoying the views over to Cardigan Bay, I descended the eastern shoulder to a col and then continued along an airy ridge that made for pleasant walking. Or at least it was pleasant until a shower arrived and I had to crouch down in the lee of the hill to quickly pull on my waterproofs. The positive was a rainbow that appeared in the sky, arching over the brow of the hill ahead and framing the evergreen forest beautifully.

To my surprise, I bumped into a large group of schoolchildren wearing matching dark green waterproofs and carrying luminous bag covers.

Their teachers barked at them to get out of the way and they obedi-
ently moved to the sides of the path, parting like the Red Sea. I passed
through, trying my best to look like a seasoned adventurer, and then
climbed steeply over tussocky grass to the 2,188ft summit of Tarren y
Gesail. Forty-five minutes later, after a descent to an old quarry and a
trudge through fields trampled into a muddy quagmire by hundreds
of bovine hooves, I was back at my car shovelling Haribo sweets into
my mouth.

I drove to Corris Uchaf, where Joe had booked an Airbnb cottage
for the night, and parked up off the main road. I located the correct
building and looked through the window. Joe appeared to be in his
element: sitting in a large leather armchair in front of a traditional
fireplace, poring over a map of Snowdonia and, I presumed,
daydreaming of the adventures that were just around the corner.
I knocked on the door and entered. We performed a man-hug – a
handshake that transitions into a semi-embrace – and spent the next
hour or so catching up on each other's exploits.

Joe quizzed me on every aspect of my challenge. 'You're so close
to the end – how does it feel?'

'Kind of unreal, I guess. I can't quite believe it. Peak-bagging has
taken over my life for the past six months. It's been incredible, but
I'm ready to finish now.'

'You've come a long way from those days when we used to drive
from Birmingham to Snowdonia and just look up at a peak and
decide to climb it,' Joe said, reminiscing about our adventures of old.

I'd met Joe in 2005, playing 11-a-side non-league football for
the same team in Birmingham. He was the creative midfielder who
played inch-perfect through balls for me to finish off as the striker.
We clicked on the pitch and off it, and somewhere along the line we
realised we shared a love of climbing mountains. It was perhaps the
first and, I imagine, only case of two people meeting in the macho
world of non-league football and then becoming hiking and wild-
camping buddies.

'I know,' I replied. 'We've been on so many epic adventures over the years, from those little day trips in the early days to our big trekking expeditions abroad. It's been awesome. It seems only right that you're here to be a part of my peak-bagging mission.'

'It's a pleasure, mate – but you do realise we usually make a series of schoolboy errors when we're adventuring together, right?'

'Good point. To be fair, I'd be massively disappointed if we didn't encounter at least one major calamity over the next two days.'

We spent the evening in a pub in Corris, having selected an establishment based on some wisdom Joe had learned travelling: if a pub has well-maintained flowers outside, it's worth going into. The tactic worked. We dined on a slap-up meal of double cheeseburgers with fries, salad and onion rings, while a black Labrador slept in the corner and an old lady gave a running commentary on her performance at the dartboard. It was a quirky pub with good character and, despite seemingly containing more dogs than humans, it had a lively atmosphere. Joe filled me in on his recent backpacking trip to Australia, New Zealand and Nepal, while I recounted tales of my recent peak-bagging mishaps and adventures.

Once our plates were empty, we grabbed the maps and set about making a plan for the next two days. It came together pretty quickly. We would walk a one-way 20-mile route heading west from Dinas Mawddwy to the hamlet of Llanfihangel-y-pennant, just north of Abergynolwyn. In the process we'd bag ten Nuttalls, including the mighty Cadair Idris, and sleep wild in the mountains on the Thursday night. By leaving one car at the finish and one at the beginning, we could manage the logistics easily enough too. It was a good plan – and one that would see me finally complete all 190 mountains in Wales.

Showers rolled over throughout the following morning as we climbed up a stepped forest path, emerged on to open fellside leading to contoured grassy slopes and, after an hour or so, gained the ridge above the near-vertical cliffs of Craig Maesglase. A fast-flowing waterfall plunged over the rocky precipice, plummeting hundreds of feet down to the forested valley. It had a shallow V-shaped lip in which a small pool of water collected, before spurting over smooth slabs of rock into the abyss. I could tell that Joe, ever the adrenalin junkie, fancied a quick dip. But it looked just a tad too dangerous, as if one false move might send you nose-diving over the edge in a fatal version of a water slide.

Instead we sat at the head of the waterfall, enjoying the views, drinking bottles of water and tucking into our mid-morning snacks. The valley below looked deserted and the walk in had been characterised by a real sense of isolation. Joe, a fan of George Monbiot and a vocal advocate of rewilding – a conservation approach that allows nature to take back control of landscapes – was mesmerised.

'If I won the lottery,' said Joe, 'I'd buy this valley, build a log cabin to live in and rewild the landscape – native trees, more birds, more animals.'

'Just live in a bivvy, mate – that would be the only true way to be connected to the landscape,' I joked.

Joe opened a multi-pack of Snickers, a look of disappointment etched on his face. It was his number-one mountain snack. I'd never been on a mountain with Joe when he didn't have at least two or three bars in his bag. But clearly something was bothering him.

'I swear Snickers keep getting smaller.'

'So true, mate. I reckon you'd have to eat two of these bars to get the same energy hit we used to get from one bar back in 2005, when we started adventuring.'

'Thieving corporates thinking only about their profit margins, not the needs of mountaineers.'

We chatted away about rewilding and chocolates and adventure and travel and football and the friends we used to know – and much more besides. After solo-climbing more than 400 mountains, it was a novelty for me to have someone to talk to. I was no longer restricted to the internal dialogue of my mind. Now I had a real living, breathing human to converse with. And I enjoyed it. It helped the miles and the peaks pass by quicker than usual.

We bagged Maesglase, making sure we visited the official summit at Craig Rhiw-erch, and continued west along a fence in ever-changing conditions. We stuck to the high ground, skirting around forests, and ticked off Cribin Fawr and Waun-oer before dropping west to the road at Bwlch Llyn Bach. We turned right and picked up a track to the left that slowly looped through boggy fields to the base of Gau Graig's northern ridge. Ahead lay a steep climb towards the main tops of the Cadair Idris range, but we were running out of time. Dusk was descending and we needed to set up camp. A charming little forest would have been perfect but for a complete lack of flat land, so we settled for a spot higher up in the lee of a rocky outcrop.

Sadly the weather was poor: low cloud, rain showers and just a bit dreary. But we made the most of it. We stayed outside, wrapped up in down jackets, waterproofs, hats and gloves, and busied ourselves all evening erecting tents, organising bags, cooking dinner, trying and failing to start a fire, sipping on hot chocolate, blowing on our cupped hands to warm our fingers, and laughing at how ridiculously small Joe's new super-lightweight one-man backpacking tent was.

'How was the tent?' I shouted from the shelter of Dennis the following morning, as raindrops pattered all around.

'Like sleeping in a coffin,' replied Joe between yawns.

An hour later we were fully packed up. The number seven was on my mind. Seven more tops to complete and all 190 Nuttalls in Wales would be in the bag. I couldn't quite believe it. But there was still a sense of so near, yet so far. We had a tough walk in gnarly weather ahead of us. Joe needed to set off home at a reasonable hour and I had a long drive back to the Lake District, so we were both in agreement. We would stride out with the bit between our teeth, and get it done efficiently.

Powering our arms and legs, we climbed above cliffs to the prominent cairn of Gau Graig and continued west through a white-out to tick off the 2,831ft summit of Mynydd Moel. Joe took a photo of me on each summit, as if it was a countdown to a celebratory finale. He had a spring in his step, clearly buoyed by the sheer joy of spending a day in the mountains. That used to be me. But after so many peaks, I felt somewhat jaded. My love for the mountains was still there but it was somehow different. It was a deeper, closer, more intimate love, rather than one of uncontrollable excitement and butterflies in your stomach. I'd gone from having one-night stands with the mountains to being in a happy, loving marriage.

The clouds suddenly lifted and we were treated to a fleeting glimpse of the range's highest peak. Cadair Idris, or Cader Idris to traditionalists, is a mountain shrouded in myth. It derives its name, meaning 'Chair of Idris', from the Welsh legend of a giant who created a mountainous seat for stargazing. As clouds swirled over the summit, it certainly felt mystical.

'I feel like I've got a connection with Cadair Idris,' said Joe, as we stood at the OS trig point. 'It's a special place to me: I know the mountain and the mountain knows me. It's a close bond.'

'We both talk about mountains in the language of relationships – is that weird?' I replied, chuckling.

'As long as the language doesn't turn sexual, then it's fine.'

We had lunch in the summit refuge, chatting about the time years ago I'd dropped my car key in the snow ascending Cadair Idris, only to miraculously find it again on the descent. Feeling refreshed, we dropped south on a rocky path and feasted on commanding views of the cliffs and crags above Llyn Cau, the most riveting scenery of the past few days. We ticked off the top of Craig Cwm Amarch, retraced our steps towards Cadair Idris and then veered north-west to the 2,661ft cairn of Cyfrwy on the edge of some cliffs. That was the high mountains of Cadair Idris completed. All that was left was a gentle two-and-a-half-mile ramble west over grassy, heather-clad terrain to two outlying Nuttalls. I was so close now.

We arrived at the rather boring top of Tyrrau Mawr without incident and, anticipating the imminent end of my Wales adventure, followed a fence south-west aiming for the 2,041ft Craig-y-llyn. We made quick progress, and it didn't take long to get there. But where exactly was the summit?

'Not exactly a smooth crossing of the finish line,' I said, dropping my backpack to the ground and loading up my OS Maps app.

'It's appropriate for your adventure, though, pal. This is real life, not a Hollywood movie.'

We figured it out and found the small pile of rocks that marked the top. I hopped over the fence and placed my foot on the cairn.

'Congratulations, mate – a brilliant achievement.'

I nodded in a slightly embarrassed way, and smiled. A hundred and ninety mountains in Wales were done and dusted.

'How does it feel?' asked Joe.

'Good,' I replied. And so, with that wild understatement, my peak-bagging adventure in Wales was over.

At 10am the next day, after a painful four-and-a-half-hour drive home to Cockermouth the previous evening, followed by a fitful night's sleep, I parked up at the green in Wasdale, stunned by the sheer number of minibuses, vans and cars already filling the grassy car park. I got out of the Golf, slid my feet into my boots, pulled on my Berghaus jacket, grabbed my backpack, and glanced up at the surrounding mountains. This was it. My final walk. The final leg of a long journey. The final nine Nuttalls. It felt unreal. I'd dreamed of this day for so long – and now it was here.

I was in go-slow mode for most of the hike, like an exhausted marathon runner staggering through his last mile. I was determined to give it one final big push, but I felt fatigued, as if the psychology of seeing the finish line had caused my body to switch off and say, 'Enough is enough, no more hiking, I'm spent.' I battled onward, nonetheless, taking heart from the blue skies and fine weather.

From Wasdale Head I took the Breast Route up Lingmell, crossed the ravine of Piers Gill to bag the knolls of Middleboot Knotts and Round How, and veered east to tick off the 2,986ft summit of Great End, the fell that accurately described what today was all about for me. Next I turned south to a col and took the main highway heading towards England's highest mountain, turning off it twice to visit Ill Crag's summit of naked rock and Broad Crag's rough top of gigantic, jumbled boulders. That was six Nuttalls completed by lunchtime. Not bad.

But I didn't, as logic would dictate, visit Scafell Pike's summit next, despite being so close to it. I wanted England's highest mountain to be my final mountain and, therefore, needed to tick off Sca Fell and Symonds Knott first. It was irrational route-planning, but I couldn't change it now. So, feeling teased by the proximity of my finish line, I took a wide loop around the summit, which appeared to be about 100ft above my contour and was absolutely heaving with charity walkers. Maybe it was a blessing in disguise to be delaying my arrival.

Accidentally disturbing a woman squatting for a wee among the rocks, I slowly turned south-west for the pass of Mickledore as clouds began to shroud the tops. Lacking the climbing skills to take on the Broad Stand route straight ahead, I was forced to walk a long and arduous route to bag my next two Nuttalls. The out-and-back to Sca Fell and Symonds Knott seemed to take for ever: I descended steep scree, turned up a wet rocky gully, arrived at Foxes Tarn, plodded on to the two 3,000fters, returned to Foxes Tarn, scrambled down the wet gully, clambered up the shifting scree and, finally, made it back to Mickledore in a total white-out.

I plodded on for ten minutes, climbing gently on a clear path through low cloud. The rocks crunched under my boots, the wind inflated the hood pulled over my head, and my walking poles clinked with each placement on the rough terrain. I felt cold and tired, but I knew I was incredibly close. The cloud lifted slightly and I could see the large summit cairn, maybe 100ft away. I took ten slow steps. And another ten. And another ten. And another ten. And then I'd made it. I was standing on top of Scafell Pike, England's highest mountain and my 446th Nuttall.

There was no fanfare – no friends, no balloons, no champagne bottles. I stood alone in quiet contemplation. A couple sitting below the cairn packed up their bags and headed down towards Wasdale. Miraculously, I had the summit all to myself, a brilliantly appropriate way to end an adventure of silence and solitude. An intoxicating wave of emotion swept over me: a mixture of relief, elation, gratitude, excitement, joy, inspiration, determination and hope. I had a lump in my throat. I'd actually done it. I'd bagged myself a peak-bagging record and, perhaps even better, proved that it really was possible to integrate an epic adventure into my everyday life.

As I stood in silence, I thought about the tough times, the low moments when I'd almost given up; and I thought about the good times, the isolation, the escapism, the beauty, the freedom, the happiness that came with detaching myself from my phone and the internet. The mountains had given me so much and taught me so much. I felt reborn, as if the challenge had injected me with a love of life and an excitement about what the future might hold. It was my 446th summit but it didn't feel like an ending. It felt like a beginning – the start of my new adventurous life.

The words of Alfred Wainwright raced through my mind. 'I was to find ... a spiritual and physical satisfaction in climbing mountains – and a tranquil mind upon reaching their summits, as though I had escaped from the disappointments and unkindnesses of life and emerged above them into a new world, a better world.'

I turned away from the summit and started walking down, feeling overwhelmingly happy to have experienced that better world.

CHAPTER 22

AFTERWARDS

Comically, the first thing that happened to me after completing my record-breaking peak-bagging feat was failing to get a table for dinner in the Wasdale Head Inn. On the one occasion in my life when I truly needed and deserved a slap-up meal I was categorically denied it by a grumpy manager. I was half tempted to exclaim, 'Do you know who I am? Can you even comprehend how far I've journeyed for this meal?' But, of course, I didn't. In fact, it was the perfect opportunity to demonstrate how the mountains had changed me. James of old would've been angry and frustrated by the situation, overwhelmed by a sense that this should not be happening. But new James was unfazed and relaxed, making a simple decision not to get annoyed. He had a more philosophical and positive perspective on life – and calmly travelled to Nether Wasdale where the pubs were less busy. No drama.

The first few weeks after summiting my 446th peak were a blur of exhaustion. Although hit by a wall of fatigue, I was straight back into everyday life – catching up with household chores, putting in the hours in the office and grappling to get my life back in order. I was so tired I didn't go anywhere near a mountain. I kept my feet squarely at sea level. And the longest hikes I did were to-ing and fro-ing from the sofa to the fridge. However, I was relieved and happy to be back living a normal, everyday existence. It felt comforting and soothing.

And my mood was constantly boosted by messages of support and by the press interest I was receiving.

John and Anne Nuttall, whom I later met at an event and who were just as sweet and kind in person as I'd imagined, sent me a lovely email. They congratulated me on an 'exceptional' and 'unique' achievement, confirming that my time of six months was the fastest-known completion of the Nuttalls. Their website detailed almost 300 hikers who had bagged all 446 mountains, but no one had ever done it so quickly. That made me very proud. But the mountains, not the record, were my prize, as Anne wisely reminded me with the words, 'We are sure that you will come to look at the summits, like we do, as very special friends.' On social media, numerous similar comments poured in: 'Congrats, your adventure has inspired me to climb more mountains'; 'Love that you fitted your challenge around your job'; and 'What an incredible achievement, such an inspiration'. Each and every message brought a big smile to my face.

On top of the wave of social-media support, the mainstream media also got hold of my story. *The Times* printed a half-page picture spread about my peak-bagging exploits, the *Sunday Telegraph* referred to me as 'Mountain Man' in a double-page feature, and I was filmed by ITV for a special news piece. Other publications seemed to be on a mission to come up with the cheesiest headline: 'Peak of his powers' (*News & Star*), 'High achiever' (*Birmingham Mail*), and the bizarre 'James and the giant mountains' (*Cumbria Life*), while most journalists seemed less interested in my mountain exploits than they were in the fact that I'd completed the challenge in a pair of my wife's old hiking boots.

But I didn't let myself get too carried away with the merry-go-round of self-indulgent publicity. Don't get me wrong, I enjoyed my moment in the spotlight and I was proud of my achievement, but I hadn't started my peak-bagging mission in a calculated ploy to become a Z-list outdoors celebrity. I'd done it for precisely the opposite reason – to indulge in the freedom of the mountains and to escape the social-media-obsessed, give-me-attention trappings of modern life. And so, as the media frenzy calmed down, I was happy to be out of the limelight and to have the time to meditate upon my challenge.

I started by crunching the numbers, and it made for interesting reading. I'd climbed 446 mountains in just six months, completing 82 days of walking in total and sleeping wild in the mountains 27 times. It had rained heavily on 48 per cent of my days in the mountains, virtually every other day, while my stats for distance and ascent surpassed 1,000 miles and 150,000ft (over five times the height of Everest), respectively. Alongside all of this, I'd churned out 91 days of work over the six months, just one day shy of four days per week on average; and I'd taken only 17 days off from either hiking or working. No wonder I was knackered. In terms of cost, my big adventure had come with a pretty small price tag – just £1,100. I'd spent £250 on hostel accommodation, £80 on equipment, £20 on my OS Maps subscription, and roughly £750 on fuel. I was pleased with that. It was definitive proof that you didn't have to break the bank to have an amazing expedition.

After I finished analysing the stats, I found myself contemplating more subjective questions about my challenge. What was the most difficult part? What was the most memorable moment? And, importantly, what on earth was I going to do next? I thought long and hard about each question and my answers changed virtually every time I did so. But these were the conclusions I came up with. The toughest part? The mental challenge of constantly climbing mountains in torrential rain, strong winds and low cloud – that had been seriously draining. The best moment? Getting to the final summit, perching atop Scafell Pike and knowing I'd achieved what I'd set out to do. It was a moment of sheer joy. And my next expedition? It had to be the Munros in Scotland and the 2,000fters in Ireland. If I kept plodding on, I might just be able to climb every mountain in the British Isles.

Annoyingly, more than any other question, there was one thing everyone wanted to know – what were my favourite mountains? It was incredibly difficult to answer. So many were in contention: Blencathra, Helvellyn, Steeple, Great Gable, Yewbarrow, Rhinog Fach, Snowdon, Crib Goch, Glyder Fawr, Cadair Idris and many more. And it was impossible to be objective. So many factors affected my enjoyment of each walk: the weather (it was difficult to fully appreciate a peak when being battered by dire conditions and the views were non-existent), my mood (was I feeling cold, fatigued and miserably wet at the time? Or inspired, motivated and happy?), and myriad other features such as luck, wildlife, fellow hikers, the proximity of roads, the weight of my bag, my wild-camping set-up, the presence or lack of mobile phone reception, the quality of the paths, and the number of syrupy flapjacks in my rucksack. But if I was forced under duress to name my top two, this would be my answer: Tryfan in Wales, because it is so striking and emotive; and Hopegill Head in England, because it is prominent on the skyline near my home and, on an almost spiritual level, I always feel like it's calling me to the mountains.

My favourite ranges were definitely those in the Lake District and Snowdonia. For beauty and drama, they were unrivalled – their naked cliffs, knife-edge ridges, towering summits and gleaming lakes always set my heart racing. Conversely, I hadn't particularly warmed to the more rounded, rolling landscapes of the North Pennines or the Brecon Beacons, but perhaps the inclement weather had warped my feelings, while the Peak District, Central Wales, the Cheviots and the Berwyns had been good but not spectacular. To my surprise, however, the rural charm of the Yorkshire Dales had utterly captivated me, while I'd also really enjoyed Dartmoor and the Black Mountains. But was I able to be objective in my thinking? Definitely not. My memories were significantly affected by the lottery of the weather. When my post-challenge tiredness finally subsided, I headed back into the mountains of the Lake District yet again for solo walks. It felt like returning home, as if I was back in my happy place. The time alone allowed me to continue meditating on my challenge, with the new perspective of hindsight. What had I learned? Was I a changed person? Had I had any epiphanies?

I thought about one of my favourite mountain quotes, by French writer René Daumal: 'You cannot stay on the summit for ever; you have to come down again. So why bother in the first place? Just this: what is above knows what is below, but what is below does not know what is above. One climbs, one sees. One descends, one sees no longer, but one has seen. There is an art of conducting oneself in the lower regions by the memory of what one saw higher up. When one can no longer see, one can at least still know.'

My mountain challenge had changed me for good. I had seen what was above. And I was now better equipped to conduct myself in the 'lower regions' of everyday life. I was more positive, happier and less addicted to my phone. I was excited about my adventurous future, filled with a newfound delight in the world, and utterly enchanted by the wild places of Britain. I no longer felt navigationally challenged in life. I was no longer stressed, depressed or anxious. Instead I knew what I wanted from my short time on this planet. I wanted to live as adventurous and epic an existence as possible; to collect memories not things; and to spend less time on the internet and more time in the hills. The mountains had improved and enhanced my life – and I was happy and grateful for the experiences my challenge had provided. As Alfred Wainwright put it, those who seek out the mountains will be 'blessed both in mind and body'. That's exactly how I felt.

However, I was still the same old James who had started the challenge. There was nothing extraordinary about me. I hadn't transformed into a super-human, all-action adventurer. I still had no idea how to abseil down a cliff, or forage for berries, or navigate in cloud. Dark nights still freaked me out and, sadly, climbing 446 mountains hadn't gifted me the ability to grow a rugged beard.

I still had rubbish credentials for an adventurer. But it really didn't matter. Despite my lack of technical skills, I'd managed to integrate something truly adventurous into my everyday life – and I'd done it simply by choosing to do so. That's all it was, a choice. And that was the most empowering lesson I learned from my challenge. Anyone can live adventurously, you just have to choose to do so. Will you?

EPILOGUE

As I'm writing this new epilogue, the world is going through a strange, unsettling time. The coronavirus crisis has curbed everyone's freedom to enjoy the countryside. We are all adapting to a new, unfamiliar 'normal'; a socially-distanced, housebound, hermit-like existence. I haven't left my home town of Cockermouth for almost two months, let alone climbed a single mountain. I'm no longer Mountain Man; I'm Lockdown Lad – or maybe Covid Chap?

But there is one thing I'm grateful to lockdown for. Cabin fever has inspired me to reminisce longingly of those halcyon days back in 2017 when I climbed 446 mountains. Sometimes, as I'm wallowing in a Netflix-induced coma of laziness and boredom, my mind will wander to my Nuttalls challenge. I think about the times I slept wild under the stars, stood triumphantly atop soaring summits, scrambled saw-toothed ridges, and – above all else – hiked myself happy. They are fond memories; memories that put a smile on my face and fuel the fire within me to continue living as adventurously as I can.

Lockdown has taught me to never take such freedom for granted again. Our time in the mountains is precious – and we should savour it, protect it and celebrate its contribution to our physical and mental wellbeing. But, simultaneously, lockdown has reminded me that adventure is, at its heart, just a mindset: a way of thinking and a way you choose to live your life. It doesn't matter that I haven't been able to travel, or climb mountains, or exercise more than once a day. I've still been able to live adventurously by camping in my garden, pushing myself to run a 5km personal best, and discovering local trails – a disused railway and a riverside path – I didn't even know existed, despite being on my doorstep. Adventure is just about stretching yourself, going outside your comfort zone, doing stuff you don't normally do, and overcoming your fears.

That adventurous spirit has been at the forefront of every decision I've made over the past few years. It has shaped and moulded my future, and transformed my life quickly and dramatically yet again. Sometimes for the better, sometimes not; but I've consciously chosen to prioritise adventure whenever I've found myself at one of life's many crossroads. It's never been 'should I fork left or right?', it's been 'which path is the most adventurous option? I'll take that one'.

Since completing my 446-mountain challenge in September 2017, my journey through life has encountered a few heartbreaking bumps and unexpected twists and turns along the way. The biggest, and most tragic, change was to my relationship status. Becky and I separated in 2018 and, while I don't feel particularly comfortable talking about something so private and personal in public, I will say that I've never known pain and grief like it – and an incomparable sense of sadness hung over me for much for 2018.

I was still working for Fix the Fells then, as well as writing this book, and somehow I managed to muck my way through the first half of 2018. I found solace in the mountains during those traumatic times. Walks around Loweswater soothed my troubled soul, and evening strolls up Watch Hill on the outskirts of Cockermouth helped me forget my sorrows, if only momentarily. As always, I saw the hills and mountains as my saviour: a place I could turn to for healing and therapy.

In my darkest moments, however, I began to doubt the veracity of that conviction. Had the Nuttalls challenge really brought happiness and meaning to my life? Or was it just some elaborate ruse for running away from my everyday problems? Did I really love adventure, or was it simply the antidote for my inability to cope with normal life? And could the mountains really bring mental relief and personal growth, or were they the equivalent of a plaster over a gaping wound, incapable of dealing with the root problems?

The foundations of my personal philosophy had been rocked. Doubts and anxieties plagued my mind – and it was upsetting. But I knew, in my heart, that this scepticism was simply negative-spiralling, a mental by-product of a painful episode in my life. The doubts weren't real. They were nebulous and emotional, born out of insecurity and low self-esteem, and all I needed to do was banish them from my head.

Conversely, the joys of walking felt anything but nebulous. They were well-defined and sharply-focused, and so real I could almost taste them on my lips. Every walk I completed in early 2018, every step I took on a mountainside, every ridge I traversed and every summit I perched upon, brought me a small sense of restoration and replenishment. Little by little, drip by drip, the cleansing and curing powers of the mountains washed over me – and, like a religious zealot whose faith in God is strengthened by tragedy, I realised that hardship and heartache had solidified my faith in the mountains too.

Forging new friendships with a motley crew of outdoor-lovers also helped me to rediscover my mojo and rekindle my love for the mountains. In mid-2018, I started attending 'Instameets' – group walks organised through Instagram – and it immediately made me feel part of a supportive, like-minded community, as if we were one big happy family. So, ironically, after 446 mountains of solo hiking and six months of living like a reclusive oddball, I went full circle and became a social butterfly, relishing the banter and camaraderie of group hikes and new friends.

Brought together by Nic Hardy (@adventurer.nic on Instagram), we were a gang of misfits and mavericks; male and female, old young, seasoned pros and total beginners, but all with a passio the great outdoors. Nic organised walks almost every weekend, mostly in the Lake District, and together we relished the blue skies and hazy sunshine of a glorious summer. As a crew, we bagged Wainwrights, wild camped high in the fells, scrambled up gnarly ridges, swam in lakes, and even danced to Mel C singing old-school Spice Girl hits at Keswick Mountain Festival. They felt like care-free, hedonistic days, as if we were kids drunk on the freedom of the seven week summer holidays.

The group was full of characters. Carl Edwards (@carl_adventurer) was like an excitable schoolchild with ADHD: he swore profusely, had no understanding of political correctness and dressed like he was colour-blind, but somehow managed to dodge being an obnoxious douche-bag by having a heart of gold. Like the father of the crew, Aidan Clarke (@aidiclarkeloveroflife) reminded me of the Big Friendly Giant: larger than life, paternal, protective, with a booming laugh and an uncanny ability to catch dreams with a butterfly net (OK, I made the last bit up). Matt Watson (@mountainswithmatt) was shy and quiet but the perfect antidote if you'd just spent too much time with Carl; and bubbly Jess Grzybowski (@jessg_outdoors) was the David Attenborough of the group, regularly pointing out weird and wonderful aspects of the natural world, such as spittlebug secretions and bird of prey regurgitated pellets. And then there was Graham Ambridge, like a wise, enlightened monk, who didn't even have Instagram, but somehow still knew about the get-togethers.

The babies of the group were David Woodward (@davidwoodward26), a tall, lanky 20-year-old of Italian heritage who loved sushi and could get a tan in the shade; and Saul Darlington (@summits_with_saul), a baby-faced outdoor instructor and part-time fire-fighter from Wrexham who – in a worrying show of fire-related incompetence considering his vocation – melted my spork over a barbecue within minutes of meeting me for the first time. Ryan Codling (@vanilakodey) was so Brummie I had to translate his accent, and so under-the-thumb he had to apply for a formal permit to go hiking from his wife; and Liz Preston (@liz_marie_preston) was a student nurse from Billinge, Merseyside, like an armadillo with a tough, guarded exterior, but once you got to know her had a soft, kind centre with a wickedly-dry sense of humour. Many more came later too, including Adam, Anna, Bryony, Becky, Ellie, Aggie and Andy – and I apologise in advance to anyone I've rudely missed out. Please don't hate me.

Some of the group also inspired me with uplifting stories of how the mountains had changed their lives. Harrison Ward (@fellfoodie), a dude with a towering physique far more worthy of the title 'Mountain Man', had overcome self-destructive alcoholism and suicidal thoughts by moving to the Lakes and finding healing in the mountains and fitness. Ditzy Jessica Mather (@jessicamather91), who'd discovered her love for hiking after winning a competition to climb Mt Kilimanjaro (which she thought was in Wales), used the outdoors as a poignant way of paying tribute to her best friend Vicky, who tragically died in a fall on Haystacks. And postwoman Laura Doling (@lauradoling), an Essex girl with the prettiest face but the foulest potty mouth, had transformed her life aged just 24, bravely moving from Jaywick to Cumbria for a fresh start.

But the person who had the biggest impression on me was Nic, the organiser of all this socialising. We seemed to gravitate towards each other, like an inexorable coming together. We'd start a group walk apart, hanging out with other friends, but by the end of it we'd have accidentally spent the past two hours together, side by side, chatting about everything and nothing. We became close friends over several months and, very slowly, despite neither of us really looking for it, the friendship naturally morphed into a fledgling romance.

For me it felt like a miracle. If I'd plugged my criteria for a woman into Tinder – mid-30s, no children, obsessed with peak-bagging, loves wild camping, willing to put up with Mountain Man's non-conformist lifestyle, slim, pretty, athletic and no major psychological abnormalities – I imagine it'd crash the app, or at very least return: 'no matches found, you're not handsome enough to be that fussy'. But, somehow, even without the help of a dating app's love-finding algorithm, I'd met Nic, we'd hit it off, and it was the start of something special.

All these new friendships, romantic or otherwise, helped me smile and laugh during 2018 – but I still worked incredibly hard during that year. I juggled my Fix the Fells job alongside writing this book and building up my freelance work as an adventurer and writer. It was hectic and exhausting and by autumn I was ready for a proper break. Weekend hikes and evening excursions into the hills had just about kept my wanderlust at bay, but I longed to re-taste that dizzying sense of adventure I'd experienced on my 446-mountain challenge. I wanted to go on another grand expedition, to be footloose and free, alone in the mountains with nothing but the open trail ahead of me. I wanted to emancipate myself from the shackles of a taxing year of bewildering change and to see, again, if time in the hills would rejuvenate my spirit.

Clearly, my Nuttalls adventure hadn't cured me of itchy-feet syndrome. It hadn't permanently appeased my restlessness or adequately scratched the wanderlust itch. Instead it had opened my eyes to endless adventurous opportunities and sparked a burning, if slightly masochistic, desire to continue taking on grand challenges. So, with some careful tactical manoeuvring and politicking, I convinced my bosses to grant me two months of unpaid leave and I set my sights on the peaks of Ireland. *Mountain Man 2: The Sequel*. The difficult second album – could I pull it off?

With my car rammed full of expedition meals, hiking clothes and camping gear galore, I took the ferry from Liverpool to Dublin ready to begin my epic hill-walking adventure, a peak-bagging record firmly in my sights. My self-imposed mission was to climb all 273 mountains in Ireland and Northern Ireland. The so-called Vandeleur-Lynams – Irish mountains over 600m with a minimum prominence of 15m – were my goal. And I wanted to be the fastest person ever to complete them and the first person ever to do so in a single-round.

In true Calamity James style, things kicked off in incongruous style. It was as if I'd learned nothing from the mishaps and errors of my 446-mountain challenge. On my very first wild camp of the whole Irish adventure, I forgot to pack a lighter, was unable to boil water and consequently had to make my freeze-dried expedition meal with cold water. Suffice to say, cold beef and potato stew is stodgy and gloopy, with a gag reflex-inducing texture. Pedigree Chum would've been more palatable. A week or so later I fell violently ill, to the point where my total mountain count was easily surpassed by my daily-visits-to-the-toilet count, and a few days after that I came very, very close to having to sleep in a squalid road-side ditch due to a hitch-hiking cock-up. Not long after that I slept in the urine-scented toilet of a youth hostel to avoid the thunderous snore of an Irish lad in my dorm room, and the run of misfortune finally ended with a bizarre incident in which I lost my wallet late one evening in a supermarket, met a van full of Irish Gardaí (police) in a dark car park to discuss the 'crime', only for a ghostly female figure to emerge out of the shadows and hand over said wallet, dubiously claiming, 'I just found this on the floor'. Either she was the kindest, sweetest, most selfless of old ladies, who didn't believe in finders keepers. Or a conniving, devious, wily old hag, who heartlessly stole my wallet and then pragmatically feigned innocence once the police van showed up. One of the two, anyway.

But it wasn't all schoolboy errors and weird experiences. In the Knockmealdowns my faith in humanity was restored when Tom, a grey-haired, smiley, chatty 82-year-old, not only responded to my thumb-wagging, hitch-hiking pleas, but also inspired me with his effervescent approach to life; in Mangerton I wild-camped with graceful panoramas over layers of distant, hazy mountains; and in the Mourne Mountains I felt like a king proudly surveying his realm, as I stood atop a dramatic summit that crescendoed with a near-vertical granite tor.

My favourite moment in that first month in Ireland, however, came on my 100th summit. I went to sleep on the side of a misty, drizzly peak called Knockowen, a 658m mountain in the Caha Mountains of the Beara Peninsula, an area of wild and rocky uplands in south-west Ireland – and my expectations for the morning were non-existent. Hence, when I unzipped my tent at 7am after a good night's sleep, I simply couldn't believe my eyes. Was I still dreaming? It felt like I'd woken up in heaven, emerging from my one-man tent into an untouched paradise above the clouds. It was the most perfect inversion I'd ever witnessed. Craggy mountaintops pierced majestically through a sea of fluffy white clouds, like the fins of dolphins breaking the waves; while the sun painted a Brocken Spectre masterpiece on the cloud canvas, a double-rainbow halo forming around my shadow. This was what I'd come to Ireland for – a wilderness experience to match my Nuttalls adventure.

Sadly, though, the good times didn't last – and for the next century of mountains I encountered the full wrath of the Irish weather, courtesy of Ali. Storm Ali, that is, who ensured the proverbial well and truly hit the fan. As I looped anti-clockwise through the north, north-west and west of Ireland, I was battered by gusting winds, torrential rain, and atrocious visibility. The storm lashed into the west coast of Ireland, really putting the wild into the Wild Atlantic Way, and high in the mountains I was dealt a severe beating. I felt like a drowned rat for about three weeks: cold, wet and miserable.

At one point I'd hiked up 53 mountains in 11 days – and not enjoyed the view from a single summit. I never saw the volcano-like pyramid of Errigal in Glenveagh National Park, one of Ireland's most dramatic peaks; my hike up Croagh Patrick, a sacred and holy mountain with the power to cleanse the souls of pilgrims, was completed in hellish rather than divine weather; and the only thing memorable of my climbs in the cloud-cloaked Ben Gorm and Partry mountains was fearing for my life atop Devilsmother, as I desperately hung to a fence in an attempt to stop 60mph gusts blowing me off a ridge and into the abyss.

Exhausted and crestfallen, I felt like giving up. I can vividly remember lifting my head to the heavens during one walk and laughing maniacally, like an evil villain. I felt like I was losing my mind. The relentless rain had left me on the brink of madness. 'Arrrggghhhh, is that all you've got?' I screamed, a deranged war cry taunting the weather gods. My Irish adventure had morphed into something horrific and demoralising and joyless – and I began to question, yet again, my life choices. Why hadn't I remembered the hardships of the Nuttalls? Only a fool repeats the same mistake twice.

But, thankfully, Storm Ali eventually passed and the final two weeks of my challenge were a sun-drenched dream. I was in the right place too. Kerry, in the south-west of Ireland, is the promised land of Irish hill-walking. The MacGillycuddy's Reeks are the star attraction: a chaotic, gnarly mountain range of inter-connecting knife-edge ridges, soaring rocky summits, and domineering cliff-faces – and home to Carrauntoohil, Ireland's highest peak at 1,039m. But Kerry is so much more than just the Reeks. To the north, the Dingle Peninsula serves up endless skies, sparkling ocean views and pristine beaches, while the Dunkerrons to the south are wild, remote and rugged; a place of tough, pathless walking for tough, fearless walkers.

It was a spectacular place to explore and the perfect way to end my adventure on the Emerald Isle. With renewed energy and determination, I powered through mile after mile, until eventually I finally found myself standing next to the trig pillar of Knocknadobar on the Inveragh Peninsula, my final Vandeleur-Lynam. I couldn't comprehend it. I'd travelled a long, long way to get there: walking 1,129km, ascending the height of Everest every week for 8 weeks in a row, and climbing 273 mountains in 56 days, another record. *Mountain Man 2: The Sequel* completed.

At the finish line, I felt close to the brink; deeply fatigued and mentally broken, but immensely proud and happy too. It had been yet another momentous, awakening journey. In many ways it was a carbon copy of my 446-mountain Nuttalls challenge; in others it was completely different. My Ireland trip was a single, continuous expedition, with no breaks – and I preferred that. The Irish hills felt quieter and remoter too, their pathless slopes untainted by stone-pitched bridleways and untouched by human interference like their English and Welsh counterparts. That was a double-edged sword: I loved the genuine escapism, emptiness and wildness of the ranges, yet slogging through knee-deep heather and clambering over boulder-strewn, ankle-jarring terrain for hours on end was physically exhausting. But I couldn't pick a favourite trip. Both adventures were unique and extraordinary – and both hold a special place in my heart.

I returned home, back to reality and routine – and it was a shock to the system. The post-adventure blues slapped me in the face and, with my immune system evidently weak and worn down, I fell ill with tonsillitis. Like a shadow of my former intrepid self, I lay in bed for days, wallowing in malaise mixed with self-pity, dreaming fondly of the Irish hills and quickly forgetting the sheer levels of suffering and torment I'd endured.

Luckily, Laura Doling – the Essex postwoman – had moved into my house as a lodger while I was in Ireland, and she was around to nurse me back to health with bowls of soup served with extra helpings of good-humoured banter. Before long, I was fighting fit and back to work with Fix the Fells for three days a week, with a new routine to give my life focus and structure. Generally on Tuesdays to Thursdays I commuted to the Lake District National Park Authority offices in Kendal or Threlkeld, working at my laptop like a million other workers in a thousand other generic offices across the country. I sent emails, wrote funding applications, filled in spreadsheets, attended meetings and sent more emails. In all honesty, I wanted out from the 9 to 5 grind, albeit a part-time one, and was desperate to quit and dedicate 100 per cent of my energy to my writing and adventure career. But the Ireland expedition had depleted my bank balance, I needed the money and a regular pay-cheque felt reassuring.

The next six months from October 2018 to March 2019 were pretty understated, yet enjoyable nonetheless. I plodded along with my Fix the Fells job and spent my weekends with Nic, bimbling around the countryside, hanging out with friends, visiting family, and chilling on the sofa watching Netflix true crime documentaries. But, most of all, I used those six months to pour every ounce of creativity, determination and skill I had into expanding my fledgling freelancing career.

I wanted to make adventuring and outdoors writing my full-time occupation, not just a side gig, and to do so I needed to earn more money from it. My living expenses were very low, thanks to my frugal lifestyle, super-cheap house in West Cumbria and lack of children, pets or expensive hobbies, so my income target wasn't unattainable. I was already halfway there, after a few years of dipping my toes in the freelancing water, but now it was time to dive head-first into the deep end. Would I sink or swim?

Building on the stable foundation I'd already laid, things progressed positively and began to skyrocket. I pitched ideas to editors left, right and centre, and some of the lines I cast got a bite. I secured more commissions from outdoor magazines and newspapers, such as *Trail*, *The Great Outdoors* and the *Sunday Telegraph*, writing features about wild camping adventures and long-distance trails, as well as basic descriptions of walking routes, and several of these opportunities became regular jobs. Plunging my fingers into numerous pies, I supplemented this base income with any and every gig I could get my hands on: writing gear reviews for outdoor websites, speaking at adventure festivals, featuring in promotional videos for outdoor companies, Instagram influencing, and acting as a brand ambassador. Much of this work fell into my lap due to my 446-mountain adventure. That challenge gave me clout and standing, increased my public exposure and helped me rise above the noise. It opened doors that otherwise might have been closed – and sent me down the road to irreversibly changing my life yet again.

It felt awesome to be making my dreams come true. I always wanted to create a life that was flexible, adventurous, outdoorsy and focused around my passion for the mountains – and I could now taste it. It was close to becoming a reality. But I knew it wasn't going to be some heal-all panacea. There would always be downsides: the freelance life felt insecure and anxiety-inducing; I was never going to get rich; and I'd have to hustle and graft in order to just scrape by. It was going to be a tough existence. But, for me, the pros far outweighed the cons.

By the end of March, I'd crunched the numbers and knew that financially I could now survive without my Fix the Fells job. So I handed in my notice and said goodbye to that chapter in my life. I didn't have any regrets and I was excited about the future. But, as is my modus operandi, there was a nagging thought at the back of my mind. There was something I wanted, nay needed, to do. It felt like the last piece of the puzzle; the final leg of the journey of my life's adventurous transformation.

I needed to complete what I'd started with the Nuttalls. All 446 mountains across England and Wales were already in the bag; every one of the 273 peaks in Ireland and Northern Ireland were ticked off; but I hadn't yet been to Scotland. I felt utterly compelled to turn my duo of peak-bagging expeditions into a trilogy, as if it was my destiny, or perhaps my moral duty. Failure to do so would be a cop out, whereas going for it would be evidence of my blinkered devotion to this new way of life. I'd be practising what I preached: walking the walk (literally), not just talking the talk.

Like all the best film trilogies – *The Lord of the Rings* and *Back to the Future* – I was confident my series would crescendo with an epic finale. The last battle to end all battles; one final quest for the protagonist to overcome; a very last journey to tie up loose ends, draw conclusions and crystallise lessons learnt. My self-chosen mission would be to bag the Munros, the popular peak-bagging list of 282 Scottish mountains over 3,000ft named after 19th-century peak surveyor extraordinaire

Sir Hugh Munro. By a beautiful quirk of mathematics, it meant that – if I made it – I'd have bagged 1,001 mountains across the UK and Ireland in just three years. England and Wales in 2017; Ireland and Northern Ireland in 2018; and Scotland in 2019. I loved the sound of that. It had a wonderful ring to it.

This time around, however, I wouldn't be alone on my mountain climbing exploits. Nic, who'd spent the past six months on her own life-changing journey, had (perhaps foolishly) agreed to join me. After 15 years in high-pressured public sector jobs, she was taking a career break, with her sights set on fulfilling her dream to walk 3,000km across New Zealand on the Te Araroa trail. But, first, she was going to be my trusted companion on our Scottish hillwalking pilgrimage – and I just hoped she could put up with exhausted, grumpy, foul-smelling James, the peak-bagging dirtbag.

It all began with Ben More on the Isle of Mull on April 16, 2019, and from there our lives quickly descended into an abnormal, transient type of existence, somewhere between intrepid wanderers and deranged vagrants. We spent our days tramping for all we were worth, blasting out the miles and the ascent in an exhausting schedule; and our nights feasting on expedition meals and sleeping rough in our tent, wherever we could wild camp. We washed with a cursory spray of Lynx, lived out of the boot of our car, and spent every other waking minute concocting elaborate and intricate strategies for avoiding the dreaded Scottish midge.

Our aim was to bag the Munros in an intensive, six-month round. Strictly speaking, it wasn't a continuous round. We'd return home every few weeks to recuperate, relax and catch up with work. I still had numerous writing commissions to fulfil and was eager to retain the positive momentum and regular income I'd built up over the past six months. It seemed like an ideal halfway house, striking a good balance between work and play – and I felt happy that I was staying true to the philosophy of my original Nuttalls challenge, integrating a grand adventure around an everyday existence.

In the first two weeks we bagged 30 Munros around the Crianlarich area, and then a date circled in my diary for well over a year came around – the publication date of this book. There was no elaborate press launch for *Mountain Man*; no swanky publication party with champagne and canapés; and no fans-queuing-around-the-block book signing event at the Waterstones in Piccadilly Circus. Instead, wearing a dodgy tracksuit and looking like I'd been dragged through a hedge backwards, I sat in a weird pub in the village of Killin, near Ben Lawers, nibbled on a foul-tasting bacon butty and watched the reaction come through online.

Despite the ignominy of the way I was celebrating the launch, I was thrilled and humbled by the response – and it felt like a real life goal achieved. Hundreds of positive messages flooded through on social media and, to top it all off, my book made it onto the Amazon bestseller lists. For a while it outsold the likes of Tommy Caldwell and Alex Honnold in the climbing and mountaineering category, which I couldn't quite believe, and for several weeks it was number 1 in the mountaineering holidays category. It was such a niche list, perhaps it was akin to calling myself an 'award-winning writer' because I'd won the 'best effort' prize in the Astwell Primary School Year Five creative writing competition in 1992, or a 'medal-winning athlete' because I'd finished bronze in the egg and spoon race at my Sunday School's garden party in 1989. But I didn't really care – I was happy with my new title of '#1 Amazon Bestseller'.

Once the buzz from the book release died down, Nic and I slipped back into our daily routine of bagging Munros. We made good progress with the peaks in the southern and central Highlands, before getting unceremoniously pummelled by incessant rain for at least two weeks in the Cairngorms to the east. But our tally kept increasing and we were getting it done, no matter what Mother Nature threw at us.

Scotland was proving a gruelling undertaking with pitfalls and traps everywhere we turned. The bloodthirsty midges were unbearable, as if God had consciously designed them to be as infuriatingly annoying as possible; the terrain was ankle-breakingly rough and soul-destroyingly steep; and the weather was often so apocalyptically atrocious we quickly learnt the meaning of the Billy Connolly quote, 'there are two seasons in Scotland: June and winter'.

It was exhausting work. With the Munros classified as over 3,000ft, compared to the 2,000ft marker for the Nuttalls, there were no freebies in Scotland. Every summit was the equivalent of a Snowdon or Scafell Pike, and the sheer distances and ascents involved were daunting. Many remote Munros weren't accessible by car either, so at times you'd have a 15km plus hike just to get to the base of the mountain. On several occasions we felt sapped of energy, gnawed by self-doubt and bereft of motivation to keep going. It was as if the 446 Nuttalls and 273 Vandeleur-Lynams were but a gentle stroll in the park, a leisurely warm-up for the real hiking challenge of Scotland.

But, as with all of my expeditions, it wasn't just suffering and displeasure. Scotland had a multi-faceted identity and I had a love-hate relationship with it. When the weather conspired against us, it was hell on earth; when the sun shone, it was paradise, a rugged nirvana of hillwalking hedonism. And, joyously, we experienced the latter in some of the most classic landscapes of Scotland: Torridon's trio of sandstone behemoths; Fisherfield's untamed, far-flung wilderness; An Teallach's terrifyingly-sheer brutality; and Knoydart's fiercely remote and hard-won summits.

Some of my best memories were in Glen Coe. There I felt like a traveller on an epic quest, exploring a fabled glen of razor-toothed ridges, lush hidden valleys and impossibly craggy peaks. Basing ourselves at the idyllic, white-washed mountaineering hut of Lagangarbh, every walk was breathtaking and every mountain awe-inspiring. Buachaille Etive Mor (*Big Herdsman* in Gaelic) was a domineering mass of knobbly outcrops and precipitous rock-faces, gashed by vertical gullies. Closeted and grand, Bidean nam Bian (*Chief of the Hills*) was the overlord of the glen, Glen Coe's highest peak and a dark, mysterious place, loyally guarded by the craggy domes of the

Three Sisters. But perhaps most striking of all was Aonach Eagach (*Notched Ridge*), a serrated, knife-edge arête – a spine of rocky turrets and craggy towers, rising and falling like the waves of a raging sea – linking two Munro summits.

No matter how superlative Glen Coe was, however, it couldn't quite compete with the Isle of Skye. The Misty Isle is home to the Black Cuillin: a spiky, barbed ridge of legendary alpine proportions, a 12km-long labyrinth of monstrous turrets, razor-thin arêtes and precipitous craggy obstacles with 11 Munro summits – the UK's most iconic ridge and the Holy Grail for the British scrambler. Nic and I both knew it was going to test our mettle and push our limits, and be the physical and emotional crux of the whole challenge. But we couldn't wimp out. If we wanted to be Munro 'compleators' we had no choice but to climb all 11 Munros on the Black Cuillin, including the most technically difficult one.

The Inaccessible Pinnacle – or Sgurr Dearg, to use its Sunday name – is a spectacular blade of rock with knee-wobbling, nerve-jangling, the-end-is-nigh levels of exposure. It reminded me of a shark's dorsal fin: sharp, narrow and a sign of impending doom. But, to my immense surprise, when I took on the In Pinn, a calmness and composure descended over me, perhaps induced by the nirvana-like artistry all around.

After weeks of grey cloud and measly weather, I found myself balanced on that serrated, fin-like rocky spine above the most perfect cloud inversion I'd seen since that morning on Knockowen in Ireland. I was floating above a sea of clouds, the blanket of white pierced only by the jagged ridge below my feet. It felt like I was surfing the clouds, riding the knobbly, gnarled backbone of a flying dragon. It was a joyous moment that made all the agony and torment and misery of the challenge worth it. Just like my Nuttalls expedition, in Scotland the lows were crushingly low, but the highs were unfathomably high.

With Skye's mountains in the bag, we had 60 Munros left to complete in four weeks to hit our self-imposed six month target.

Blood was shed, tears were cried and sweat was secreted by the gallon, but eventually we made it to within 20 metres of the summit of Ben Lomond, our final Munro. We'd travelled to hell and back to get there. It'd taken 109 days of walking, covering 2,015km and ascending 151,464m – and now we had just a few steps to go. Our friends and family, including both sets of parents, formed a human archway for us to walk through, as they clapped and cheered and hollered. We neared the summit, ready to triumphantly place our hands on the trig pillar, and then out of nowhere a random couple appeared, stopped us in our tracks and asked, 'Can you take a photo of us please?' Denied at the very last second. I felt like Taylor Swift at the VMA awards when Kanye West snatched her mic; like a lover cruelly denied just before the moment of ecstasy; or a kid whose swirl of teetering Mr Whippy callously plunged to the floor nano-seconds before their tongue got to touch the sweet white nectar. But we obliged, in a show of true English politeness, and at least it gave everyone a good laugh as we celebrated Munro number 282.

For Nic, it was the end of her Scottish adventure, her first ever major expedition. For me, it was the culmination of a three-year mission, a crazy experiment in how to make my life as adventurous as possible. I'd walked 5,000km, ascended the height of Everest from sea level over 30 times, slept wild under the stars on more than a century of occasions, and climbed 1,001 mountains across the UK and Ireland. My triple-crown of peak-bagging adventures was over and a defining chapter in my life was coming to an end. But another chapter would soon start. What did it hold in store? Where would life take me next? What grand adventures and epic expeditions were around the corner? I honestly didn't know – and that was an exciting thought.

HOW TO PLAN YOUR OWN EPIC ADVENTURE

I hope my book has convinced you that an adventurous life is within your grasp, even if you've got a 'normal' job and everyday responsibilities such as a mortgage or children. Perhaps you're wondering, *What epic adventure could I go on?* or thinking, *How could I be more adventurous on my days off?* If you are, that's awesome. You're at the beginning of an amazing, life-changing, memory-forging, happiness-inducing journey.

But, more than likely, you're probably also pondering the practicalities of turning your adventure dreams into reality. Questions are racing around your mind: What could I do? Where could I go? How do I overcome the barriers in my way? How much will it cost? How much time do I need? What equipment will be useful? Have I got the right skills? Am I brave enough? How do I plan everything? It might well feel overwhelming, but answers are out there.

Whole books have been written on the topic of planning adventures, in more detail than I have space for. These are a valuable resource and I can wholeheartedly recommend a few: *Microadventures* by Alastair Humphreys (for cheap, simple, quick everyday adventures); *Grand Adventures* by, again, Alastair Humphreys (for bigger expeditions at home and abroad); *Amazing Family Adventures* by Jen and Sim Benson (for adventurous days out and weekends with the kids), and *The Girl Outdoors* by Sian Lewis (for the female would-be adventurer). Read them, cherish them, absorb the wisdom – and then forge your own adventurous path.

But before you go on a book-buying spree, I will try and impart some of my – albeit limited – insight into the topic and offer my top tips and advice on integrating more adventures into your everyday life. It has been difficult to write this section because of the myriad scenarios that could be relevant: you might never have been on an adventure before or you might be a seasoned adventurer looking to take things up a notch or two; you might have £5,000 in the bank or be totally penniless; you might be young and single or be married with seven children, two dogs and a cat. I have tried to provide an overview for everyone.

No matter who you are, the good news is that if you genuinely want to go on more adventures, then you can. It's not rocket science. There are always ways around the obstacles in your path and a truly awe-inspiring adventure is never out of reach. If I could do it – an everyday guy with bad map-reading skills, a rubbish beard and a fear of the dark – then so can you. Definitely.

I've never been on an adventure – how do I start?
You don't have to begin with a trek to the North Pole or a backpacking trip around the world. Simply start small: climb your local hill on a Saturday, cycle to a village pub after work, or visit the coast for a weekend. Go solo, take a friend or join a more formal gathering such as Explorers Connect, The YesTribe, Adventure Queens, Love Her Wild or local Ramblers groups. And then, as your confidence grows, progress to wild camping, bigger mountains, longer trails, or whatever takes your fancy. For more beginner-adventure inspiration, *Microadventures* by Alastair Humphreys is essential reading.

Everyday life is so busy – how do I find time for adventures?
It is an empowering thought that the average UK worker has over 130 days off a year. Even if you set aside only a small proportion of

those days for adventure, you could still achieve something special. Why not start by pencilling in one weekend a month in your diary for 'adventure' and booking one week of annual leave for 'adventure travel'? That is almost certainly feasible for most people. If not, can you squeeze in a microadventure from 5pm to 9am on a weekday?

What adventures could I go on? And where could I go?

There are many places you could visit and many adventurous activities you could take up in Britain, from mountain biking in the Scottish Highlands to wild camping in the Dales to surfing on the South Coast. Or you could flee the nest and head abroad for your adventures – do you fancy trekking in Nepal, diving in Thailand, backpacking in Australia or skiing in the Alps? The best approach is to focus on places and activities that excite you. Don't try and imitate others. Be yourself and focus on your own adventure passions – or be inspired by my selection of example adventure ideas below.

How can I improve my adventure skills and confidence?

Practice makes perfect. The more adventures you undertake, the more your skills and confidence will improve, and learning as you go is perhaps the best approach. Studying books, reading blogs, watching YouTube videos and buddying up with more experienced friends are great ways to upskill too. But you could also complete formal training, such as a navigation course or a climbing qualification, to boost your abilities in your chosen activity.

I want to go on a bigger, grander adventure – how can I find the time?

Time is a precious commodity and it might feel like you don't have enough of it to commit to a grand adventure. But there are options. Can you go part-time at work? Will your employer offer you an unpaid career break with your role secured on your return? Are you between jobs, with the opportunity to take a gap year?

Depending on your circumstances, there are two approaches available. If you can take a bigger chunk of time off work, such as three, six or 12 months, then the world is your oyster – you could go backpacking through Europe, or hike the Pacific Crest Trail, or cycle across the world, or whatever other crazy idea you can dream up. Long-distance and long-term journeys are a possibility for you. Alternatively, if – like me – you can dedicate only smaller chunks of time, can you come up with an overarching mission to unite your separate trips? Perhaps you could walk the 630-mile South West Coast Path over 25 weekends, or cycle the North Coast 500 ride in Scotland in ten legs, or complete every Grade 1 and 2 scramble in the Lake District in a year. With a bit of creative thinking the possibilities are endless.

How much will it cost?

How long is a piece of a string? Obviously, some adventures will be more expensive than others. Hiring a professional mountaineering guide to take you up Everest is going to cost a fortune, whereas wild camping on a trail in your local area will cost next to nothing. The good news is that you can definitely go on a long-term, amazing adventure for about £1,000, especially if you're sleeping wild and undertaking a self-propelled journey. Cut out the daily coffee or cancel the gym membership you never use, and you'll quickly be able to save up a healthy adventure fund. After all, being frugal in everyday life is a vital skill for every adventurer – the less money you spend at home, the more money you have for adventures.

It feels like there are so many reasons not to go on a big adventure – why is that?

None of us is ever as free or footloose as perhaps we'd like, so inevitably there will be obstacles in your way – time, money, family and/or work. Sometimes these obstacles might seem insurmountable but, trust me, they aren't. There are innumerable examples of everyday people with full-time jobs, or three children, or marriages, or big mortgages, who still manage to fit a grand adventure into their lives. You just have to be determined and resourceful in finding a way to joyously leap over the hurdles in your path, rather than falling over them. If you've got a partner and kids, can you go on an adventure with them? If you're struggling for money, can you go on a cheap adventure in Britain? Or, if you're super busy with work and short on time, can you simply use your annual leave to go on a two-week adventure abroad?

I want to start wild camping – how can I get into it?

First build up your confidence by camping in official campsites. Learn to set up your tent quickly and correctly; get used to your sleeping mat and sleeping bag system; and practise cooking hearty meals on your stove. Once you feel happy and proficient, then you're ready to dip your toes into the glorious world of wild camping. Before you start, make sure you read up about the do's and don'ts. The internet is awash with useful advice, *The Book of the Bivvy* by Ronald Turnbull and *Wild Camping* by Stephen Neale are superb resources, and I've outlined the basics in Chapter 7. They are quite simple: leave no trace, set up late, leave early, and be discreet. If you're of a nervous disposition, why not do a test run in your garden or in your local countryside, or take a friend (or friends) on your first trip? If you're not nervous, then there's no need for the test run – you're good to go. Do your research, pack your bags, and enjoy the life-affirming experience of sleeping wild under the stars.

I want to take on a peak-bagging challenge – how can I start?

It's easy – just choose a list, buy the guidebook and start ticking them off. You could go for a classic list, such as the Wainwrights in the Lake District or the Munros in Scotland, or something more obscure like the Marilyns in Wales or the Vandeleur-Lynams in Ireland. You could set yourself a time target, or simply go with the flow, and either way it will give a bigger purpose to your weekend trips.

How can I tick off the peaks as quickly as possible?

Obviously, you could just walk faster, or for longer, but I found the best tactic for bagging peaks quickly was completing multi-day wild-camping trips. That way you can combine several day-walks into your own bespoke long-distance routes, cutting out long hikes back to your car every evening and ensuring instead that you wake up in the middle of the mountains, ready to bag that next top. Using this approach, I was regularly able to complete two so-called day-walks in a single day.

Can I get more advice?

Visit www.jamesmforrest.co.uk and drop me an email – I will endeavour to reply as soon as I can. I'm always happy to help out a fellow adventurer.

Example Adventures

The one for all the family

What?   Ticking off a child-friendly bucket list of 50 fun outdoors activities, based on the book *Amazing Family Adventures* by Jen and Sim Benson. The list includes everything from exploring rock pools and flying a kite to watching the sunrise and going on a wildlife safari. The activities are split by age as follows: 0–4, 5–7, 8–11 and 11+.

Why?   This is your chance to bond positively as a family unit, to engage your children in healthy activities in the great outdoors, and to fit fun, simple adventures around your everyday life.

Where?   It is very flexible. Many of the activities – such as follow a waymarked trail or go on a night walk – can be completed locally to you, while others – such as climb a mountain or explore a castle – may require travelling away from home.

When?   All year, depending on the activity.

Duration Set your own timeline – six months, one year, two years, the next decade. It doesn't really matter. Choose whatever works for you and your children.

Kit   Jen and Sim Benson's book; spare dry and warm clothes for your children (they will get wet and muddy!); a good off-road buggy with rugged tyres or soft rucksack-style baby carriers for younger children; lots of food and drink; and other outdoors gear suitable for each individual activity.

Skills   Basic outdoors confidence and know-how, but very few technical skills are required – you can learn as you go.

Tips   ▶ Involve your children in the planning of adventures: this can get them excited and help them learn about maps and navigation.

▶ Share the experience: invite other friends or family members to get involved in your family adventures.

▶ Make it fun and be flexible: if you plan to climb a hill but find that the kids are loving skimming stones and paddling in a stream at the bottom, that's still a successful adventure.

▶ Tie in your adventure with a topic the children are studying at school, thus stimulating their learning in a practical way.

The one for a night away or a wild weekend

What?   An overnight bike-packing microadventure from your front door: start pedalling from home on Saturday morning, get as far as you can, wild camp under the stars, and cycle back on Sunday. A simple but epic adventure.

Why?   This is a cheap, quick, no-frills way of escaping the stresses and anxieties of everyday life, getting a much-needed dose of outdoorsy adventure in a short space of time, and exploring the beauty of your local area. Everybody loves cycling – the open road, the wind in your hair, the exercise. Perfect.

Where?   Anywhere within pedalling distance of your home. Pore over some maps and see what you can find – a beach, a forest, a hill, the mountains, a river, or a national park.

When?   All year, although April to September will offer a better chance of good weather.

Duration A one-night, two-day adventure that fits perfectly into Saturday and Sunday. If you're short on time, try to squeeze it into the 5pm-to-9am slot on a school night. Or, if you're in no rush, you could extend your trip into a long weekend with two nights of wild camping.

Kit   Bike with panniers, bivvy bag, sleeping mat, sleeping bag, camping stove, outdoors clothes, and maps. See below for full adventure kit list.

Skills Basic fitness levels for cycling, basic bike maintenance skills and the confidence and ability to wild camp.

Tips   ▶ Use a mountain bike so you can head off-road.

        ▶ Pack light to avoid weighing your bike down unnecessarily.

        ▶ Wear a decent pair of padded cycling shorts to avoid the dreaded saddle-sore arse.

        ▶ Practise your wild-camping set-up before you set off.

The one for the peak-bagger

What?   Walking the Wainwrights, the list of 214 Lakeland fells detailed in the seven pictorial guides by iconic writer Alfred Wainwright. The 214 mountains feature numerous Lake District classics, including Scafell Pike, England's highest mountain, Helvellyn, Blencathra, Skiddaw, Great Gable, Cat Bells and many more.

Why?   This is your chance to indulge in the delights of the Lake District, the prettiest corner of England, and to claim a classic peak-bagging accolade.

Where? The Lake District in north-west England, surprisingly. The 214 fells are spread pretty evenly across Lakeland.

When?   All year, depending on your confidence and skills. The weather for fellwalking is, naturally, far better from April to September. From November to March, crampons, ice axes and technical skills may be required to be safe in the snow-covered high fells.

Duration It depends. Some people take a lifetime; ultra-runner Steve Birkinshaw completed them all in under a week. Anything from six months to two years seems like a reasonable target.

Kit   Wainwright's guidebooks, walking boots, hiking gear, map and compass. See below for full adventure kit list.

Skills   Basic fitness levels for hillwalking and the ability to navigate safely in the mountains using map and compass.

Tips   ▶ Don't be tempted by other guidebooks. Buy the seven-book set of *The Pictorial Guides to the Lakeland Fells* by Alfred Wainwright: their poetic descriptions, beautiful drawings, hand-drawn maps, and walk details will be the perfect companion to your peak-bagging mission.

           ▶ Use a mobile app or website such as www.hill-bagging.co.uk to track your progress.

           ▶ Get involved with a Wainwright-bagging Facebook group for advice from fellow enthusiasts.

           ▶ Join the Wainwright Society to claim your place on the completers' hall of fame once you've climbed number 214.

The one for an epic overseas expedition

What?   Thru-hiking the Pacific Crest Trail (PCT), a world-famous 2,650-mile walk across America from the Mexico border to the Canada border, passing through the states of California, Oregon and Washington and the stunning Sierra Nevada and Cascade mountain ranges.

Why?   This is your chance to take on a truly grand journey, completing one of the world's great long-distance routes and embracing the back-to-nature simplicity of trail life. If you want to 'find yourself' or overcome personal problems, a long-distance trail might just be right for you.

Where?   The western states of America – most hikers journey north, walking from the Mexican border to the Canadian border.

When?	Snow, ice and dangerous winter conditions in the high mountains mean there is a specific window for thru-hiking the PCT. Most northbound thru-hikers start sometime between mid-April and early May, while southbound hikers generally start between June and early July.
Duration	According to the Pacific Crest Trail Association, most hikers take about five months to complete the trail. Very fit hikers, capable of walking 30 miles per day, can complete the trail in about 100 days.
Kit	Lightweight walking gear, lightweight camping kit, water-filtration system, and bear canister and spray!
Skills	Good fitness levels for long-distance hiking; camping skills and knowledge; and the ability to navigate safely in the mountains using a map and compass.
Tips	▶ Build up your wilderness skills, camping experience and hiking fitness in advance – the PCT is not to be underestimated.
	▶ Plan, plan, plan: significant research will be needed in advance on lightweight kit, route-planning, maps, safety, bear encounters, water purification, permits and much more.
	▶ Read *Wild* by Cheryl Strayed (or watch the Hollywood film version starring Reese Witherspoon) – a classic account of hiking the PCT. My other favourite PCT book is *The Last Englishman* by Keith Foskett.

KIT LIST

It might seem as if you need to spend a fortune to get started in adventure. But you don't. Retailers such as Go Outdoors and Alpkit have some very competitively priced gear and, unless you're undertaking a particularly technical or hardcore adventure, you don't need super-expensive gear. Below are my suggestions on a basic starter kit list for a would-be adventurer:

- large backpack – up to 65L, with a good hip belt to reduce backache
- daypack – about 30L, with sturdy straps and ideally a hip belt
- boots – waterproof boots with good grip for rough terrain
- walking poles – for balance and to take pressure off your joints
- waterproofs – Gore-Tex outer layers for the inevitable rain
- down jacket – an insulated jacket for when it's cold
- base layers – underlayers to keep you warm
- hat, gloves and neck-warmer – for those inevitable cold days
- sun hat, sunglasses and sun cream – for those rare hot days
- outdoors trousers – lightweight, breathable and weatherproof
- sleeping mat – a foam or inflatable mat to sleep on
- sleeping bag – a warm bed for a night under the stars
- bivvy – a lightweight waterproof cover for when pitching a tent is a hassle
- tent – a portable home you can pitch wherever you want
- camping stove – a gas-powered stove for hot meals and drinks
- cooking utensils – pans, titanium spork and mug for mealtimes
- dry bags – waterproof, sealable bags to safely store your gear
- headtorch – for navigating or reading after dark
- compass – a crucial tool for navigating safely in the mountains
- maps – hard-copy maps are indispensable for navigation
- OS Maps app – for navigation and pinpointing your location
- water containers – holding up to three litres
- Water To Go bottle – a bottle with an in-built filtration system

- first-aid kit – plasters, painkillers and basic medical supplies
- phone – for calling mountain rescue services in an emergency
- powerpacks and cables – for recharging your phone
- emergency shelter – a life-saving shelter for emergencies
- emergency rations – high-energy gels and snacks
- safety whistle – for drawing attention in an emergency
- accessories – Ziploc bags, multi-tool, penknife, spare shoelaces

Obviously, more technical equipment – such as ropes and a harness for climbing, a kayak for, well, kayaking (incredible advice, James), or ice axe and crampons for winter walking – might be required, depending on your chosen adventure activity.

GLOSSARY

Arête – a sharp mountain ridge

Bothy – a simple shelter in remote country for the use and benefit of all

Bwlch – the Welsh word for a col (see below)

Clag – low cloud or fog

Col – the lowest point of a ridge or saddle between two peaks, typically providing a pass from one side of a mountain range to another

Corbetts – the mountains in Scotland between 2,500ft and 3,000ft high, with at least 500ft of drop on all sides

Corrie – a circular hollow in the side of a mountain

Crevasse – a deep, open crack

Gill – a narrow mountain stream

GPS (Global Positioning System) – a system that shows the exact position of a person or thing by using signals from satellites

Grough – a natural channel or fissure in a peat moor

Grahams – the mountains in Scotland between 2,000ft and 2,500ft high, with at least 150m of drop on all sides

Hewitts – the mountains in England, Wales and Ireland of 2,000ft or more, with at least 30m of drop on all sides

Marilyns – the hills and mountains of Britain of any height, with at least 150m of drop on all sides

Munros – the mountains in Scotland of 3,000ft or more

Nuttalls – the mountains in England and Wales of 2,000ft or more, with at least 50ft of drop on all sides

OS Maps app – a mapping app for smartphones that uses GPS to pinpoint your exact location or record your route

Peak-bagging – the act of ticking off – or 'bagging' – a set list of mountains

Peat hag – an overhang of peat

Saddle – a low part of a ridge between two higher points or peaks

Trig point – a reference point on high ground used in surveying, typically marked by a small pillar

Wainwrights – the 214 mountains in the Lake District featured in the seven pictorial guides by iconic writer Alfred Wainwright

Wild camping – sleeping overnight in the great outdoors, but not in an official campsite